Richard Manning Smith

STUDY GUIDE AND WORKBOOK FOR

MODERN ELEMENTARY STATISTICS

Seventh Edition

John E. Freund
Arizona State University

PRENTICE-HALL / Englewood Cliffs, New Jersey 07632

Editorial/production supervision and
    interior design: Benjamin D. Smith
Manufacturing buyer: Paula Massenaro

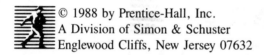
Printed in the United States of America

10 9 8 7 6 5 4 3 2 1

ISBN: 0-13-593617-9

Prentice-Hall International (UK) Limited, *London*
Prentice-Hall of Australia Pty. Limited, *Sydney*
Prentice-Hall Canada Inc., *Toronto*
Prentice-Hall Hispanoamericana, S.A., *Mexico*
Prentice-Hall of India Private Limited, *New Delhi*
Prentice-Hall of Japan, Inc., *Tokyo*
Simon & Schuster Asia Pte. Ltd., *Singapore*
Editora Prentice-Hall do Brasil, Ltda., *Rio de Janeiro*

TABLE OF CONTENTS

HOW TO USE THIS BOOK

This STUDY GUIDE AND WORKBOOK is designed to accompany the 7th Edition of <u>Modern Elementary Statistics</u> by John E. Freund. It is intended to help you increase your understanding of the textbook and, at the same time, increase your likelihood of obtaining high grades on tests in a basic statistics course.

The Format of Each Chapter

The CHAPTER OBJECTIVES provide a list of nearly all topics covered in the corresponding textbook chapter, with an emphasis on those that involve solving problems. The numbers enclosed in parentheses to the right of each objective are numbers of exercises in the textbook. These exercises are intended to help you master the given objective.

The KEY POINTS OF THE CHAPTER, the core of the Study Guide section, provide a comprehensive summary of the significant concepts and definitions in the chapter.

The section AVOIDING COMMON ERRORS (contained in almost all chapters) is intended to alert you to several errors that I have observed many students make in the past. My experience suggests that an awareness of these common errors will make it more likely that you will avoid them.

The section containing KEY SYMBOLS is provided for chapters in which there are many new symbols.

The section containing KEY FORMULAS is given as a reference for the important formulas of the chapter.

The workbook part of each chapter begins with three sections of "short-answer" questions of the MODIFIED TRUE/FALSE, MULTIPLE CHOICE, and COMPLETION types. These sections test your understanding of concepts, definitions, and symbols in the textbook chapter, and often are considered in the KEY POINTS OF THE CHAPTER section of the Study Guide.

The final section of each chapter contains PROBLEMS which test whether you have achieved important chapter objectives. Since the problems are not necessarily in any particular order, they also test your ability to do problems when they are out of the context of a particular textbook section.

The ANSWER KEY at the end of the book provides answers to all questions and problems in the book, including detailed solutions to all problems.

Advice on Preparing for Tests

1. From your teacher, determine which chapters and CHAPTER OBJECTIVES within each chapter are eligible for the test. If entire chapters are assigned without qualification, then all CHAPTER OBJECTIVES within each chapter must be considered.

2. For each relevant chapter, read in the Study Guide and Workbook KEY POINTS OF THE CHAPTER, AVOIDING COMMON ERRORS, KEY SYMBOLS (if contained in the chapter), and KEY FORMULAS. Special emphasis should be placed on the KEY POINTS OF THE CHAPTER and AVOIDING COMMON ERRORS, which should be read at least three times.

3. For each relevant CHAPTER OBJECTIVE write out solutions to several problems from the textbook that deal with the topic. Do not look at a solution until you finish attempting the problem.

4. After finishing each problem, think of specific questions that are answered by the solution to the problem. In addition, think of possible errors you have to avoid in solving such problems.

5. Solve and think about enough problems on a topic so that you can confidently call the topic a strength rather than a weakness. To evaluate your mastery of an objective, answer to yourself the following questions after you have worked out the solutions to several problems dealing with the objective:

    (i) What are the main issues involved in solving problems concerned with this objective?

    (ii) How good am I at solving these kinds of problems?

    For any objective that your answer to (ii) is less than "very good," write out more problems (or redo those you have done) until you can answer "very good" to (ii).

    Do this for all the relevant CHAPTER OBJECTIVES, until all these topics become strengths so that, then you will have no weaknesses among the topics.

6. In the Study Guide and Workbook, answer the MODIFIED TRUE/FALSE, MULTIPLE CHOICE, and COMPLETION questions for each chapter that is eligible for the test. Check your answers in the back of the book, only after you have finished each of the three sections, not after each question. If you do not understand why a certain answer is correct, check the KEY POINTS OF THE CHAPTER or AVOIDING COMMON ERRORS sections, or the textbook chapter.

7. For each eligible chapter, <u>write out</u> the PROBLEMS in the Study Guide. Try working each problem through the first time, before checking the completely worked out answers in the back of the book. Do each of the problems two or three times.

8. To give you more practice in solving problems when they are out of context, work out the review exercises at the end of each of the relevant chapters in the textbook.

<u>Additional Strategies for Test Preparation</u>

For a greater depth of understanding and for more of a guarantee that you will be successful on tests, you should try some of the following activities:

1. <u>Explain to another student</u> how to solve a typical exercise relating to an objective. Compare and check answers and methods of solution. Make up questions and problems for each other.

2. (a) <u>Describe alterations in a problem</u> on an objective that might make it different or more difficult.

   (b) <u>Solve problems</u> which contain such alterations.

3. Finally, in order to achieve a greater confidence in your success, I recommend that your <u>writing study time</u> be at least one-and-a-half times as much as you think is necessary. (e.g., if you feel that you know it all after six hours, spend at least three more hours writing out problems and answering short answer questions.)

Finally, I wish you success with your course and the use of this study guide and workbook.

Richard Manning Smith

CHAPTER 1

INTRODUCTION

This chapter provides an introduction to statistics. It discusses:

(1) the recent growth of statistics and its ever-widening range of applications.
(2) the distinction between descriptive statistics and statistical inference.
(3) the restrictions on the indiscriminate mathematical treatment (addition, multiplication, etc.) of statistical data.

CHAPTER OBJECTIVES: By the end of this chapter, you should be able to:

1. Explain why a given study will not yield the desired information. (1.2 - 1.4)

2. Identify conclusions from data that can be obtained by purely descriptive measures and those that require generalizations. (1.5 - 1.8)

3. Identify data as nominal, ordinal, interval, or ratio data. (1.9 - 1.12)

KEY POINTS OF THE CHAPTER:

1. The results of costly surveys can be useless if questions are ambiguous or asked in the wrong way, if they are asked of the wrong persons, in the wrong place, or at the wrong time.

   A. Begging the Question

      If an interviewer leads a person to respond to a question in a particular way, it is "begging the question" and may lead to misleading results.

      Example

      Asking the question "Do you feel that this wasteful program should be stopped?" suggests that the program is, in fact, wasteful.

   B. Not Obtaining the Desired Sample

      Example

      In studying consumer reaction to a new convenience food, a house-to-house survey is conducted during weekday mornings, with no provisions for return visits in case no one is home. Such a survey is likely to be misleading, since the people who are most likely to use the product are not likely to be at home: single persons, and husbands and wives who are both employed.

2. Since statistical methods are widely applicable, all the exercises can be rephrased so that they would be of special interest to someone in any particular field of application.

3. Descriptive statistics includes anything done to data which is designed to summarize, or describe, without attempting to infer anything that goes beyond the data themselves.

1

4. Methods which serve to make <u>generalizations</u> come under the heading of <u>statistical inference</u>.

5. Probability theory is applied to descriptive statistics in making the generalizations of statistical inference.

6. <u>Nominal data</u> (i.e., categorical, qualitative, or descriptive) is coded or put into categories. They are numerical in name only because they do not share any of the properties of the numbers we deal with in ordinary arithmetic. For instance, if we record marital status as 1, 2, 3, or 4, we cannot write 3>1 or 2<4, and we cannot write 2-1=4-3, 1+3=4, or 4÷2.

7. For <u>ordinal data</u> we can

    (i) set up inequalities

but not form differences or multiply or divide with ordinal data. The symbol > may mean "greater than," "happier than," "preferred to," "more difficult than," "tastier than," and so forth.

8. For <u>interval data</u> we can

    (i) set up inequalities

    (ii) form differences

but not multiply or divide.

<u>Example</u>

We can write

    (i) 107° > 98°

and also

    (ii) 68° - 63° = 131° - 126°

but it does not mean anything to say that 80° is twice as hot as 40°. (i.e., 80 ÷ 40 = 2 is meaningless.)

9. For <u>ratio data</u> we can

    (i) set up inequalities

    (ii) form differences

(iii) multiply or divide

<u>Example</u>

Measurements of length, height, money amounts, weight, volume, area, pressure, elapsed time, sound intensity, density, brightness, velocity, etc.

The reason we can multiply or divide here is that for these measurements the number 0 is indicative of the absence of the quantity we are trying to measure. However, Fahrenheit temperature readings are not ratio data because 0° does not mean no temperature.

MODIFIED TRUE/FALSE: If the statement is true, write true. If false, change the underlined words to make the statement true.

_____ 1. For an interviewer who wants accurate information, it is undesirable to "beg the question."

_____ 2. "Begging the question" is involved when the sample of people is not appropriate for the study.

_____ 3. Descriptive statistics involves making generalizations.

_____ 4. The art of describing the data belongs under the heading of statistical inference.

_____ 5. For nominal data we cannot set up inequalities.

_____ 6. Nominal data is also called categorical data.

MULTIPLE CHOICE: Write the letter of the best answer in the given space.

___ 1. When using interval data, one cannot:

   (a) set up inequalities   (c) divide
   (b) form differences   (d) do any of the above

___ 2. When using ratio data, one cannot do which of the following:

   (a) set up inequalities   (c) divide
   (b) form differences   (d) can do any of the above

___ 3. A type of data that does not allow inequalities to have meaning is _____ data.

   (a) nominal   (c) interval
   (b) ordinal   (d) ratio

___ 4. A type of data in which zero indicates the absence of certain property is _____ data.

   (a) nominal   (c) interval
   (b) ordinal   (d) ratio

___ 5. Measurements of height involve which kind of data?

   (a) nominal   (c) interval
   (b) ordinal   (d) ratio

___ 6. If the apartment numbers in a large building are looked upon as data, they would fall into the _____ category.

   (a) nominal   (c) interval
   (b) ordinal   (d) ratio

COMPLETION: Complete each of the following sentences by filling in the given blanks.

1. With ordinal data we are allowed to _____.

2. For interval data, we can _____, but for ordinal data we cannot.

3

3. For ordinal data, we can _____, but for nominal data we cannot.

4. For ratio data, we can _____, but for interval data we cannot.

5. If an interviewer asks the question "Do you approve of the President's big spending policy?", he is making the error of _____.

6. If the difficulty level of books is ranked from 1 to 10, a set of data rankings of books falls into the category of _____ data.

PROBLEMS:

1. The annual sales for a manufacturing company for each of the past 5 years were $600,000, $721,000, $138,000, $621,000, $865,000. Which of the following conclusions can be obtained from these figures by purely descriptive methods and which require generalizations?

   (a) Among the 5 years, the highest sales were in the 5th year.

   (b) The sales exceeded $800,000 in one of the 5 years.

   (c) The sales increased from the fourth to fifth year because of increased advertising expense.

   (d) Sales were low in the third year because of the recession.

2. Are the following nominal, ordinal, interval, or ratio data? Explain your answers.

   (a) Scores of a basketball team in each of 10 games

(b) Social Security numbers.

(c) Responses to a question concerning the evaluation of the service at a particular restaurant in which the categories are 5 (excellent) to 1 (poor).

(d) Grades on a test in which the lowest grade is 0.

3. Explain why each of the following data may fail to yield the desired information:

   (a) To predict a local election, a pollster samples only people who are leaving an expensive restaurant.

   (b) To determine students' opinion concerning the construction of a new school building, an interviewer asks students "Do you want the school to construct a new building, which will have the effect of raising tuition?"

4. On a statistics test 6 students in a large class obtained the grades 75, 84, 92, 87, 84. Which of the following conclusions can be obtained by purely descriptive methods and which require generalizations? Explain your answers.

(a) None of the grades differs from 83 by more than 8 points.

(b) The most common grade is 84.

(c) The most common grade in the whole class is 84.

(d) If another 6 students are selected all grades will be between 75 and 92.

5. Explain why the following may lead to useless data:

(a) To predict the public view of a proposed gun control law, a poll taker interviews people walking out of a local gun club.

(b) A teacher evaluation form is administered to a class of students immediately after the whole class failed a test given by the teacher.

6. Are the following nominal, ordinal, interval, or ratio data? Explain your answers.

(a) Credit card numbers

(b) Stock prices

(c) Telephone numbers

(d) Supermarket customers rank order their preferences for 10 products.

CHAPTER 2

SUMMARIZING DATA: FREQUENCY DISTRIBUTIONS

This chapter discusses methods of summarizing or presenting data by
using either tables or charts.

<u>CHAPTER OBJECTIVES</u>: By the end of this chapter, you should be able to:

1. Indicate possible limits for a given range of data. (2.1 - 2.3)

2. Given class limits of a frequency distribution, determine (if
    possible) the frequency of items in a given interval. (2.4 - 2.6)

3. Given classes of a frequency distribution, determine:
    a. the class limits and/or boundaries.
    b. the class marks.   (2.7, 2.8)
    c. the class intervals.

4. Given the class marks of a frequency distribution, find:
    a. the class boundaries.
    b. the class limits.   (2.9, 2.10)

5. Given raw data, construct a frequency distribution.
    (2.13, 2.16, 2.19, 2.21, 2.23, 2.24)

6. Convert a frequency distribution into a percentage distribution.
    (2.14, 2.17, 2.20a, 2.35a)

7. Construct a cumulative distribution from a frequency distribution.
    (2.15, 2.18, 2.20b, 2.22, 2.25)

8. Construct a categorical distribution from given data. (2.26, 2.27)

9. Draw a histogram of a frequency distribution.
    (2.30, 2.33, 2.36, 2.40)

10. Draw an ogive of a cumulative distribution.
    (2.32, 2.35b, 2.39, 2.41)

11. Draw a bar chart of a distribution.
    (2.31, 2.34, 2.35, 2.38, 2.45, 2.46)

12. Construct a pie chart of a distribution. (2.43 - 2.46)

13. Construct a stem-and-leaf display for given data.
    (2.48 - 2.52, 2.55 - 2.58)

<u>KEY POINTS OF THE CHAPTER</u>:

1. A <u>frequency distribution</u> is a table showing the classes and the
    number of values falling in each class.

2. Frequency distributions are of two types:

    (i) <u>numerical</u> or <u>quantitative distributions</u>--data are grouped
         according to numerical size.

    (ii) <u>categorical</u> or <u>qualitative distributions</u>--data are grouped
          into categories which differ in kind rather than in degree.

3. Some disadvantages that a frequency distribution has compared to raw data are the following: In a frequency distribution

    (i)   We can find neither the highest nor the lowest value in the data.

    (ii)   We cannot find the total of all values of the data.

    (iii) We cannot find the average of all data values.

4. In choosing a classification scheme for constructing a frequency distribution, we usually choose from between 6 to 15 classes; the exact number we use in a given situation will depend mainly on the number of measurements or observations we have to group.

5. We always make sure that each item (measurement or observation) will go into one and only one class.

6. Whenever possible, we make the classes the same length; that is, we make them cover equal ranges of values.

7. Any class of the "less than," "or less," "more than," or "or more" type is called an open class. We can use an open class if the data contains a few values which are much greater than or much smaller than the rest, so that the number of required classes is reduced.

8. The class limits are the smallest and largest values that go into any given class.

9. The class boundaries are midpoints between successive class limits. Such boundaries cannot possibly be values from the original data.

10. The class marks are the midpoints of the classes. Each class mark is the sum of the lower and upper class limits divided by 2. The class mark is the number in the class that best represents that class.

11. A class interval is the length of the class, or the range of values it contains. It is given by the difference between the class boundaries. If the classes of a distribution are all equal in length, their common class interval is called the class interval of the distribution.

12. A percentage distribution shows the percentage of items in each class of a distribution.

13. A cumulative distribution divides the data into any of the following categories: "less than," "more than," "or more," or "or less." The headings for a cumulative "less than" or "or more" distribution are given by the lower class limits. The headings for a cumulative "more than" or "or less" distribution are given by the upper class limits.

14. A histogram is a picture of a frequency distribution that is constructed with the grouped observations or measurements in a horizontal scale, the class frequencies on a vertical scale. Rectangles are drawn whose bases equal the class interval and whose heights are determined by the corresponding class frequencies. The markings on the horizontal scale can be the class limits, the class boundaries, or arbitrary key values. Histograms cannot be used with frequency distributions having open classes.

15. A <u>frequency polygon</u> is a picture of a frequency distribution in which class frequencies are plotted at the class marks and the successive points are connected by means of straight lines.

16. An <u>ogive</u> is a frequency polygon of cumulative distribution.

17. A <u>pie chart</u> is a picture of a percentage distribution. In such a representation, a circle is divided into sectors (pie-shaped pieces) which are proportional in size to the corresponding frequencies of percentages.

18. In a histogram for a frequency distribution having unequal intervals: If an interval is twice as wide as the normal interval, the height of the bar is one-half the size of the frequency value; if the interval is three times as wide, the height of the bar is one-third the size of the frequency. value, etc.

19. A relatively new method of grouping mass data involves what are called <u>stem-and-leaf plots</u>. In such a plot, each line is a <u>stem</u> and each digit on a stem to the right of the vertical line is a <u>leaf</u>. To the left of the vertical line are the stem labels.

KEY FORMULAS:

1. Class Mark = $\dfrac{\text{Lower Class Limit + Upper Class Limit}}{2}$

2. Class Interval = Upper Class Boundary - Lower Class Boundary

3. Percentage of Items in a Class of a Percentage Distribution

   $= \dfrac{\text{Class Frequency}}{\text{Total Number of All Frequencies}} \cdot 100$

MODIFIED TRUE/FALSE: If the statement is true, write true. If false, change the underlined words to make the statement true.

_____ 1. One of the advantages of <u>frequency distributions</u> is that we can find the exact highest value in the data.

_____ 2. The sum of the frequencies in a frequency distribution is <u>equal to</u> the number of elements in the sample.

_____ 3. An ogive of a cumulative "less than" distribution <u>always</u> decreases as we move from left to right.

_____ 4. For a frequency distribution, we can <u>never</u> find the total of all the original scores.

_____ 5. It is <u>possible</u> for the class boundaries of an interval to be <u>the same</u> as its class limits.

_____ 6. A <u>frequency polygon</u> is a line graph of a cumulative frequency distribution.

_____ 7. A stem-and-leaf display contains <u>no more</u> information than a frequency distribution.

_____ 8. A frequency distribution <u>always</u> has equal class intervals.

10

_____ 9. Frequency distributions are of two types: <u>quantitative</u> and <u>qualitative</u>.

_____ 10. If two consecutive class intervals of a frequency distribution are 60-67 and 68-75, the class boundaries of the second interval are <u>68.95-75.95</u>.

<u>MULTIPLE CHOICE</u>: Write the letter of the best answer in the given space.

Questions 1-4 refer to the frequency distribution at the right.

Scores	Frequency
24-30	4
31-36	2
37-43	1
44-50	6

____ 1. The class boundaries of the second class are:

    (a) 30.5-36.5   (c) 31-26.5
    (b) 31-36   (d) 30.5-36

____ 2. The numbers 37 and 44 are examples of:

    (a) class marks   (c) class limits
    (b) class boundaries (d) class intervals

____ 3. The numbers 27 and 47 are examples of:

    (a) class marks   (c) class limits
    (b) class boundaries (d) class intervals

____ 4. If a cumulative "less than" distribution were constructed from the above frequency distribution, the cumulative frequency in the third row down would be:

    (a) 1   (c) 6
    (b) 9   (d) 7

____ 5. In a cumulative "less than" distribution, the classes are labeled using:

    (a) class marks   (c) upper class limits
    (b) lower class limits (d) class boundaries

____ 6. In a cumulative "more than" distribution, the classes are labeled using:

    (a) class marks   (c) upper class limits
    (b) lower class limits (d) class boundaries

____ 7. We can show the proportion of values falling into various class intervals by using a _____ distribution.

    (a) frequency   (c) quantitative
    (b) cumulative   (d) percentage

____ 8. In order to present numerical categories of a variable with their corresponding frequencies, we use a _____ distribution.

    (a) cumulative   (c) qualitative
    (b) quantitative   (d) percentage

____ 9. Which of the following would be a desirable property of a frequency distribution?

   (a) contains open end classes
   (b) contains more than 15 classes
   (c) contains exactly 4 classes
   (d) contains equal class intervals

____ 10. Given the frequency distribution:

Scores	Frequency
20-29	8
30-59	18

For the histogram of this distribution, the height of the 30-59 interval should be:

   (a) 18   (c) 54
   (b) 9   (d) 6

COMPLETION: Complete the following sentences by filling in the given blanks.

1. In constructing a frequency distribution from raw data, there will usually be between _____ and _____ classes.

2. The single number that best represents a given interval of a frequency distribution is called the _____.

3. In a stem-and-leaf display each digit to the right of the vertical line is called a _____.

4. Pie charts are graphical representations of _____ distributions.

5. If categories of a distribution differ in kind rather than degree, the resulting table is called a _____.

6. A bar chart of a frequency distribution is called a _____.

7. A class mark is defined as the average of _____.

8. A class interval can be defined as _____.

9. For an ogive, the horizontal axis should contain the class _____.

10. A numerical distribution is the same as a _____ distribution.

PROBLEMS

1. A sample of 80 company employees is grouped into a table based on their weekly salaries:

Salary	Frequency
100.00-149.99	15
150.00-199.99	10
200.00-249.99	30
250.00-299.99	25

Make a table providing the class limits, the class boundaries, the class marks, and the class intervals.

class limits	class boundaries	class marks	class intervals

2. From the data in Problem 1, construct a percentage distribution.

3. From the data in Problem 1, construct the following distributions.

   (a) cumulative "less than"

   (b) cumulative "greater than"

(c)   cumulative "or less"

4.   From the data in Problem 1, construct:

(a)   a histogram

(b)   an ogive for a cumulative "less than" distribution

5.   A Personnel Department has given a placement exam to 60 job applicants.   Here are the scores:

88	86	89	90	75	98
93	78	72	85	80	88
97	96	100	72	85	86
79	91	89	95	92	74
93	88	75	73	88	77
65	81	68	84	90	53
80	87	55	96	80	94
89	70	81	45	72	89
79	68	76	62	70	72
82	60	68	48	83	71

(a) Group these figures into a table having the classes 41-50, 51-60, 61-70, 71-80, 81-90, 91-100.

Scores	Tally	Frequency
41-50		
51-60		
61-70		
71-80		
81-90		
91-100		

(b) Convert the distribution of part (a) into a percentage distribution.

6. For the distribution in Problem 5, construct:

(a) a histogram

(b) a frequency polygon

7. (a) For the distribution in Problem 5, construct a cumulative "more than" distribution.

(b) Construct an ogive for the distribution in part (a).

8. (a) Given the class marks: 22, 30, 38, 46, provide (i) class boundaries and (ii) class limits for this frequency distribution.

class marks	class boundaries	class limits
22		
30		
38		
46		

(b) Given the class boundaries 30.95, 42.95, 54.95, 66.95, 78.95, provide (i) class limits and (ii) class marks for this frequency distribution.

class boundaries	class limits	class marks
30.95-42.95		
42.95-54.95		
54.95-66.95		
66.95-78.95		

9. The federal budget for a certain year designated $250 billion going for Social Security, $240 billion for defense, $30 billion for veterans' benefits, $11 billion for unemployment, $30 billion for other benefits, $7.5 billion for interest payments, and $135 billion for "other" expenses. Present this information in:

   (a) a bar chart.

   (b) a pie chart.

10. The following are the daily pizza sales in units for a local pizza restaurant for the past two weeks: 228, 252, 310, 305, 165, 182, 312, 182, 171, 285, 307, 281, 234, 175. For this data:

    (a) Construct a stem-and-leaf display with the stem labels 1, 2, and 3 (and, hence, with two-digit leaves).

    (b) Construct a stem-and-leaf display with one-digit leaves.

11. To group data on the number of potential buyers entering an automobile dealer's showroom for a given week, the sales manager uses the classes 25-49, 51-75, 75-99, 100-124, 125-149. Explain what difficulties might arise.

12. In a graph of a frequency distribution with classes 10-19, 20-29, 30-59, 60-69, explain why a histogram of the data might be misleading if all the heights of the rectangles are equal to the class frequencies. (See textbook, exercise 2.42.)

13. List the data which correspond to the following stem-and-leaf displays.

(a) 3 | 6 2 5 7 2

(b) 4** | 72, 51, 36, 23, 95

(c) 51. | 12 34 57 25 17

CHAPTER 3

SUMMARIZING DATA: MEASURES OF LOCATION

This chapter is concerned with the calculation and interpretation of
measures of location.

CHAPTER OBJECTIVES: By the end of this chapter, you should be able to:

1. Give an example of a situation in which we might consider given
    data to be (a) a population or (b) a sample. (3.1 - 3.3)

2. Find the mean for raw data. (3.4 - 3.10, 3.12, 3.16)

3. Given the mean of data and all but one of the values, find that
    value. (3.11)

4. Apply Markov's theorem. (3.15)

5. Find a geometric mean. (3.17)

6. Find an harmonic mean. (3.18)

7. Find a weighted mean. (3.19 - 3.24)

8. Find the median's position for a given sample size. (3.25, 3.26)

9. Find the median for raw data. (3.27, 3.28, 3.29b, 3.37a, 3.38a)

10. Find the median for raw data by first constructing a stem-and-leaf
    display. (3.30b, 3.31)

11. Determine the more reliable average for given data between the mean
    and the median. (3.32 - 3.34)

12. Identify the most reliable "average" in a given situation. (3.35)

13. Find the midrange for raw data. (3.36)

14. Find the two hinges for raw data. (3.37b, 3.38b, 3.39, 3.41)

15. Find the position of the two hinges for raw data. (3.40)

16. Find the mode for: (a) raw data. (3.46 - 3.49)
                        (b) categorical data.(3.50, 3.51)

17. Given grouped data, decide if the mean and/or median can be
    calculated. (3.52)

18. Find the mean for grouped data. (3.53, 3.56, 3.59, 3.62 - 3.64)

19. Find: quartiles, percentiles, deciles. (3.54b, 3.57b, 3.60b),
           (3.55b, 3.58b), (3.55a, 3.58a)

20. Rewrite a summation without the summation sign. (3.65)

21. Rewrite a sequence of terms as a summation. (3.66)

22. Evaluate a summation for particular values of the variables.
    (3.67 - 3.71)

KEY POINTS OF THE CHAPTER:

1. A population is a set of data which consists of all conceivably possible (or hypothetically possible) observations of a certain phenomenon.

2. A sample is a set of data which contains only part of the observations in the population.

3. A parameter is a description of a population. An example of a parameter is the population mean, μ.

4. A statistic is a description of a sample. An example of a statistic is the sample mean, $\bar{x}$.

5. The mean has the following desirable properties:

    (i)   It can be calculated for any set of data; it always exists.

    (ii)   A set of data has one and only one mean, so it is always unique.

    (iii) The means of many samples drawn from the same population usually do not fluctuate very widely.

6. An undesirable property of the mean is that it can be greatly affected by extreme values.

7. The median of n values is found by first arranging the data according to size and then it is defined as follows:

    The median is the middle item when n is odd, and the mean of the two middle items when n is even.

8. An advantage of the median over the mean is that it is not as affected by extreme values as is the mean. A disadvantage that the median has compared to the mean is that the medians of many samples drawn from the same population usually vary more widely than the corresponding sample means. (To obtain a clarification of this point, do exercises 3.33 and 3.34.)

9. The mode is the data value having the highest frequency.

10. A weighted mean is used when averaging quantities in which not all of them are equally important in the phenomenon being described.

11. The geometric mean of a set of n positive numbers is the nth root of their product. It is always less than the arithmetic mean unless all the numbers are equal. The geometric mean is used mainly to average ratios, rates of change, and index numbers.

12. Fractiles are numbers which divide data into two or more parts as nearly equal as they can be made. Examples of fractiles are quartiles, deciles, and percentiles.

13. There are three quartiles, Q_1, Q_2, and Q_3, which are intended to divide the data into four nearly equal parts.

14. There are nine deciles, D_1, D_2, ..., D_9, which are intended to divide the data into ten nearly equal parts.

15. There are ninety-nine <u>percentiles</u>, P_1, P_2, ..., P_{99}, which are intended to divide the data into one hundred nearly equal parts.

16. The <u>lower hinge</u> is the median of all the values less than or equal to the median of the whole set of data; the <u>upper hinge</u> is the median of all the values greater than or equal to the median of the whole set of data.

17. The <u>midquartile</u> is the mean of Q_1 and Q_2.

18. The <u>midrange</u> is the mean of the highest and lowest values in the data.

AVOIDING COMMON ERRORS:

1. <u>Finding the median</u>. Be sure to first rearrange the numbers in order of magnitude. For example, the numbers 13, 10, 20, 17, 19 must be reordered as 10, 13, 17, 19, 20 to identify 17 as the median.

2. <u>Finding the weighted mean</u>. If you want to find, say, the average price <u>per pound</u>, the sum of the weights (Σw) in the weighted mean formula is the sum of the <u>pound</u> values in the problem. This value is placed in the denominator.

KEY SYMBOLS:

$\bar{x}$ = sample mean Q_1, Q_2, Q_3 are 1st, 2nd, and 3rd quartiles.

μ = population mean

$\tilde{x}$ = sample median D_1,..., D_9 are 1st,..., 9th deciles.

$\bar{x}_w$ = weighted mean P_1,..., P_{99} are 1st,..., 99th percentiles.

KEY FORMULAS:

1. <u>Sample mean</u>   n = number of items in the sample

   $$\bar{x} = \frac{\Sigma x}{n}$$

2. <u>Population mean</u>   N = number of items in the

   $$\mu = \frac{\Sigma x}{N}$$ population

3. <u>Position of median in the data</u>   The data is arranged in numerical

   $$\frac{n+1}{2}$$ order. Then $\frac{n+1}{2}$ gives the <u>position</u>

   of the median, <u>not</u> its value.

4. <u>Weighted mean</u>

   $$\bar{x}_w = \frac{\Sigma w \cdot x}{\Sigma w}$$ The w's are the weights.

5. Geometric mean

$$g.m. = \sqrt[n]{x_1 \cdot x_2 \cdot x_3 \cdots x_n}$$

This formula is applied when the interest is in finding the average of ratios or rates of change.

6. Harmonic mean

$$h.m. = \frac{n}{\Sigma 1/x}$$

7. Grouped data

mean $\bar{x} = \dfrac{\Sigma xf}{n}$

x values are class marks.

8. Grouped data with coding

mean $\bar{x} = x_o + \dfrac{\Sigma uf}{n} \cdot c$

x_o = class mark in the original scale to which o was assigned in the new scale
c = class interval
n = number of items grouped
u = new coded class marks

9. Median for grouped data

(begin counting at bottom)

$$\tilde{x} = L + \frac{j}{f} \cdot c$$

L = lower class boundary of median class
c = class interval
j = number of items we lack when we reach L
f = frequency of median class

or

(begin counting at top)

$$\tilde{x} = U - \frac{j'}{f} \cdot c$$

U = upper class boundary of median class
j' = the number of items we lack when we reach U

10. midquartile

midquartile $= \dfrac{1}{2} (Q_1 + Q_3)$

This is a measure of central location.

11. midrange

$$\text{midrange} = \frac{(\text{highest data value} + \text{lowest data value})}{2}$$

This is a measure of central location.

MODIFIED TRUE/FALSE: If the statement is true, write true. If false, change the underlined words to make the statement true.

_____ 1. The mean of a list of numbers is <u>more</u> likely to be affected by extreme values than the median.

_____ 2. In a list of 9 numbers, the median is <u>always</u> the 5th number from either end of the list.

_____ 3. If some of the frequencies are greater than 1, the number of rows in the frequency distribution is <u>equal to</u> the size of the sample.

_____ 4. The <u>means</u> of many samples drawn from the same population usually do not fluctuate widely.

_____ 5. When calculating the mean for grouped data, the denominator is equal to the <u>number of rows</u> in the table.

_____ 6. A stem-and-leaf display is especially helpful when finding the <u>mean</u> of a set of data.

_____ 7. If the data consists of all possible observations of a certain phenomenon, it is called a <u>sample</u>.

_____ 8. The symbols $(\sum_{i=1}^{n} x_1)^2$ and $\sum_{i=1}^{n} x_1^2$ are <u>always</u> equal.

_____ 9. The midquartile is <u>always</u> equal to the median.

_____ 10. For a sample size of 15 values, if the largest value is increased, the midquartile is <u>increased</u>.

MULTIPLE CHOICE: Write the letter of the best answer in the given space.

____ 1. For a set of data which contains extreme values, the best measure of central location among the following is the:

(a) mean   (c) mode
(b) median   (d) midrange

____ 2. A stem-and-leaf display is especially helpful in finding:

(a) the mean   (c) the midrange
(b) the midquartile (d) the median

____ 3. The mean of Q_1 and Q_3 equals the

(a) midrange   (c) median
(b) the midquartile (d) mean

____ 4. When no two values are the same, which measure is exceeded by as many values as it exceeds?

(a) the median (c) the first quartile
(b) the mean   (d) the midrange

____ 5. The _____ is not a measure of central location.

(a) mean   (c) first quartile
(b) second quartile (d) midquartile

____   6. The 65th percentile is always less than:

   (a) Q_3 (c) the mean
   (b) the midquartile   (d) the median

____   7. When data contains extreme values, which of the following
           is the poorest measure of location?

   (a) the median   (c) the midrange
   (b) Q_2 (d) the midquartile

____   8. For the data 2, 10, 20, 15, 100, 30, and 90, which of the
           following measures would be changed if the 90 were changed
           to 70?

   (a) the mean   (c) the mode
   (b) the median   (d) the midrange

____   9. Which of the following measures is not equal to the other
           measures?

   (a) D_5 (c) the median
   (b) Q_3 (d) P_{50}

____ 10. For the data, 1, 2, 4, 6, 8, 12, and 15, which of the
           following measures of location is not changed if either
           the 4, 6, or 10 is removed?

   (a) the mean   (c) the midrange
   (b) the median   (d) the midquartile

COMPLETION: Complete the following sentences by filling in the given
             blanks.

1. A parameter is a value obtained from a _____ .

2. The mean is _____ larger than the median.

3. In calculating a weighted mean, the denominator is given by
    _____ .

4. The median of an odd number of values is _____ the middle
    number in the list.

5. The number which appears most often in a data set is called
    the _____ .

6. If coding is used to calculate the mean more easily for a frequency
    distribution with 7 classes, the coded value of the second lowest
    class is _____ .

7. If the mean of a set of raw data is subtracted from each of the
    numbers, the mean of the new set of data is _____ .

8. To determine the quartiles of a set of raw data, the first step
    is to _____ the data _____ .

9. The measure of location that is used to average rates of change
    is the _____ .

10. The two measures that are needed to calculate the midquartile are
    the _____ and the _____ .

24

1. The grades on a test obtained by twelve students in a class are:

   66, 70, 68, 75, 80, 86, 64, 73, 80, 94, 72, 91. For this data:

   (a) Construct a stem-and-leaf display.

   (b) Find the mean.

   (c) Find the median.

   (d) Find the mode.

2. The frequency distribution of grades on a test for a class of 30 students is given below:

grades	f
51-60	4
61-70	6
71-80	8
81-90	10
91-100	2

   Find:

   (a) the median

   (b) Q_3

25

3. Ten dieters entering a weight loss program have the following weights (in pounds) at the start of the program:

182, 160, 120, 140, 155, 136, 115, 190, 144, 200.

For this data:

(a) Construct a stem-and-leaf display.

(b) Find the median.

4. The number of sales of homes having two bedrooms or less in a state for a ten-week period in 1987 is given in the following table:

Price (in dollars)	Number of homes sold
95000-109999	233
110000-124999	204
125000-139999	71
140000-154999	18
155000-169999	9

For a two-bedroom or less home in this state during the given period, find:

(a) the mean price.

(b) the median price.

5. An investor purchased a particular stock on several occasions at different prices:

Number of shares	Price per share
100	$5
200	4
400	2

What is the investor's breakeven price? (i.e., what is his average price per share?)

6. The prices (in dollars) of 16 film video casettes on sale at a video store are:

38, 32, 38, 13, 23, 38, 32, 28, 27, 32, 23, 27, 25, 32, 27, 30.

For this data, find:

(a) the mean.

(b) the median.

(c) the mode.

(d) the midrange.

7. The following is the distribution of weights (in pounds) of
    40 students entered in a hamburger eating contest:

weights (lbs.)	frequency
100-120	3
121-140	8
141-160	10
161-180	9
181-200	10

Find:

(a) D_7

(b) P_{30}

8. Suppose your capital today is $1000 and in each of the following
    four years your capital increases to $1600, $2000, $2400, and
    $2640, respectively. Find the average yearly percentage increase.
    (Hint: First find the percentage that each succeeding year is
    based on the value in the preceding year. Then find the geometric
    mean of the percentages.)

9. If an investor buys $1000 worth of stock at $20 per share,
    $1000 worth at $15 per share, and $1000 worth at $30 per share,
    what is the average price per share?

10. Write each expression as a summation:

(a) $x_1^2 + x_2^2 + \ldots + x_{15}^2$

(b) $2y_3 f_3 + 2y_4 f_4 + 2y_5 f_5 + 2y_6 f_6$

11. Write each expression without summation signs:

(a) $\displaystyle\sum_{i=2}^{5} x_i y_i$

(b) $\displaystyle\sum_{i=1}^{3} (y_j - z_j)$

12. If $x_1=3$, $x_2=4$, $x_3=1$, $x_4=5$, $f_1=1$, $f_2=2$, $f_3=2$, $f_4=1$, find:

(a) $\displaystyle\sum_{i=1}^{4} x_i f_i$

(b) $\displaystyle\sum_{i=2}^{4} x_i^2$

13. Determine which of the three properties of quartiles listed on page 52 of the textbook are satisfied by the hinges and the median when:

(a) n = 15

(b) n = 16

CHAPTER 4

SUMMARIZING DATA: MEASURES OF VARIATION

This chapter is concerned with the calculation and interpretation of
measures of variation.

CHAPTER OBJECTIVES: By the end of this chapter, you should be able to:

1. Find the range for raw data. (4.1 - 4.4, 4.6, 4.8)

2. Find the interquartile range. (4.5, 4.7)

3. Using a stem-and-leaf display, find the semi-interquartile range.
    (4.9)

4. Find the standard deviation of a sample using the definition or
    computing formula. (4.10 - 4.15)

5. Find the standard deviation of a population. (4.18)

6. Using Chebyshev's theorem, find:

    (a) the fraction of data contained in a given interval.
         (4.22 - 4.24, 4.26, 4.27)

    (b) the interval which contains a given fraction of data. (4.25)

7. Apply the empirical rule. (4.26, 4.28b)

8. Compare the relative values of data using z-scores. (4.29 - 4.32)

9. Find the coefficient of variation. (4.33 - 4.36)

10. Find the standard deviation for grouped data.
     (4.40b, 4.42, 4.44, 4.46, 4.48)

11. Calculate the Pearsonian coefficient of skewness.
     (4.41, 4.43, 4.45, 4.47, 4.49)

12. Draw a boxplot. (4.50 - 4.54, 4.56, 4.58)

KEY POINTS OF THE CHAPTER:

1. The range is a measure of variation which equals the highest
    number minus the lowest number.

2. The standard deviation is a measure of variation which gives the
    spread of the data about the mean.

3. The variance is the square of the standard deviation.

4. A distribution with a tail to the left is negatively skewed; if
    it has a tail to the right, it is positively skewed.

5. A z-score is the number of standard deviations that a data value
    is above or below the mean.

6. Chebyshev's theorem states that for any set of data and any constant $k > 1$, at least $1 - \dfrac{1}{k^2}$ of the data must lie between $\bar{x} - ks$ and $\bar{x} + ks$.

7. The empirical rule says that if a distribution has the general shape of the cross section of a bell, approximately:

   (1)   68% of the data lies between $\bar{x} - s$ and $\bar{x} + s$.

   (2)   95% of the data lies between $\bar{x} - 2s$ and $\bar{x} + 2s$.

   (3)   99.7% of the data lies between $\bar{x} - 3s$ and $\bar{x} + 3s$.

8. The coefficient of variation gives the dispersion of the data relative to the level of magnitude of the data.

9. An outlier is a value so far removed from the body of the data that it may be due to extraneous causes, such as an error in measurement or errors in recording the data.

10. A boxplot consists of a rectangle which extends from the lower hinge to the upper hinge, or from Q_1 to Q_3, lines drawn from the smallest value to the lower hinge and from the upper hinge to the largest, and a line at the median which divides the rectangle into two parts.

AVOIDING COMMON ERRORS:

Finding the standard deviation for grouped data:

   (i)   A column for xf must be computed by multiplying each data value by the corresponding frequency.

   (ii)   A column for $x^2 f$ must be computed by multiplying the square of each data value by the corresponding frequency.

   (iii)   The n value in the computing formula is equal to the sum of the frequencies (not the number of rows unless all frequency values are 1).

KEY SYMBOLS:

σ^2 = population variance	s^2 = sample variance
σ = population standard deviation	s = sample standard deviation
z = z-score	SK = Pearsonian coefficient of skewness

31

KEY FORMULAS:

1. Range

   Range = highest data value – lowest data value

2. Population variance

   $\sigma^2 = \dfrac{\Sigma(x-\mu)^2}{N}$

3. Population standard deviation

   $\sigma = \sqrt{\dfrac{\Sigma(x-\mu)^2}{N}}$

4. Sample variance

   $s^2 = \dfrac{\Sigma(x-\bar{x})^2}{n-1}$

5. Sample standard deviation

   $s = \sqrt{\dfrac{\Sigma(x-\bar{x})^2}{n-1}}$

6. Sample standard deviation (computing formula)

   $s = \sqrt{\dfrac{n(\Sigma x^2) - (\Sigma x)^2}{n(n-1)}}$

7. z-score (converting to standard units)

   $z = \dfrac{x-\bar{x}}{s}$ or $z = \dfrac{x-\mu}{\sigma}$

8. Coefficient of variation

   $V = \dfrac{s}{\bar{x}} \cdot 100$ or $V = \dfrac{\sigma}{\mu} \cdot 100$

9. Standard deviation for frequency distributions

   $s = \sqrt{\dfrac{\Sigma(x-\bar{x})^2 f}{n-1}}$

10. Standard deviation for frequency distributions (computing formula)

$$s = \sqrt{\frac{n(\Sigma x^2 \cdot f) - (\Sigma x f)^2}{n(n-1)}}$$
n = sum of the frequencies (the total number in the sample)

11. Standard deviation for frequency distributions (grouped data with coding - computing formula)

$$s = c\sqrt{\frac{n(\Sigma u^2 \cdot f) - (\Sigma u \cdot f)^2}{n(n-1)}}$$
n = number of items grouped
u = new coded class marks

12. Pearsonian coefficient of skewness

$$SK = \frac{3(\text{mean} - \text{median})}{\text{standard deviation}}$$
The closer to 0 the value is, the more symmetric the distribution is.

13. Interquartile range

$$Q_3 - Q_1$$
This is a measure of variation which is an improvement on the range.

14. Semi-interquartile range

$$\frac{1}{2}(Q_3 - Q_1)$$
This is a measure of variation which is an improvement on the range.

15. Coefficient of quartile variation

$$\frac{Q_3 - Q_1}{Q_1 + Q_3} \cdot 100$$
This is a measure of relative variation which can replace the coefficient of variation.

MODIFIED TRUE/FALSE: If the statement is true, write true. If false, change the underlined words to make the statement true.

_____ 1. A measure of variation that is greatly affected by extreme values is the standard deviation.

_____ 2. Distributions having a tail to the right are called negatively skewed.

_____ 3. The midrange is a measure of variation.

_____ 4. The standard deviation of the numbers 7,7,7,...,7 is zero.

_____ 5. In a boxplot, if the median is close to the left side of the box, the data is symmetric.

_____ 6. An outlier is an extreme value in the data that may be due to an error in measurement.

_____ 7. A measure of variation that depends on all the data is the range.

_____ 8. The symbol s represents the <u>population</u> standard deviation.

_____ 9. If the mean of a set of data is negative, then the standard deviation is <u>negative</u>.

_____ 10. If the mean and standard deviation of a set of data are 60 and 5, respectively, then the values 50 and 70 have <u>z-scores</u> which are equal in magnitude, but opposite in sign.

<u>MULTIPLE CHOICE</u>: Write the letter of the best answer in the given space.

____ 1. Which of the following is a measure of variation?

    (a) the mean   (c) the midquartile
    (b) the median   (d) the semi-interquartile range

____ 2. In order to compare the values of two numbers which belong to different sets of data, we use:

    (a) z-scores   (c) the coefficient of variation
    (b) Chebyshev's theorem   (d) the semi-interquartile range

____ 3. The measure of variation among the following that is most affected by outliers is the:

    (a) range   (c) standard deviation
    (b) interquartile range   (d) variance

____ 4. The _____ is not a measure of variation.

    (a) range   (c) semi-interquartile range
    (b) midrange   (d) mean deviation

____ 5. A set of data has a mean of 80 and a standard deviation of 5. To determine two values that contain at least 8/9 of the data, we use:

    (a) Chebyshev's theorem   (c) z-scores
    (b) the coefficient of   (d) the empirical rule
        variation

____ 6. In order to measure the dispersion of a set of data relative to its level of magnitude, we use:

    (a) z-scores   (c) the coefficient of variation
    (b) Chebyshev's theorem   (d) the empirical rule

____ 7. Which of the following symbols represents a sample value, not a population value?

    (a) μ (c) σ

    (b) $\bar{x}$ (d) N

___ 8. The degree of symmetry of a distribution is given by:

       (a) the standard deviation   (c) SK
       (b) the interquartile range   (d) Q_3

___ 9. Which of the following does not provide an application of the standard deviation?

       (a) z-scores   (c) the coefficient of variation
       (b) Chebyshev's theorem   (d) the midquartile

___ 10. The interquartile range is a better measure of variation than:

       (a) the range   (c) the standard deviation
       (b) the mean deviation   (d) the variance

COMPLETION: Complete the following sentences by filling in the given blanks.

1. One advantage of the computing formula for the standard deviation is that it does not require calculating the _____.

2. The number of standard deviations a value lies above or below the mean is given by a _____.

3. The symbol σ denotes the _____.

4. A denominator of (n - 1) in the defining formula for a standard deviation indicates that the formula measures the variation of a _____.

5. A disadvantage that the range has compared to the standard deviation is that the range is _____.

6. If a distribution has the general shape of the cross section of a bell, then the _____ allows for a stronger statement than Chebyshev's theorem.

7. In order to compare the variability of several populations having different magnitude levels, we should use the _____.

8. The closer the Pearsonian coefficient of skewness is to _____, the more symmetric the distribution is.

9. When drawing a boxplot, we usually omit _____ from the data.

10. The three measures that are needed to calculate the Pearsonian coefficient of skewness are the mean, the median, and the _____.

PROBLEMS:

1. The grades on a test of twelve students in a class are:

    66, 70, 68, 75, 80, 86, 64, 73, 80, 94, 72, 91

    Find:

    (a) the range of the grades.

    (b) the standard deviation of the grades.

    (c) the variance of the grades.

2. The frequency distribution of grades on a test for a class of
    30 students is given below:

grades	f
51-60	4
61-70	6
71-80	8
81-90	10
91-100	2

    Find:

    (a) the variance of the grades.

    (b) the standard deviation of the grades.

3. Ten dieters entering a weight loss program have the following weights (in pounds) at the start of the program:

182, 160, 120, 140, 155, 136, 115, 190, 144, 200.

For this data:

(a) Find the hinges.

(b) Construct a boxplot.

(c) Using the hinges as quartiles, find the interquartile range.

4. For the data in Problem 3:

(a) Find the variance (if the data is viewed as a sample).

(b) Find the range.

5. The number of sales of homes having two bedrooms or less in a state for a ten-week period in 1987 is given in the following table:

Price (in dollars)	Number of homes sold
95000-109999	233
110000-124999	204
125000-139999	71
140000-154999	18
155000-169999	9

For a two-bedroom or less home in this state during the given period, find:

(a) the variance of the prices.

(b) the standard deviation of the prices.

6. Two companies have the following sales results for a particular month.

		Company 1	Company 2
(average sales per worker)	$\bar{x}$	$8000	$7500
(standard dev. of sales)	s	500	300

(a) A salesperson with $6000 of sales has lower sales relative to the mean in which of the two companies?

(b) In company 1, at least what percentage of salespersons have sales between $7000 and $9000?

(c) In company 1, between what values does at least 35/36 of the salespersons' sales fall?

(d) Give the coefficient of variation of the sales of each of the two companies.

7. The prices (in dollars) of 16 film video casettes on sale at a video store are:

38, 32, 38, 13, 23, 38, 32, 28, 27, 32, 23, 27, 25, 32, 27, 30.

For this data, find:

(a) the range.

(b) the standard deviation (if the data is viewed as a population).

(c) the Pearsonian coefficient of skewness.

8. Draw a boxplot for the data in Problem 7.

9. The following is a list of the numbers of dollars a sample of students say they are willing to spend for a present for a close friend:

       Males: 25, 80, 30, 50, 45, 30, 260, 60, 50

     Females: 15, 35, 60, 55, 40, 90, 100, 25, 30

(a) Find the range for the entire group.

(b) Find the standard deviation for the females.

(c) Find the interquartile range for the males.

10. A sample of college sophomores, juniors, and seniors were asked how many hours per week they spend daydreaming during their waking hours. Here are the results:

	Sophomores	Juniors	Seniors
mean	10 hrs.	14 hrs.	24 hrs.
standard deviation	2 hrs.	4 hrs.	6 hrs.

(a) One of the juniors daydreams for 8 hours per week, one of the seniors 18 hours. Which of the two students, the junior or the senior, daydreams for more time relative to his/her classification?

(b) At least 8/9 of the sophomores must daydream between what two numbers of hours?

(c) At least what percent of the juniors daydream between 6 and 22 hours?

11. For the data in problem 10, if the distribution has approximately the shape of a cross section of a bell, approximately 68% of the seniors daydream between what two numbers of hours?

12. For the data in problem 10, for which of the three classifications, sophomores, juniors, or seniors, does the data have the greatest variability relative to its own average number of daydreaming hours?

13. The mean, median, and standard deviation of a list of numbers are 128, 160, and 8.2. Suppose that the number 25 is added to each number. What are the new values of the following descriptive measures?

    (a) the mean

    (b) the median

    (c) the standard deviation

    (d) the variance

14. How does the interquartile range compare to the range when the distribution is shaped like:

    (a) the cross section of a bell?

    (b) a U?

CHAPTER 5

POSSIBILITIES AND PROBABILITIES

This chapter introduces the subject of probability with the following topics:

    (1) counting problems

    (2) elementary probability problems

<u>CHAPTER OBJECTIVES</u>: By the end of this chapter, you should be able to:

1. Construct a tree diagram to represent different possibilities. (5.1 - 5.6)

2. Apply the multiplication of choices principle to count the number of possibilities. (5.7 - 5.15)

3. Evaluate statements involving factorials. (5.16, 5.17)

4. Find the number of permutations. (5.18 - 5.25)

5. Find the number of permutations when some of the digits are identical. (5.26, 5.27)

6. Find the number of permutations in which n distinct objects can be arranged in a circle. (5.28)

7. Find the number of combinations. (5.29 - 5.39)

8. Find probabilities using the classical probability concept. (5.46 - 5.55)

9. Find probabilities involving combinations and the classical probability concept. (5.56 - 5.60)

10. Find probabilities using the frequency concept of probability. (5.61 - 5.67)

<u>KEY POINTS OF THE CHAPTER:</u>

1. <u>Multiplication of Choices (generalized)</u>. If a choice consists of k steps, the first of which can be made in n_1 ways and for each of these the second can be made in n_2 ways..., and for each of these the kth can be made in n_k ways, then the whole choice can be made in $n_1 \cdot n_2 \cdot \ldots \cdot n_k$ ways.

2. When using the multiplication of choices principle, the n values are the number of choices at each step. The k value is the number of steps. For example, for 7 multiple choice questions with 3 choices each there are $3 \cdot 3 \cdot 3 \cdot 3 \cdot 3 \cdot 3 \cdot 3 = 3^7$ ways of answering the questions (7 <u>steps</u>, 3 <u>choices</u> each), <u>not</u> $7 \cdot 7 \cdot 7 = 7^3$.

3. Permutations. When we count objects where order makes a difference, we are counting permutations, and so we use ${}_nP_r$.

Example: When we count the number of 3 letter words that can be formed from the 6 letters a, b, c, d, e, f, we are counting permutations. (e.g., the word abc is different from the word bac.)

4. Combinations. When we count objects without concern for order, we are counting combinations.

Example: When we count the number of 3 person committees that can be formed from the 6 people whose names are a, b, c, d, e, f, we are counting combinations. (e.g., the committee abc is the same as the committee bac.)

5. The Classical Probability Concept. If there are n equally likely possibilities, one of which must occur, and s possibilities are regarded as favorable, or as "successes," then the probability of a success is given by the ratio $\frac{s}{n}$.

6. The Frequency Interpretation of Probability. The probability of an event is the proportion of the time that events of the same kind will occur in the long run.

7. The Law of Large Numbers. If a situation, trial, or experiment is repeated again and again, the proportion of successes will tend to approach the probability that any one outcome will be a success.

8. Random Selection Example. If 3 of 20 tires are defective and 5 of the 20 are randomly chosen for inspection, what is the probability that exactly 2 of the defective tires will be chosen?

Solution: We use the classical probability formula $\frac{s}{n} = \frac{\text{number of successes}}{\text{number of trials}}$. The number of ways of selecting 5 tires from 20 is $\binom{20}{5}$. The number of ways of selecting 2 defectives from 5 defectives is $\binom{5}{2}$. The number of ways of selecting 3 nondefectives from the 15 nondefectives is $\binom{15}{3}$. Thus, the number of ways of selecting 5 tires, 2 of which are defective and the remaining 3 are not defective is $\binom{5}{2} \cdot \binom{15}{3}$ (by the multiplication of choices principle).

Then our final answer in symbols is $\dfrac{\binom{5}{2}\binom{15}{3}}{\binom{20}{5}}$

AVOIDING COMMON ERRORS:

1. When using the multiplication of choices principle, it is correct to multiply, and not add the individual numbers of choices. For example, in Exercise 5.7, the answer is 6·5, not 6+5.

2. It is important to place the base and exponent in the correct place in certain applications of the multiplication of choices principle. For example, in Exercise 5.14 the answer is 2^{12}, not 12^2.

3. It is important to distinguish correctly between a permutations and a combinations problem.

    Example: Exercise 5.23 is a permutations problem, since order is relevant, so the answer is $_9P_3 = 9 \cdot 8 \cdot 7$ and not $\binom{9}{3} = \frac{9 \cdot 8 \cdot 7}{3 \cdot 2 \cdot 1}$. Exercise 5.29 is a combinations problem, since order is not relevant, so the answer is $\binom{13}{2} = \frac{13 \cdot 12}{2 \cdot 1}$ and not $_{13}P_2$.

KEY FORMULAS:

1. The number of permutations of r objects chosen from n distinct objects

    $$_nP_r = n(n-1)(n-2)\ldots(n-r+1)$$

    or

    $$_nP_r = \frac{n!}{(n-r)!}$$

2. The number of permutations of n objects taken all together

    $$_nP_n = n!$$

3. The number of combinations of r objects chosen from n distinct objects

    $$\binom{n}{r} = \frac{n(n-1)(n-2)\ldots(n-r+1)}{r!}$$

    or

    $$\binom{n}{r} = \frac{n!}{r!(n-r)!}$$

4. Rule for binomial coefficients

    $$\binom{n}{r} = \binom{n}{n-r}$$

MODIFIED TRUE/FALSE: If the statement is true, write true. If false, change the underlined words to make the statement true.

_____ 1. An accounting firm is selecting 3 accounts to audit out of a total of 11 accounts. The number of ways the firm can select the 3 accounts is given by $\underline{11 \cdot 10 \cdot 9}$.

_____ 2. The number of 3 person committees that can be formed from 8 people is <u>the same as</u> the number of 3 letter words that can be <u>formed from</u> the letters a, b, c, d, e, f, g, h with no repetitions.

_____ 3. The probability of rolling a three in one roll of an ordinary die is 1/6. This is an example of the <u>frequency</u> interpretation of probability.

_____ 4. The expression 7!3! is <u>equal to</u> 10!

_____ 5. The expression 11! is <u>equal to</u> $\frac{12!}{12}$.

_____ 6. The number of 6 letter words that can be formed from the word OBJECT is <u>6!</u>.

_____ 7. The <u>multiplication of choices principle</u> states that if an experiment is repeated again and again, the proportion of successes will tend to approach the probability that any one outcome will be a success.

_____ 8. A magazine reader wants to select 3 magazines to subscribe to from a choice of 8 magazines. The number of ways that this can be done is $\underline{\frac{8 \cdot 7 \cdot 6 \cdot 5 \cdot 4 \cdot 3 \cdot 2 \cdot 1}{3 \cdot 2 \cdot 1}}$.

_____ 9. The number of 7 digit phone numbers that can be formed that begin with 353 with not all of the last 4 digits zero is $\underline{9^4}$.

_____ 10. The number of ways that 4 students can be selected from 30 students in a class to fill 4 seats (if order matters) is $\underline{\frac{30 \cdot 29 \cdot 28 \cdot 27}{4 \cdot 3 \cdot 2 \cdot 1}}$.

<u>MULTIPLE CHOICE</u>: Write the letter of the best answer in the given space.

____ 1. Which of the following is false?

(a) $13! = 13 \cdot 12 \cdot 11 \cdot 10$ (c) $\binom{5}{2} = 10$

(b) $_8P_2 = 28$ (d) $\binom{15}{4} = \frac{15 \cdot 14 \cdot 13 \cdot 12}{4 \cdot 3 \cdot 2}$

____ 2. A multiple choice test has 10 questions with 4 choices for each question. The number of ways a student can answer all 10 questions is:

(a) $10 \cdot 4$ (b) 4^{10} (c) 10^4 (d) $10+4$

____ 3. Two restaurants are to be built at locations selected from a choice of 11 locations. The number of ways of selecting the locations for the two restaurants is:

(a) $\frac{11!}{2}$ (b) $11 \cdot 11$ (c) $\frac{11 \cdot 10}{2}$ (d) $11 \cdot 10$

____ 4. In an 8 horse race, the number of ways that 3 horses can finish first, second, and third (order matters) is given by:

(a) $8 \cdot 3$ (b) 8^3 (c) $8 \cdot 7 \cdot 6$ (d) $\frac{8 \cdot 7 \cdot 6}{3 \cdot 2 \cdot 1}$

5. The probability of selecting a defective component from 20 components, 3 of which are defective, is 3/20. This is an example of:

   (a) the classical probability concept
   (b) the frequency interpretation of probability
   (c) the law of large numbers
   (d) subjective probability

6. A company employs 40 skilled and 30 unskilled workers. Twenty-five of the skilled workers and 17 of the unskilled are college graduates. If an employee of the company is selected at random, the probability that the person picked will not be a college graduate is:

   (a) $\frac{2}{5}$ (b) $\frac{25}{70}$ (c) $\frac{12}{28}$ (d) $\frac{17}{70}$

7. Which of the following is not true of the symbol $\binom{11}{3}$?

   (a) It is used when order does not matter.
   (b) Its value is less than $_{11}P_3$.
   (c) It is the number of 3 letter words that can be formed from 11 letters.
   (d) It is the number of 3 person committees that can be formed from a group of 11 people.

8. In the past 8 Friday nights, a student has gone to the same rock music club on 5 occasions. The claim that the probability is 5/8 that the student will attend the same club next Friday is based on:

   (a) the classical probability concept
   (b) the frequency interpretation of probability
   (c) the law of large numbers
   (d) subjective probability

9. A student has time to see 4 films on his vacation. If he is selecting the movies from a total of 9 choices, how many ways can he choose the films?

   (a) $9 \cdot 4$ (c) $\frac{9!}{4!}$
   (b) $9 \cdot 8 \cdot 7 \cdot 6$ (d) $\frac{9 \cdot 8 \cdot 7 \cdot 6}{4 \cdot 3 \cdot 2 \cdot 1}$

10. A student has 7 items of living room furniture and room for 5 items in his living room. Assuming that any of the 7 items can be placed in any of the 5 locations, in how many ways can the student arrange his living room with the furniture?

    (a) $\binom{7}{5}$ (c) $7 \cdot 6 \cdot 5 \cdot 4 \cdot 3$
    (b) $7 \cdot 6$ (d) $7 \cdot 5$

: Complete the following sentences by filling in the given
              blanks.

1. The number of 5-player basketball teams that can be formed from
    a group of 11 players is _____.

2. The value of $\binom{7}{3}$ is _____.

3. The value $_7P_3$ is _____.

4. The symbol $\binom{20}{13}$ can be rewritten symbolically as _____.

5. The probability of selecting a face card in one draw of a card from
    an ordinary deck is _____.

6. The factorial notation for $_7P_7$ is _____.

7. The factorial notation for $_8P_5$ is _____.

8. A restaurant menu has 8 main courses, 5 appetizers, 6 desserts,
    and 4 beverages. The number of ways that a patron can select
    a meal with one appetizer, one main course, one dessert, and
    one beverage is _____.

9. If the President is considering the elimination of 7 federal
    programs but is selecting only 3 of the 7 to eliminate, the
    number of ways he can select the programs is _____.

10. A woman who is furnishing her apartment is selecting a sofa, a
     lounge chair, and a bookcase. If she has 5 sofas, 8 lounge chairs,
     and 3 bookcases to choose from, the number of ways that she can
     select the furniture is _____.

PROBLEMS

1. A student can play 0, 1, or 2 hours of racquetball on any given
    night. Construct a tree diagram to determine the number of ways
    that in 3 nights he can play for a total of:

    (a) 4 hours

    (b) 5 hours

2. Give the number of ways a student can mark her answers to a multiple choice test if there are:

   (a) 8 questions with 3 choices each

   (b) 3 questions with 8 choices each

   (c) 10 questions, with 4 choices each for the first 3 questions and 5 choices each for the next 7 questions

3. There are 6 baseball teams in the American League's eastern division. In how many ways can:

   (a) 3 teams finish first, second, and third?

   (b) all 6 teams finish first through sixth?

4. A new campus project requires a committee of 5 students which will include 2 seniors and 3 juniors. There are 6 available seniors and 8 available juniors. In how many ways:

   (a) can the students be chosen?

   (b) can the required committee be chosen?

(c) can the committee be chosen from the same available students if there are no restrictions on the number of juniors or seniors on the committee?

5. A shipment of 12 television sets contains one that is damaged. In how many ways can an inspector choose 3 of the televisions to inspect so that:

(a) the defective is not included?

(b) the defective is included?

6. A balanced die is rolled. Find the probability of getting:

(a) a value of at least 2

(b) an odd number

7. Two cards are drawn from a well-shuffled deck of 52 playing cards. What are the probabilities of getting:

(a) two jacks?

(b) two clubs?

(c) an ace and a king?

8. A student is planning the music she will play at a party she will have. If she has 15 record albums and wants to select 6 to play, in how many ways can she select the albums if she believes that:

    (a) the order of the records matters?

    (b) the order of the records does not matter?

9. If 3 of 16 tax returns contain errors, and 7 of them are randomly chosen for audit, what is the probability that:

    (a) exactly 2 of the returns with errors are audited?

    (b) all 3 of the returns with errors are audited?

    (c) none of the returns with errors is audited?

10. (a) Two vice presidents are to be selected from the division managers in a certain company. If there are 9 division managers, in how many ways can the vice presidents be selected?

(b) After the vice presidents are selected, 3 other promotions will be granted. From the remaining division managers, in how many ways can the new promotions be granted?

11. (a) How many permutations are there of the letters in the word "distinction"?

(b) In how many ways can 12 persons be arranged in a circle?

12. Two families, each consisting of a husband, a wife, two sons, and one daughter, are planning to see a movie together and sit together in the same row. In how many ways can they be seated if:

(a) each family is to sit together?

(b) all the males are to sit together?

(c) all the children are to sit together?

13. A Cable TV Company has 10 channel offerings. One option is that a subscriber may select any 4 channels. In how many ways may a subscriber make his/her selection?

14. I have 11 shirts, but only 4 hangers. In how many ways can I choose 4 of the shirts to hang in which the arrangement of the shirts in my closet makes a difference to me?

15. A group of investors wants to hire a team of 4 accountants and 2 financial planners. If the investors are considering 8 accountants and 5 financial planners:

    (a) How many 6-person teams can be hired under the given conditions?

    (b) How many 6-person teams can be hired if no attention is paid to profession?

51

CHAPTER 6

SOME RULES OF PROBABILITY

This chapter deals with the following topics of probability:

(1) what we mean by statements involving probabilities

(2) how probabilities are determined

(3) how to apply the mathematical rules of probability

CHAPTER OBJECTIVES: By the end of this chapter, you should be able to:

1. Express an event in symbols and also in words.
    (6.1, 6.3 - 6.5, 6.7, 6.12)

2. From pairs of events, recognize those pairs which are mutually
    exclusive. (6.2, 6.6, 6.8, 6.11, 6.13c, 6.16)

3. List the elements of a sample space. (6.9, 6.10)

4. Draw a diagram to represent a sample space. (6.10a, 6.13a)

5. List the elements of an event. (6.5, 6.10b, 6.12, 6.13b, 6.14, 6.15)

6. Given a Venn diagram, express in words which events are represented
    by given regions. (6.17 - 6.20, 6.24)

7. From a verbal description of regions in a Venn diagram, indicate
    the regions described. (6.23, 6.25)

8. Prove a set equality using Venn diagrams. (6.27)

9. State in words what probabilities are described by a given
    probability symbol. (6.28, 6.30)

10. Rewrite a verbal description of a probability situation in
    symbolic form. (6.29, 6.31)

11. Recognize violations of elementary probability laws from given
    probabilities. (6.32 - 6.35)

12. Calculate probabilities using one or more of the addition rules
    and complement rule if the problem is given (a) verbally or
    (b) symbolically. (6.39, 6.42, 6.44, 6.56 - 6.75)

13. Convert a given probability to odds. (6.46 - 6.48)

14. Convert odds to a probability. (6.49, 6.50, 6.54 - 6.56)

15. State the meaning of given symbolic statements of conditional
    probabilities. (6.77, 6.79, 6.81)

16. Express given descriptions of conditional probabilities in
    symbolic form. (6.76, 6.78, 6.80)

17. Calculate conditional and other related probabilities.
    (6.82, 6.84, 6.86 - 6.89)

18. Calculate probabilities in "and" questions using the multiplication formulas. (6.90 - 6.97, 6.101 - 6.108)

19. Determine if given events are independent. (6.98 - 6.100)

20. Calculate conditional probabilities using Bayes formula. (6.109 - 6.119, 6.121)

KEY POINTS OF THE CHAPTER:

1. An experiment refers to any process of observation or measurement. The results one obtains from an experiment are called the outcomes of the experiment.

2. The set of all possible outcomes of an experiment is called a sample space. Any subset of a sample space is called an event.

3. Two events are called mutually exclusive if they cannot both occur at the same time.

4. The union of two events X and Y, denoted by X∪Y (read "X or Y") is the event which consists of all elements either in event X or in event Y, or in both.

5. The intersection of two events X and Y, denoted by X∩Y (read "X and Y") is the event which consists of all the elements (outcomes) contained in both X and Y.

6. The complement of X, denoted by X' (read "not X") is the event which consists of all the elements (outcomes) of the sample space that are not contained in X.

7. A Venn diagram is a method of pictorially representing a sample space by means of a rectangle. Events are represented in the Venn diagram by means of circles or parts of circles within the rectangle.

8. The probability of any event must be at least 0 and at most 1.

9. The probability of any sample space is equal to 1; symbolically, $P(S) = 1$ for any sample space S.

10. If two events A and B are mutually exclusive, then $P(A∩B) = 0$.

11. If two events A and B are independent, then $P(A∩B) = P(A)P(B)$. The $P(A∪B) = P(A) + P(B) - P(A)P(B)$ if A and B are independent.

12. The probability of at least one of two events A and B occurring can be written $P(A∪B)$.

AVOIDING COMMON ERRORS:

1. The union of two events is often confused with the intersection of the two events.

   (a) A∪B is the collection of all elements in A together with all elements in B.

   (b) A∩B is the collection of all elements that are present in both A and B simultaneously.

Example:

If A = {1, 2, 3, 4}   B = {3, 4, 5, 6}
Then A∪B = {1, 2, 3, 4, 5, 6}
        A∩B = {3, 4}

2. If two events are independent, then they cannot be mutually exclusive.

    Example: If A is the event that the Yankees win a baseball game and B is the event that the Celtics win a basketball game, A and B are presumably unrelated, and so are independent events. Since they can both occur at the same time, they are not mutually exclusive.

3. If two events are mutually exclusive, they cannot be independent.

    Example: If A occurs, B cannot, so that A affects B. Then A and B are not independent.

4. If you are asked an "and" question, the general multiplication rules may be appropriate. The conditional formula is not appropriate for an "and" question.

5. If you are asked a conditional question (e.g., one that has "given that" in the question part of the problem) the conditional formula may be appropriate. The general multiplication rule ("and" formula) is not appropriate here.

6. It is acceptable to add the probabilities of two events when:

    (a) you are asked an "or" question, and
    (b) the two events are mutually exclusive.
         Then use $P(A∪B) = P(A) + P(B)$

7. It is acceptable to multiply the probabilities of two events when:

    (a) you are asked an "and" question, and
    (b) the two events are independent.
         Then use $P(A∩B) = P(A)P(B)$.

KEY FORMULAS:

Basic Probability Facts

1. $P(A) \geq 0$ for any event A

2. $P(S) = 1$ for any sample space S

3. $P(A) \leq 1$ for any event A

4. $P(\phi) = 0$

Mathematical Rules of Probability

1. Special Addition Rules

    $P(A∪B) = P(A) + P(B)$ if A and B are mutually exclusive.

54

2. Complementary Events

$$P(A') = 1 - P(A)$$

3. Addition Rule--any two events (used in an "or" question)

$$P(A \cup B) = P(A) + P(B) - P(A \cap B)$$

4. Addition Rule--k mutually exclusive events

$$P(A_1 \cup A_2 \cup \ldots \cup A_k) = P(A_1) + P(A_2) + \ldots + P(A_k)$$
for any mutually exclusive events A_1, A_2, ..., A_k

5. Conditional Probability Definition Formula (used in conditional questions containing expressions such as "given that" and "if..., find the probability...")

$$P(A/B) = \frac{P(A \cap B)}{P(B)} \quad \text{if } P(B) \neq 0$$

6. General Multiplication Rules

$$P(A \cap B) = P(B)P(A/B)$$
$$P(A \cap B) = P(A)P(B/A)$$
(used in an "and" question)

Independent Events

7. $P(A \cap B) = P(A)P(B)$ if A and B are independent events

8. $P(A/B) = P(A)$ if A and B are independent events

9. $P(A \cup B) = P(A) + P(B) - P(A)P(B)$ if A and B are independent events

Miscellaneous Probability Facts

10. $P(A \cap B) = 0$ if A and B are mutually exclusive events

11. $P(A \cap B) + (P A \cap B') = P(A)$ for any events A and B

12. $P\{(A \cap B)'\} = P(A' \cup B')$

13. $P\{(A \cup B)'\} = P(A' \cap B')$

14. The Relationship of Odds to Probabilities

If the probability of an event is p, the odds for its occurrence are a to b, where $\frac{a}{b} = \frac{p}{1-p}$

15. Formula Relating Probabilities to Odds

If the odds are a to b that an event will occur, the probability of its occurrence is $p = \frac{a}{a+b}$

MODIFIED TRUE/FALSE: If the statement is true, write true. If false, change the underlined words to make the statement true.

_____ 1. The probability of A given B can sometimes be expressed as P(A∩B) .

_____ 2. If P(A) = $\frac{2}{5}$ and P(B) = $\frac{4}{5}$, then P(A∪B) must be greater than 1.

_____ 3. Two events are independent if they cannot both occur at the same time.

_____ 4. If A and B are two events, the probability that at least one of the two events occurs can be represented by P(A∪B).

_____ 5. The expressions A∪B and (A∩B)' are equal.

_____ 6. The expressions A'∩B' and (A∩B)' are equal.

_____ 7. To calculate the probability that both of two events will occur, we would most likely use the conditional formula.

_____ 8. If the probability of an event A is unaffected by the probability of an event B, then the events A and B are mutually exclusive.

_____ 9. The events of drawing a ten and a jack on a single draw of one card from an ordinary deck of fifty-two cards are independent events.

_____ 10. If A is the event of rolling a 3 on a roll of a die and B is the event of rolling at least a 3 on a second roll of the die, then the events A and B are independent.

MULTIPLE CHOICE: Write the letter of the best answer in the given space.

____ 1. The expression P(A∩B) = P(A)P(B/A) is valid if:

(a) A and B are independent
(b) A and B are mutually exclusive
(c) only if A equals B'
(d) for any events A and B

____ 2. If A and B are independent events, with P(A) = $\frac{1}{5}$, P(B) = $\frac{2}{5}$, then P(A∪B):

(a) equals $\frac{3}{5}$ (c) equals $\frac{3}{25}$

(b) equals $\frac{13}{25}$ (d) cannot be determined from the given information

____ 3. If the odds in favor of an event occurring is 9 to 2, then the probability that the event will not occur is:

(a) $\frac{2}{11}$ (c) $\frac{2}{9}$

(b) $\frac{9}{11}$ (d) $\frac{9}{2}$

____ 4. The expression $P(A \cup B) = P(A) + P(B)$ is valid if:

    (a) A and B are independent
    (b) A and B are mutually exclusive
    (c) A and B are dependent
    (d) none of the above

____ 5. If A and B are mutually exclusive events with $P(A) = \frac{1}{7}$, $P(B) = \frac{2}{7}$, then $P(A \cap B)$ equals:

    (a) $\frac{3}{7}$ (c) $\frac{2}{47}$

    (b) $\frac{19}{49}$ (d) 0

____ 6. Which of the following may be true if A and B are dependent events?

    (a) $P(A \cup B) > 1$ (c) $P(A \cap B) < 0$
    (b) $P(A) + P(B) > 1$ (d) $P(A/B) = P(A)$

For Problems 7 and 8 refer to the table at the right:

	(T) Teachers	(S) Students	
(M) Men	15	40	55
(W) Women	25	20	45
	40	60	100

____ 7. The probability expressed by $P(S \cup W)$ equals:

    (a) $\frac{85}{100}$ (c) $\frac{20}{45}$

    (b) $\frac{20}{100}$ (d) $\frac{40}{60}$

____ 8. The probability that a person is a woman, given that the person is not a teacher is:

    (a) $\frac{20}{100}$ (c) $\frac{20}{60}$

    (b) $\frac{25}{40}$ (d) $\frac{25}{100}$

____ 9. Two probabilities may be added when we are asked:

    (a) an "or" question and the events are independent
    (b) an "or" question and the events are mutually exclusive
    (c) an "and" question and the events are independent
    (d) an "and" question and the events are mutually exclusive

____ 10. Two probabilities may be multiplied when we are asked:

    (a) an "or" question and the events are independent
    (b) an "or" question and the events are mutually exclusive
    (c) an "and" question and the events are independent
    (d) an "and" question and the events are mutually exclusive

COMPLETION: Complete the following sentences by filling in the given blanks.

1. If the probability that a company will make a profit or break even is $\frac{2}{7}$, then the odds in favor of the company losing money are
    _____.

2. If A and B are mutually exclusive events with P(A) = .15, P(B) = .45, then P{(A∪B)'} equals _____.

3. If A and B are independent events with P(A)=.25 and P(B)=.30, then P{(A∩B)'} equals _____.

4. Given the sample space S = {1, 2, 3, 4, 5, 6, 7, 8} with A = {3, 5, 7}, B = {2, 3, 4, 5, 6}, then A'∩B = _____.

5. Given the Venn diagram at the right, in terms of circles A and B, the region R_1 can be written symbolically as _____.

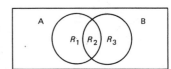

6. If C is the event that a student buys a stereo and D is the event that the student buys a personal computer, then P(C∪D') can be described in words as the probability that _____.

7. A vocational counselor believes that the probability that interest rates will go up is .40. He further believes that the probability that a particular student will get a job at the end of the year if interest rates go up is .30. Based on these estimates, the probability that both interest rates will go up and that the student will get the job is _____.

8. If A is the event that a product will be a financial success and B is the event that production will be preceded by a marketing study, then the probability that the product will be a financial success if production will be preceded by a marketing study can be expressed symbolically as _____.

Use the table at the right for Questions 9 and 10.

	Teachers	Students	
Males	15	40	55
Females	25	20	45
	40	60	100

9. The probability that the person is both male and a teacher is
    _____.

10. The probability that the person is a male given that the person is a student is _____.

58

PROBLEMS:

1. In the following diagram, G is the event that a student graduates this year, and C is the event that the student's father buys him a car this year.

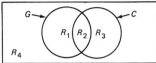

   Explain in words what events are represented by the regions:

   (a)   (i) R_1

         (ii) R_2

         (iii) R_3

         (iv) R_4

   (b) R_3 and R_4 together

   (c) R_2 and R_3 together

   (d) R_1, R_2, and R_3 together

2. In an experiment, persons are asked to pick a number from 10 to 18, so that for each person the sample space is the set S = {10, 11, 12, 13, 14, 15, 16, 17, 18}. If A = {10, 11, 15, 16, 17}, B = {10, 12, 14}, and C = {14, 16, 18}, list the elements of the sample space comprising each of the following events:

   (a)   A'   (c)   A∩C

   (b)   B∪C   (d)   A'∩B

3. A company has discovered a way of evaluating the success of both their radio and television advertising. If R and T are, respectively, the events that the radio advertising and television advertising is successful P(R) = .62, P(T) = .75, and P(R∩T) = .43, find:

   (a)   P(R')

   (b)   P(R∪T)

   (c)   P(R∩T')

   (d)   P(R∪T')

4. State in words what probabilities are expressed by each part of Problem 3:

(a)

(b)

(c)

(d)

5. A basketball coach plans to add two players from among 5 juniors and 8 seniors. What is the probability that:

(a) both people will be seniors

(b) the first will be a junior and the second will be a senior

6. A school has tabulated the favorite snacks of 1000 of its students in the two categories, males and females. Here are the results:

	(I) Ice Cream	(Z) Pizza	
(M) Males	500	125	625
(F) Females	200	175	375
	700	300	1000

If one of these terms is selected at random, find each of the following probabilities:

(a) $P(M) = $ ____   (d) $P(F/I) = $ ____   (g) $P(F \cup Z) = $ ____

(b) $P(I') = $ ____   (e) $P(Z/M') = $ ____   (h) $P(M \cap I') = $ ____

(c) $P(M'/Z) = $ ____   (f) $P(F'/Z') = $ ____   (i) $P(F \cap I') = $ ____

7. State in words what probabilities are represented by the expressions in each part of Problem 6.

(a) _____

(b) _____

(c) _____

(d) _____

(e) _____

(f) _____

(g) _____

(h) _____

(i) _____

8. A company estimates that the probability of a recession occurring in the next year is .4. The company also estimates the probability that another company distributes a competing product in the next year is .5. Finally, the company feels that the probability of both a recession occurring and a competing product being produced in the next year is .25.

   (a) If there is a recession, what is the probability that a company will distribute a competing product in the next year?

   (b) If a company produces a competing product, find the probability that there will be a recession in the next year.

   (c) Find the probability that there will be either a recession or a competing product or both in the next year.

   (d) Let R = recession occurs during the next year
          C = competing product is available in the next year

      Using an appropriate formula, determine whether the events R and C are independent.

9. Given mutually exclusive events C and D for which P(C) = .61 and P(D) = .34, find:

   (a) P(D')

   (b) P(C∩D)

(c) $P(C \cup D)$

(d) $P(C' \cup D')$

(e) $P(C' \cap D')$

10. Two options an automobile buyer may purchase are air-conditioning (C) and an automatic transmission (T). A dealer notes from his sales records that the probability of a buyer purchasing an automatic transmission is .60 and the probability that he purchased air-conditioning is .50. The probability that the buyer bought air-conditioning if he bought an automatic transmission is .70.

(a) Find the probability that a buyer purchased both an automatic transmission and air-conditioning.

(b) If a buyer purchased air-conditioning, find the probability that he bought an automatic transmission. (Use your answer to part (a).)

(c) Find the probability that a buyer purchased either air-conditioning or an automatic transmission.

(d) Find the probability that a buyer did not purchase either air-conditioning or an automatic transmission.

(e) Determine, using an appropriate formula, whether the events C and T are independent.

11. A group of 91 college students were categorized according to their classification and favorite dessert.

	(cookies) (C)	(jello) (J)	(ice cream) (I)	
(F) Freshman	9	11	6	26
(S) Sophomore	8	10	12	30
(G) Graduate Student	15	7	13	35
	32	28	31	91

One person is selected at random from this group. Find the following probabilities:

(a) P(C ∪ G)   _____

(b) P(I/F)   _____

(c) P(S ∩ C)   _____

(d) P(J/F')   _____

(e) P(G'/I')   _____

(f) the probability that the person prefers cookies if he/she is among those who are sophomores.

(g) the probability that the person is a graduate student if you know that he/she does not prefer jello.

(h) the probability that the person prefers cookies and is not a freshman.

12. Thirty percent of students attending a certain student mixer meet someone new to date. Forty percent of students attending the mixer dance at sometime during the mixer. Of those who dance, 60% meet someone new to date. A randomly selected student who attends the mixer is selected.

   (a) Find the probability that he/she either dances or meets someone new to date.

   (b) Find the probability that he/she has danced if you know that he/she has met someone new to date.

   (c) Find the probability that he/she has neither danced nor met someone new to date.

13. In problem 12, if M is the event of meeting someone new and D is the event of a student dancing, determine by calculation using a formula whether M and D are independent.

14. Three families A, B, and C are bidding on the same one-family house. If the probabilities are .20, .25, and .28, respectively, that a given family eventually moves into the house, find the probability that:

   (a) either family A or C eventually moves into the house.

   (b) none of the 3 families eventually moves into the house.

   (c) If A is the event that family A moves into the house, and B is the event that family B moves into the house, the events A and B are:

   (i)   independent   (iii) complementary

   (ii) mutually exclusive   (iv)   none of the above

15. (a) A consumer has placed two orders for a new product from two different suppliers X and Y. The probabilities that the suppliers deliver the product on time are .40 for X and .60 for Y. If the probability of one supplier delivering the product on time has no effect on whether or not the other one does, find the probability that one or both of the suppliers will deliver the product in the required time.

(b) If X is the event that supplier X delivers the product on time, and Y is the event that supplier Y delivers on time, the events X and Y are:

(i)   independent

(iii) complementary

(ii) mutually exclusive

(iv) none of the above

CHAPTER 7

EXPECTATIONS AND DECISIONS

This chapter introduces the concept of a mathematical expectation, and gives examples which show how mathematical expectations are used in making decisions.

CHAPTER OBJECTIVES: By the end of this chapter, you should be able to:

1. Find the mathematical expectation. (7.1, 7.2, 7.4 - 7.12)

2. Find a person's feeling about the probability of an event using the mathematical expectation. (7.13 - 7.17)

3. Determine the payoff that makes a game fair. (7.3)

4. Find the decision which maximizes the expected profit, minimizes expected cost, distance, etc. (7.19 - 7.27)

5. Make a decision using the following criteria:

    (a) minimax criterion
    (b) maximin criterion
    (c) minimin criterion   (7.28 - 7.30, 7.36, 7.37)
    (d) maximax criterion

6. Find the expected profit with perfect information and the expected value of perfect information. (7.31)

7. Find the prediction which maximizes the size of a reward.
    (7.33 - 7.35)

KEY POINTS OF THE CHAPTER:

1. The _mathematical expectation_ is a kind of average. It is calculated by multiplying each amount times each corresponding probability and adding the results. The amounts may be cash winnings, losses, penalties, or awards.

$$E = a_1 p_1 + a_2 p_2 + \ldots + a_k p_k$$

    where the a's are the amounts and the p's are the probabilities.

2. In _Bayesian analysis_, probabilities are assigned to the _states of nature_ about which uncertainties exist; then we choose whichever action promises the greatest expected profit or the smallest expected loss.

3. A game in which the mathematical expectation is zero and neither player is favored is said to be a _fair game_ or an _equitable game_.

4. The _minimax criterion_ is used when the payoffs are quantities such as losses or costs, which we want to make small. To apply this criterion, we look for the largest value of each column of the payoff table. Then we choose the column (action) which minimizes this maximum payoff.

5. To apply the maximin criterion, we look for the smallest value in each column of the table. Then we choose the column (action) which maximizes the minimum payoff. Such a criterion applies only when the payoffs are quantities such as profits or benefits which we want to make large. A pessimistic decision maker would apply this criterion. The maximin and minimax criteria are equivalent, since minimizing maximum losses is the same as maximizing minimum profits.

6. The maximax criterion is used when the payoffs are profits or benefits which we want to make large. To apply this criterion, we look for the largest value in each column of the table. Then we choose the column which maximizes this maximum payoff. This criterion would be used by an optimistic decision maker.

7. The minimin criterion is used by an optimistic decision maker instead of the maximax criterion when the payoffs are losses, costs, or other quantities which he wants to make small.

8. The expected profit with perfect information is found by first selecting the highest value in each row of the payoff table. Now find the mathematical expectation using the values you found for the amounts and the probabilities for the corresponding states of nature.

9. The maximum expected profit under uncertainty is found by finding the mathematical expectation of each decision or action (columns of payoff table) and then selecting the maximum of these mathematical expectation values.

10. The expected value of perfect information equals the expected profit with perfect information minus the expected profit under uncertainty.

MODIFIED TRUE/FALSE: If the statement is true, write true. If false, change the underlined words to make the statement true.

_____ 1. The maximin criterion applies only when the payoffs are quantities, such as profits or benefits, which we want to make large.

_____ 2. If the payoffs are quantities such as losses or costs, which we want to make small, we use the minimax criterion.

_____ 3. If the payoffs are losses or costs, the optimistic decision maker would use the minimax criterion.

_____ 4. The mathematical expectation is a kind of average.

_____ 5. In Bayesian analysis, probabilities are assigned to the states of nature.

_____ 6. The expected profit with perfect information is equal to the expected value of perfect information.

_____ 7. The expected profit with perfect information minus the maximum expected profit equals the expected value with perfect information.

_____ 8. The maximum expected profit in a payoff table is calculated using the row amounts.

_____ 9. In a payoff table, the <u>columns</u> indicate the decisions to be made.

_____ 10. Suppose the mathematical expectation is given with the corresponding probabilities and all amounts but one amount **a**. Solving for a requires E to be <u>multiplied</u> by a number.

<u>MULTIPLE CHOICE</u>: Write the letter of the best answer in the given space.

____ 1. A fair game is defined to be a game in which:

(a) the probabilities of all events are equal
(b) the sum of all probabilities equals 1
(c) E = 1
(d) E = 0

____ 2. For a payoff table containing company profit values, a pessimistic manufacturer would most likely use the _____ criterion.

(a) minimax   (c) maximin
(b) maximax   (d) minimin

____ 3. For a payoff table containing company profit values, an optimistic manufacturer would most likely use the _____ criterion.

(a) minimax   (c) maximin
(b) maximax   (d) minimin

____ 4. The mathematical expectation is always:

(a) a probability
(b) the most likely value to occur
(c) a long run expected average
(d) a positive value

Questions 5, 6, and 7 refer to the table at the right. You are given two states of nature S1 and S2 and two courses of action A1 and A2 with a profit payoff table.

	A1	A2
S1	40	10
S2	20	50

____ 5. If the probabilities of S1 and S2 are, respectively, $\frac{4}{5}$ and $\frac{1}{5}$, the expected profit if A1 is selected is:

(a) 36   (c) 18
(b) 34   (d) 26

____ 6. The action which maximizes expected profit is:

(a) A1 since 34>26   (c) A2 since 34>26
(b) A1 since 36>18   (d) A2 since 36>18

____ 7. The decisions A1 and A2 have the same expected profit if the probabilities of S1 and S2 are, respectively,

(a) $\frac{1}{2}$ and $\frac{1}{2}$ (c) $\frac{1}{3}$ and $\frac{2}{3}$

(b) $\frac{1}{5}$ and $\frac{4}{5}$ (d) $\frac{2}{3}$ and $\frac{1}{3}$

___ 8. If the prediction of a consultant must be exact with no reward for being close, the best prediction is:

(a) the mean   (c) the mode
(b) the median   (d) none of the above

___ 9. If the amount that the consultant is paid is reduced by a penalty which is 20 times the size of the error, the prediction which maximizes his payment is:

(a) the mean   (c) the mode
(b) the median   (d) none of the above

___ 10. If the amount that the consultant is paid is reduced by a penalty which is 20 times the square of the size of the error, the prediction which maximizes his payment is:

(a) the mean   (c) the mode
(b) the median   (d) none of the above

COMPLETION: Complete the following sentences by filling in the given blanks.

1. When applying the _____ criterion, we look for the largest value of each column of the payoff table and select the largest of these column values.

2. In order to make a decision using the minimax criterion, we select the action that gives the _____ of the _____ opportunity losses.

3. When calculating the mathematical expectation, amounts which represent losses are assigned _____ values.

4. In Bayesian analysis, we select the action which promises the _____ expected profit or the _____ expected loss.

5. A game in which the mathematical expectation of each player is zero is called a _____.

6. Calculating the mathematical expectation requires having the values for the amounts and their corresponding _____.

7. The expected profit with perfect information for a profit payoff table is calculated by using the _____ values in each _____ (row, column).

8. The expected value with perfect information is calculated by subtracting the maximum expected profit under uncertainty from _____.

9. Given the profit payoff table at the right, if we use the maximin criterion we will choose action _____.

	A1	A2	A3	A4
S1	12	30	20	8
S2	15	10	25	10

10. In the table of Question 9, if we use the maximax criterion we will choose action _____.

69

PROBLEMS:

1. (a) If 600 lottery tickets are sold for a cash prize of $150, what is the mathematical expectation of a person who buys one of these tickets for $1?

   (b) A grab-bag contains 6 packages worth $2 each, 11 packages worth $3, and 8 packages worth $4 each. Is it reasonable to pay $3.50 for the option of selecting one of these packages at random?

   (c) A real estate investor can buy a house for $70,000. He estimates that in a year he can sell it for $70,000, $72,000, $75,000, $80,000, and $82,000 with probabilities, respectively, of .15, .20, .35, .18, and .12. If he buys the house, what is his expected gain in one year?

2. Two finalists are in a tennis match with the winner to receive $40,000 and the loser $25,000. What are the two players' mathematical expectations if:

   (a) they are equally matched?

(b) their probabilities of winning are $\frac{2}{3}$ and $\frac{1}{3}$?

3. An entrepreneur is considering building a new restaurant. She knows that if the restaurant is built and the economy improves there will be a profit next year of $70,000; if the restaurant is built and there is a recession, there will be a loss next year of $10,000. If she buys a particular established restaurant and the economy improves, there will be a profit of $40,000 next year; if she buys the established restaurant and there is a recession, there will be a profit of $8000 next year.

(a) Construct a payoff table.

(b) Find the expected profit of perfect information if the probability of a recession is $\frac{1}{4}$.

(c) Find the expected profit of perfect information if the probability of a recession is $\frac{1}{3}$.

4. Using the results of Problem 3, find the expected value of perfect information when the

(a) probability of recession is $\frac{1}{4}$

(b) probability of recession is $\frac{1}{3}$

5. The following payoff table shows two surveys of data for the monthly rental prices for equivalent apartments in four different locations in a certain city.

Location

		A	B	C	D
Survey	I	$245	$260	$250	$255
	II	$230	$220	$225	$210

A builder wants to construct apartments of the type referred to above and must select one of the four locations A, B, C, or D. Which location should he choose if he wants to:

(a) maximize his minimum rental charge?

(b) maximize his maximum rental charge?

6. A speculator evaluating a particular investment concludes that if the company's balance sheet claims are true, the speculator's profit will be $15,000, and if the company's balance sheet claims are false, he will lose $5000. If he makes no investment, he has no profit or loss.

(a) Construct a payoff table for the decision problem.

(b) If the speculator feels that the probabilities are .20 and .80 that the balance sheet claims are true and false, respectively, what should he decide to do to maximize his expected profit?

(c) Suppose that the speculator's accountant feels that the speculator rates the accuracy of the balance sheet claims too low, that the probabilities of the claims being true or false are .30 and .70. Would it affect the speculator's decision if he assigned these probabilities to the two events?

7. The values in the following table are the prices charged for three menu items at three different restaurants of equal quality:

	Restaurant		
	A	B	C
Chopped Sirloin Steak	$7.00	$6.75	$7.65
Veal Parmigiana	$9.00	$8.50	$8.00
Broiled Boneless Chicken	$7.75	$7.55	$7.85

A person who has narrowed his choice of entree to one of the above three items is planning on dining at one of the above three restaurants and will make his final choice of entree after having a cocktail. Which restaurant would he go to if he applied:

(a) the minimax criterion to the amount of money he will have to pay?

(b) the minimin criterion to the amount of money he will have to pay?

8. A salesperson must choose between a straight salary of $25,000 and a salary of $20,000 plus a bonus of $8000 if his sales exceed a certain quota. How does he assess his probability of exceeding the quota if he chooses the lower salary with the possibility of a bonus?

9. A student wants to purchase a ticket from a friend to a very popular rock concert. He agrees to pay the friend $30, but will only get the ticket if he rolls a 5 or a 6 on an ordinary die, otherwise, the friend keeps the ticket and the $30. What is the ticket worth to the student if he thinks that this arrangement is fair?

10. The annual income (in thousands of dollars) of all ten entries in a lottery are 30, 25, 50, 48, 30, 30, 60, 42, 38, 15, and their chances of winning are all equal. If we want to predict the annual income of the winner, what prediction maximizes the expected reward if:

   (a) there is a reward for being right but none for being close?

   (b) there is a penalty equal to 15 times the size of the error?

   (c) the penalty is equal to 15 times the square of the size of the error?

11. What is a fair game?

12. What is Bayesian analysis?

CHAPTER 8

PROBABILITY DISTRIBUTIONS

This chapter deals with the following topics in probability distributions:

    (1)   random variables and general probability distributions

    (2)   special probability distributions including descriptions of their most important properties

CHAPTER OBJECTIVES: By the end of this chapter, you should be able to:

1. Recognize whether or not a function is a probability distribution. (8.1 - 8.4)

2. Find probabilities involving the binomial distribution by using (i) the formula or (ii) Table V.

    Some types of questions involve:

    (a) "exactly"
    (b) "no"
    (c) "at least"   (8.5 - 8.17)
    (d) "at most"
    (e) "from ... to"

3. Find probabilities involving a geometric distribution. (8.21)

4. Find probabilities involving the hypergeometric distribution. (8.22 - 8.29)

5. Find probabilities involving the hypergeometric distribution by using the binomial distribution as an approximation. (8.32 - 8.43)

6. Find probabilities involving the Poisson distribution. (8.34 - 8.44)

7. Find probabilities involving the multinomial distribution. (8.45 - 8.50)

8. Find the mean of a probability distribution. (8.51a, 8.53a, 8.55, 8.57, 8.59. 8.60, 8.63, 8.65, 8.67b)

9. For a probability distribution, find:

    (a) the variance   (8.51b, 8.52. 8.58 - 8.60)

    (b) the standard deviation(8.53, 8.54, 8.56, 8.68)

10. Find the mean and/or standard deviation of a binomial distribution. (8.57 - 8.62)

11. Find the mean of a hypergeometric distribution. (8.64, 8.66, 8.67c)

12. Calculate the mean of a Poisson distribution. (8.71, 8.72)

13. Calculate the variance and standard deviation of a Poisson distribution. (8.73)

14. Apply Chebyshev's theorem to a probability distribution. (8.74 - 8.76)

KEY POINTS OF THE CHAPTER:

1. A random variable is a quantity which can take on different values depending on chance.

2. A probability distribution is a correspondence which assigns probabilities to the values of the random variable.

3. The chapter deals primarily with calculating probabilities involving one of the following distributions:

   (a) binomial   (c) Poisson
   (b) hypergeometric   (d) multinomial

   Such problems can be solved in two steps:

   (1) Decide which of the above distributions is involved.
   (2) Apply the appropriate formula one or more times.

4. Deciding which distribution is involved

   A. If the problem has the following properties:

      (a) a sequence of a definite number n of independent trials
      (b) two possible outcomes for each trial, "success" and "failure"
      (c) the probability of success is the same for each trial, then the problem involves the binomial distribution.

      To answer probability questions involving the binomial distribution, we can

      (i)   use the binomial formula, OR
      (ii) if $n \leq 20$ and p=.05, .10, .20,..., .90, .95, use Table V, OR
      (iii) if np<5 and n is large, use the Poisson formula.

   B. If the problem has all of the following properties:

      (a) sampling from a definite number of objects without replacement
      (b) two possible outcomes, "success" and "failure," then the problem involves the hypergeometric distribution.

      To answer probability questions involving the hypergeometric distribution, we can

      (i) use the hypergeometric formula, OR
      (ii) if $n \leq .05(a+b)$, use the binomial formula as an approximation for the hypergeometric distribution.

   C. If the problem has the following property:

      a fixed number of "successes" per unit time (or for some other kind of unit), e.g., when a bank can expect to receive 6 bad checks per day, the problem involves the Poisson distribution.

   D. If the problem has all of the following properties:

      (a) a sequence of a definite number of independent trials
      (b) more than two possible outcomes for each trial
      (c) the probabilities remain the same for each trial, then the problem involves the multinomial distribution.

5. Ways to apply the distribution formulas one or more times

   Our distribution formulas in this chapter are:

   (a) the binomial formula   (c) the Poisson formula
   (b) the hypergeometric formula   (d) the multinomial formula

One application of each of these formulas gives the answer to an "exactly" question only. Here is how to apply the various formulas to different types of questions:

If the question is:

"find the probability of obtaining"	Then use
(1) exactly 5 successes	$f(5)$
(2) at most 2 successes	$f(0) + f(1) + f(2)$
(3) less than 2 successes	$f(0) + f(1)$
(4) from 4 to 7 successes	$f(4) + f(5) + f(6) + f(7)$
(5) at least 3 successes	$1 - \{f(0) + f(1) + f(2)\}$
(6) more than 3 successes	$1 - \{f(0) + f(1) + f(2) + f(3)\}$
(7) no successes	$f(0)$

AVOIDING COMMON ERRORS:

1. Do not use the formula for a distribution in a problem where it does not apply. (e.g., do not use the binomial formula when the hypergeometric formula is the correct one, or vice versa.)

2. Do not apply the <u>mean</u> of a probability distribution formula to answer a <u>probability</u> question involving the distribution. (e.g., do not use $\mu = np$ when $f(x) = \binom{n}{x}p^x(1-p)^x$ applies.)

3. Do not confuse "at least," "at most," and "exactly" questions. (e.g., do <u>not</u> answer $f(2)$ to an "at most" question when the correct answer is given by $f(0) + f(1) + f(2)$.)

4. Do not use the <u>general</u> formula for the mean of a probability distribution $\mu = \Sigma xp(x)$ when a specific formula more easily applies (such as $\mu = np$ if the distribution is binomial).

5. Note that the Poisson distribution applies not only in problems that are given as Poisson distributions, but also as an approximation in problems that are originally binomial, if $np < 5$ and n is large. (See Key Points of the Chapter 4A.)

KEY FORMULAS:

1. <u>Binomial Distribution</u>

    The probability of getting x successes in n independent trials is

    $$f(x) = \binom{n}{x}p^x(1-p)^{n-x} \text{ for } x = 0,1,2,\ldots,n$$

    where p is the probability of one success in one trial

2. <u>Hypergeometric Distribution</u>

    $$f(x) = \frac{\binom{a}{x} \cdot \binom{b}{n-x}}{\binom{a+b}{n}} \text{ for } x = 0,1,2,3,\ldots,n$$

    where a = total available number of objects which are successes
          b = total available number of objects which are failures
          n = total number of objects selected from a+b

3. Poisson Distribution

$$f(x) = \frac{\mu^x e^\mu}{x!} \quad \text{for } x=0,1,2,3,\ldots$$

where μ = the mean of the distribution
x = the number of successes

4. Multinomial Distribution

$$\frac{n!}{x_1! x_2! x_3! \ldots x_k!} \; p_1^{x_1} \cdot p_2^{x_2} \cdot p_3^{x_3} \ldots \cdot p_k^{x_k}$$

5. The Mean and Standard Deviation of a Binomial Distribution

$$\mu = \Sigma x p(x)$$
$$\sigma^2 = \Sigma x^2 p(x) - \mu^2 \quad \text{(short-cut formula)}$$

These formulas are used to determine μ and σ in most problems. However, when we are dealing with the binomial distribution, the hypergeometric distribution, and the Poisson distribution, we will use some special formulas:

6. The Mean and Standard Deviation of a Binomial Distribution

$$\mu = np$$
$$\sigma = \sqrt{np(1-p)}$$

7. The Mean of a Hypergeometric Distribution

$$\mu = \frac{na}{a+b}$$

8. The Mean and Standard Deviation of a Poisson Distribution

$$\mu = \lambda$$
$$\sigma = \sqrt{\lambda}$$

MODIFIED TRUE/FALSE: If the statement is true, write true. If false, change the underlined words to make the statement true.

_____ 1. The Poisson distribution <u>can</u> be applied in situations which do not involve the <u>binomial</u> distribution.

_____ 2. The mean of a probability distribution is <u>always</u> a value that can be obtained by the random <u>variable</u>.

_____ 3. If we want to calculate the probability of from 4 to 6 successes in a hypergeometric distribution problem, then we must use the formula <u>three</u> times.

_____ 4. The use of the <u>Poisson</u> distribution requires a value n which indicates a definite number of independent trials.

_____ 5. In a problem involving the <u>hypergeometric</u> distribution, the probability of success <u>remains the same</u> from trial to trial.

_____ 6. In a problem involving the hypergeometric distribution, the binomial distribution may <u>sometimes</u> be used as an approximation.

_____ 7. If a distribution is known to be binomial, the most convenient formula that can be used to calculate the mean is $\underline{\mu = \Sigma xp(x)}$.

_____ 8. If a distribution is known to be binomial, the most convenient formula that can be used to calculate the variance is $\underline{\sigma^2 = \Sigma x^2 p(x) - \mu^2}$.

_____ 9. To determine the mean of a binomial distribution, it is necessary to know the number of <u>successes</u> involved in the problem.

_____ 10. The <u>standard deviation</u> is a measure of the theoretical average value that a distribution is likely to assume for a large number of trials.

MULTIPLE CHOICE: Write the letter of the best answer in the given space.

____ 1. One application of the binomial distribution formula or one number in Table V is always the answer to what kind of question?

(a) exactly   (c) at least
(b) at most   (d) between

____ 2. To calculate the probability of obtaining 3 aces in 8 draws of a card with replacement from an ordinary deck, we would use the:

(a) hypergeometric distribution
(b) Poisson distribution
(c) binomial distribution
(d) multinomial distribution

____ 3. If the selection of the cards in Question 2 is without replacement, the required distribution is the:

(a) hypergeometric distribution
(b) Poisson distribution
(c) binomial distribution
(d) multinomial distribution

____ 4. If a binomial distribution problem has p=.003 and n=1000, then the answer should be approximated by using the:

(a) Table V   (c) hypergeometric distribution
(b) Poisson distribution   (d) multinomial distribution

____ 5. One application of the Poisson distribution formula is always the answer to what kind of question?

(a) exactly   (c) at least
(b) at most   (d) between

____ 6. A die is rolled 10 times. The probability of obtaining from 4 to 7 threes should be determined using the formula for the:

(a) hypergeometric distribution
(b) Poisson distribution
(c) binomial distribution
(d) multinomial distribution

___ 7. A service station receives an average of 6 customers per hour. The probability that there will be 3 arrivals in a given hour can be found by using the:

   (a) binomial distribution (c) hypergeometric distribution
   (b) Poisson distribution (d) multinomial distribution

___ 8. A multiple choice test consists of 7 questions with 5 choices each. If a student guesses on all questions, the probability that a student gets exactly 3 correct answers is given by:

   (a) $\binom{7}{3}(\frac{3}{5})^3(\frac{2}{5})^4$ (c) $\binom{7}{5}(\frac{1}{5})^3(\frac{4}{5})^4$

   (b) $\binom{7}{5}(\frac{1}{3})^5(\frac{2}{3})^2$ (d) $\binom{7}{3}(\frac{1}{5})^3(\frac{4}{5})^4$

___ 9. We want to determine the probability of obtaining at most 4 successful operations in 10 independent surgical operations where the probability of success is the same for each operation. The appropriate formula to be used is:

   (a) the binomial formula (c) the hypergeometric formula
   (b) the mean of the   (d) the mean of the hypergeometric
        binomial distribution   distribution

___ 10. Which of the following formulas, when applicable, gives <u>exact</u> answers to probability questions involving the binomial distribution?

   (a) the binomial formula (c) the hypergeometric formula
   (b) Table V   (d) the Poisson formula

<u>COMPLETION</u>: Complete the following sentences by filling in the given blanks.

1. The binomial distribution Table V can be used to solve problems involving the binomial distribution if n has the values _____, and p has the values _____.

2. Problems that involve the binomial distribution always assume that (1) _____, (2) _____, and (3) _____.

3. The sum of all the values of a probability distribution must be equal to _____.

4. The mean of a Poisson distribution is given by _____.

5. The generalization of the binomial distribution when there are _____ outcomes is called the multinomial distribution.

6. The symbol p in the binomial distribution formula means the probability of _____.

7. According to Chebyshev's theorem, the probability that a random variable will take on a value within 2 standard deviations of the mean is _____ $\frac{3}{4}$.

8. If we apply Chebyshev's theorem to the 60 to 80 interval of a distribution, with $\sigma=5$, the value of k will be _____.

81

9. In the hypergeometric distribution formula, the total number of trials is given by _____ .

10. In order to apply Chebyshev's theorem to determine the minimum fraction of data contained in a given interval, we need to know the _____ and the _____ of the distribution.

PROBLEMS:

1. Which of the following can be probability distributions? Justify your answer.

   (a) f(1)=.40, f(2)=.20, f(3)=.50 where the random variable can take on only the values 1, 2, and 3

   (b) $f(x) = \frac{x}{10}$ for x = 0,1,2,3,4

   (c) f(1)=.25, f(2)=.30, f(3)=.15, f(4)=.15 where the random variable can take on only the values 1,2,3, and 4

   (d) $f(x) = \frac{x-3}{7}$ for x = 0,1,2,3,4,5

2. Among 18 job applicants, 6 are actually qualified to do the job. If 7 applicants are randomly selected to be hired, find the probability that in this sample:

   (a) from 2 to 4 applicants are qualified

   (b) exactly 3 applicants are qualified

3. For the distribution in Problem 2, find:

   (a) the mean

   (b) the variance

   (c) the standard deviation

4. A company produces stereo components. The probability of the company producing a defective component is .003. If 1000 components are produced, find the probability that:

    (a) exactly 5 components are defective

    (b) at least 3 components are defective

    (c) at most 4 components are defective

    (d) from 4 to 6 components are defective

5. A test has 12 multiple choice questions with 4 choices for each question. If a student guesses on all questions, find the probability that:

    (a) she gets exactly 5 correct answers

    (b) she gets at least 2 correct answers

6. For the distribution in Problem 5, find:

    (a) the mean

    (b) the variance

    (c) the standard deviation

7. It has been found 40% of the employees who complete a sequence of executive seminars go on to become vice presidents. If 10 graduates of the program are randomly selected, find the probability that:

(a) exactly 5 become vice presidents

(b) no one becomes a vice president

(c) at least 3 become vice presidents

(d) at most 2 become vice presidents

(e) from 2 to 4 become vice presidents

8. Three companies share the entire market for a particular product. Company A has a 50% share, company B has a 30% share, and company C has a 20% share. If 12 people who buy the product are selected at random, find the probability that 5 buy the product from company A, 4 from company B, and 3 from company C.

9. The probabilities that a customer entering a particular bookstore buys 0,1,2,3,4, or 5 books are .30, .20, .20, .15, .10, and .05 respectively. For this probability distribution, find:

(a) the mean

(b) the variance

(c) the standard deviation

10. The daily number of people who examine cars in a particular automobile showroom is a random variable with $\mu=80$ and $\sigma=6$.

   (a) According to Chebyshev's theorem, with what probability can we claim that between 68 and 92 people will look at cars in the showroom on a particular day?

   (b) Give the interval such that there is at least a $\frac{35}{36}$ probability that the number of people who look at cars will be in that interval.

11. The editor of a particular women's magazine claims that the magazine is read by 60% of the female students on a college campus. If this claim is true, find the probabilities that in a random sample of 10 female students:

   (a) more than 2 read the magazine.

   (b) exactly 6 read the magazine.

   (c) at most 2 read the magazine.

12. If 2% of the checks received in an all night drugstore bounce, what is the probability that in the next 100 checks received by the store:

    (a) at least 3 bounce.

    (b) at most 2 bounce.

    (c) exactly 96 do not bounce.

13. Among 10 video movie tapes that a retail store has available, 4 are comedies. If a customer selects 3 video tapes at random to buy for a friend, what are the probabilities that:

    (a) none of them are comedies.

    (b) two of them are comedies.

14. Check in each case whether the given function can serve as the probability distribution of an appropriate random variable:

    (a) $f(x) = \frac{1}{5}$, for x = 0, 1, 2, 3, 4

    (b) $f(1) = .25$, $f(2) = .40$, $f(3) = .30$

CHAPTER 9

THE NORMAL DISTRIBUTION

This chapter introduces several continuous distributions, with special emphasis on the normal distribution and its applications.

CHAPTER OBJECTIVES: By the end of this chapter, you should be able to:

1. Find probabilities from the graph of a continuous curve. (9.2 - 9.4)

2. Find probabilities under a standard normal curve. (9.5 - 9.7, 9.10)

3. Find z for a given normal curve area. (9.8, 9.9)

4. Verify that a given area corresponds to a given z value. (9.11)

5. Find probabilities in a normal distribution when μ and σ are given. (9.13)

6. Find the standard deviation for a normal distribution with a given μ value corresponding to a given area. (9.14)

7. Find probabilities in a normal distribution when μ is not given. (9.15)

8. Find probabilities in an exponential distribution. (9.16 - 9.18)

9. Check whether a given distribution is normal. (9.19 - 9.22)

10. Find probabilities in a word problem involving the normal distribution. (9.26, 9.28, 9.29, 9.33, 9.34, 9.35)

11. Use the normal approximation to the binomial distribution to solve binomial distribution problems. (9.38 - 9.43, 9.46, 9.48, 9.49)

KEY POINTS OF THE CHAPTER:

1. Continuous Probability Distributions

    In Chapter 8, the probability distributions: the binomial, the hypergeometric, and the multinomial distributions were considered. Each of these distributions can arise in probability questions only when we are dealing with individual numbers or points. Such distributions are called discrete probability distributions.

    This chapter introduces the concept of continuous probability distributions, which involves situations in which we are interested in probabilities associated with intervals or regions. Probability distributions are either discrete or continuous.

2. The Normal Distribution

    The most important example of a continuous distribution is the normal distribution. The most significant properties of the normal distribution are as follows:

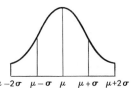

(i)   The curve is bell-shaped. $\mu-2\sigma$ $\mu-\sigma$ μ $\mu+\sigma$ $\mu+2\sigma$
(ii) The total area under the curve equals 1.
(iii) The curve is infinite in both directions without ever intersecting the horizontal axis.
(iv) The center of the curve is the mean μ. The "thickness" of the curve depends directly on the size of the standard deviation σ. Then, there are an infinite number of normal distribution curves, one for every pair of possible values of μ and σ.

3. The Standard Normal Distribution

    The normal distribution table (Table I) is based on only one of the infinite number of normal distributions: the one for which $\mu = 0$ and $\sigma = 1$. This normal distribution which has $\mu = 0$ and $\sigma = 1$ is called the standard normal distribution. The values of the standard normal variable are called z values or z-scores.

4. Calculating Probabilities Involving the Standard Normal Distribution

    Example: If z is a standard normal variable, find the following probabilities:

    (a) $P(z \geq 1)$*

         First, draw a bell curve and shade in the desired area. (See curve at right.) Next, look up z = 1 on the left side of Table I. Next to 1.00, we find .3413, but this is the area from the center line to z = 1. To determine the area (the probability) we want, we must subtract: .5 - .3413 = .1587.

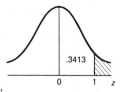

    (b) $P(z \geq -2)$

         There are no negative values of z in Table I, but since the curve is symmetric around the center line, we can look up z = 2. The number .4772 is the area between the center line and z = -2. The graph indicates that we must add .5 + .4772 = .9772.

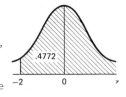

5. Calculating Probabilities in Normal Distribution Problems Involving Any μ and σ

    The standard normal distribution (Table I) is sufficient to answer probability questions involving normal distributions having any combination of μ and σ. To answer such questions, we must use the formula

    $$z = \frac{x - \mu}{\sigma}$$

    which converts any normal variable x that may have any μ and σ to the standard normal variable z having a mean 0 and standard deviation 1.

*This shorthand for probabilities is used here, but not in the textbook.

88

Example: If x is a normal variable with μ = 60 and σ = 4, find the following probabilities:

(a) $P(x \geq 66)$

Draw a normal curve with the desired area shaded. Then the x value of 66 must be converted to a z-score using $z = \dfrac{x - \mu}{\sigma}$.

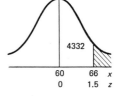

$$z = \frac{66 - 60}{4} = \frac{6}{4} = 1.5$$

Look up z = 1.5 in Table I to find .4332. Then from the curve $P(x \geq 66)$ = .5 - .4332 = .0668.

(b) $P(62 \leq x \leq 68)$

Here we must convert both 62 and 68 to z-scores.

$$z = \frac{62 - 60}{4} = \frac{2}{4} = .5, \quad z = \frac{68 - 60}{4} = \frac{8}{4} = 2$$

Looking up z = .50 in Table I, we find .1915; z = 2.00 gives us .4772 - .1915 = .2857.

6. Testing Whether an Observed Frequency Distribution Has Roughly the Shape of a Normal Distribution.

If we plot the cumulative "less than" percentages which correspond to the class boundaries of the distribution on normal probability paper and the points follow the general pattern of a straight line, we consider this as positive evidence that the distribution has roughly the shape of a normal distribution.

7. The Normal Approximation to the Binomial Distribution

(a) Suppose a problem involving probabilities has the following properties:

1. the binomial distribution is involved
2. both np>5 and n(1-p)>5.

Then the normal approximation to the binomial distribution should be applied. All of the following are needed for the application:

1. μ =np

2. $\sigma = \sqrt{np(1-p)}$

3. $z = \dfrac{x - \mu}{\sigma}$

4. the continuity correction

The continuity correction applies only to problems which involve discrete (usually binomial) distributions in which we use the normal approximation method. For example, the continuity correction does not apply to problems when presented as involving the normal distribution.

(b) Examples of How to Apply the Continuity Correction

The continuity correction is an attempt to improve the normal approximation by increasing the area that we calculate using the normal curve. Suppose a binomial distribution has 200 trials. The following table illustrates how the continuity correction applies to various binomial probability questions.

Type of question: The probability of--	binomial symbol	translates to normal approximation symbol
(1) at most 165 successes	$P(x \leq 165)$	$P(x \leq 165.5)$
(2) at least 150 successes	$P(x \geq 150)$	$P(x \geq 149.5)$
(3) between 75 and 90 successes inclusive	$P(75 \leq x \leq 90)$	$P(x \leq 74.5 < x \leq 90.5)$
(4) less than 165 successes	$P(x < 165) = P(x \leq 164)$	$P(x \leq 164.5)$
(5) more than 150 successes	$P(x > 150) = P(x \geq 151)$	$P(x \geq 150.5)$

8. Calculating Probabilities Involving the Normal Approximation to the Binomial Distribution

Example: A multiple choice test consists of 50 questions with five choices for each question. Find the following probabilities of a student guessing on all questions:

(a) at least 12 correct
(b) between 7 and 11 correct

Solution: This is a binomial distribution problem. Since n = 50 and p = .2, np = 50(.2) = 10 ≥ 5 and n(1-p) = 50(.8) = 40 ≥ 5 so the normal approximation to the binomial distribution can be applied.

(a) $P(x \geq 12)$
This can be converted to $P(x \geq 11.5)$ in applying the normal approximation. (See 7(b).)

$\mu = np = 10$

$\sigma = \sqrt{np(1-p)} = \sqrt{50(.2)(.8)} = 2.83$

$z = \dfrac{x - \mu}{\sigma} = \dfrac{11.5 - 10}{2.83} = \dfrac{1.5}{2.83} = .53$

$P(x \geq 12) = .5 - .2019 = \underline{.2981}$

(b) $P(7 \leq x \leq 11)$
This can be converted to $P(6.5 \leq x \leq 11.5)$ in applying the normal approximation.

$z = \dfrac{x - \mu}{\sigma} = \dfrac{6.5 - 10}{2.83} = \dfrac{-3.5}{2.83} = -1.24$

$P(7 \leq x \leq 11) = .3925 + .2019 = \underline{.5944}$

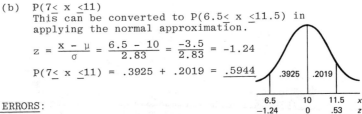

AVOIDING COMMON ERRORS:

1. The continuity correction is used in problems involving the normal approximation to the binomial distribution. (These problems involve the formulas $\mu = np$, $\sigma = \sqrt{np(1-p)}$ and $z = \frac{x - \mu}{\sigma}$.) The continuity correction is not used in problems that are presented as normal distribution problems.

A typical error is to not use the continuity correction where it belongs (normal approximation) nor to use it where it does not belong (normal distribution).

KEY FORMULAS:

1. Converting to z-scores to use the normal distribution table

$$z = \frac{x - \mu}{\sigma}$$

2. To apply the normal approximation to the binomial distribution

    (i) $\mu = np$ (mean of binomial distribution)

    (ii) $\sigma = \sqrt{np(1-p)}$ (standard deviation of binomial

    (iii) $z = \frac{x - \mu}{\sigma}$ distribution)

MODIFIED TRUE/FALSE: If the statement is true, write true. If false, change the underlined words to make the statement true.

_____ 1. The continuity correction is always used in problems involving the normal distribution.

_____ 2. The normal approximation to the binomial distribution applies in problems that originally involve the normal distribution.

_____ 3. The z value such that the area to the left of z is .05 is located to the right of zero on the z-axis.

_____ 4. The symbol μ represents the sample mean.

_____ 5. If $P(2 < x < 5) \neq P(2 \leq x \leq 5)$ then x must be a discrete random variable.

_____ 6. If the area in the standard normal distribution is on the left side of zero, then that area has a negative value.

_____ 7. It is sometimes desirable to use the normal approximation to the binomial distribution to solve binomial problems that can be solved by using Table V.

_____ 8. The formula $\mu = np$ is used to convert any normally distributed variable to one which has a mean of 0 and a standard deviation of 1.

_____ 9. The formula $\mu = \sqrt{np(1-p)}$ finds the standard deviation in problems which originally involve the binomial distribution.

_____ 10. The mean of every normal distribution is equal to 0.

MULTIPLE CHOICE: Write the letter of the best answer in the given space.

____ 1. Which of the following distributions is not continuous?

    (a) normal distribution   (c) exponential distribution
    (b) uniform distribution   (d) binomial distribution

2. Which of the following is always true for a normal distribution?

(a) $P(x>8)=P(x>9)$ (c) $P(x<5)\neq P(x<5)$
(b) $P(2 < x \leq 8)=P(2\leq x <8)$ (d) $P(x\leq 8)=P(x\leq 8.5)$

3. If we are using the normal approximation to determine the probability of at most 28 successes in a binomial distribution $(P(x\leq 28))$, the normal distribution probability that is used to make the estimate is:

(a) $P(x<27.5)$ (c) $P(x<28.5)$
(b) $P(x\leq 28)$ (d) $P(x\leq 28)$

4. For the uniform distribution pictured at the right, the probability $P(2\leq x \leq 2\frac{1}{2})$ equals:

(a) $\frac{1}{6}$ (c) $\frac{1}{3}$

(b) 1   (d) none of the above

5. The area to the right of z = 1.0 is equal to:

(a) .3413   (c) .6816
(b) .8413   (d) .1587

6. To determine the probability of obtaining exactly 20 successes in 50 trials with p = .30, we should use the:

(a) binomial formula
(b) Poisson formula
(c) normal approximation to the binomial distribution
(d) Table V

7. The probability in Question 6, $P(x=20)$:

(a) is equal to 0
(b) is found by using $P(19.5 < x < 20.5)$
(c) can only be approximated by the binomial formula
(d) cannot be found using the normal table

8. In a binomial distribution with 10 trials, which of the following is true?

(a) $P(3< x \leq 5) = P(3< x <5)$ (c) $P(x<6) = 1 - P(x>7)$
(b) $P(x\leq 4)=P(x>5)-P(x\geq 4)$ (d) $P(x>7) = P(x>8)$

9. A problem that is solved by using the standard normal table and the formula $\mu =np$:

(a) involves Table V
(b) involves the normal approximation to the binomial distribution
(c) originally involved the normal distribution
(d) originally involved the Poisson distribution

10. If x is a normal random variable with $\mu = 50$ and $\sigma =6$, then the probability that x is not between 44 and 56 is:

(a) .6826   (c) .8413
(b) .3413   (d) .3174

<u>COMPLETION</u>: Complete the following sentences by filling in the given
blanks.

1. If x is a normal random variable, the probability that x is exactly
    equal to any number is _____.

2. Distributions are of two types: _____ and _____.
    The binomial is an example of a distribution that is _____.
    The normal is an example of a distribution that is _____.

3. The total area under any normal curve is always equal to
    _____.

4. The standard normal distribution has a mean of _____ and a
    standard deviation of _____.

5. The z value such that 50% of the area is to the right of z is
    _____.

6. If a normal distribution has μ = 40 and σ = 5, the area to the
    left of x = 42 equals _____.

7. The symbol $\bar{x}$ represents the _____.

8. The binomial distribution can be approximated by the normal
    distribution when _____ and _____.

9. If the area to the left of z is .20, then z = _____.

10. The area under a normal curve between any two values a and b gives
    the _____ that a random variable having the normal
    distribution will take on a value in the interval from a to b.

<u>PROBLEMS</u>:

1. Find the probability below by using the probability distribution
    pictured at the right:

    (a) P(-1$\leq$ x $\leq$1)

    (b) P($\frac{1}{2}$$\leq$ x $\leq$$\frac{3}{2}$)

    (c) P(-2$\leq$ x $\leq$-1)

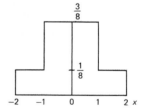

2. Find the following probabilities using the normal table:

    (a) P(-1.3$\leq$ z $\leq$-.4)

    (b) P(z<.67)

    (c) P(z<-.54)

3. If $\mu = 30$ and $\sigma = 5$, calculate

    (a) $P(x \leq 32)$

    (b) $P(31 \leq x \leq 35)$

    (c) $P(24 \leq x < 28)$

4. Find the following z values:

    (a) $z_{.05}$

    (b) $z_{.45}$

    (c) $z_{.65}$

    (d) $z_{.90}$

5. (a) Find z if the normal curve area
            (i)   between 0 and z is .4750

            (ii) to the right of z is .90

            (iii) to the left of z is .16

    (b) A normal distribution has a mean $\mu = 60$. If 15.87% of the
         area under the curve is to the left of 54, find:
            (i)   the area to the right of 64

            (ii) the area between 58 and 63

6. The number of ounces of soda that a vending machine dispenses per
    cup is normally distributed with a mean of 12 ounces and a
    standard deviation of 4 ounces. Find the probability that:

    (a) more than 16 ounces is dispensed in a cup

(b)   between   15 and 18 ounces are dispensed in a cup

7.   An electronics firm believes that 70% of the new products they
     market will be successful. If the company markets 80 products
     in the next 5 years, find the probability that in that time:

     (a)   at least 60 products will be successful

     (b)   at most 50 products will be successful

     (c)   between 55 and 59 products, inclusive, will be successful

8.   A supermarket manager has determined that the amount of time
     customers spend in the supermarket is approximately normally
     distributed with a mean of 45 minutes and a standard deviation
     of 6 minutes. Find the probability that:

     (a)   a customer spends less than 48 minutes in the supermarket

     (b)   a customer spends between 39 and 43 minutes in the
           supermarket

9.   It has been estimated that 40% of the televisions that a
     manufacturer makes need repairs in the first three years of
     operation. A new hotel buys 90 televisions from this company.
     Find the probability that in the first three years of operation:

     (a)   less than 32 of the televisions need repairs

     (b)   between 38 and 42 of the televisions, inclusive, need repairs

10. The waiting time in a doctor's office has an exponential
     distribution with $\mu = 45$ minutes. Find the probability that:

     (a)   a patient has to wait between 0 and 30 minutes

     (b)   a patient has to wait between 35 and 50 minutes

11. Use normal probability paper to check whether the following
     distribution follows a normal distribution.

Grades	Number of Students
51-60	5
61-70	8
71-80	10
81-90	6
91-100	3

12. Find the area under the standard normal curve which lies

     (a) to the left of $z = -1.5$

     (b) between $z = -1.3$ and $z = 1$

     (c) between $z = -2$ and $z = -1$

13. Find z if

     (a) the normal curve area to the left of z is 0.3.

     (b) the normal curve area to the right of z is 0.35.

14. A salesperson knows that 20% of her presentations result in sales. Find the probabilities that in the next 60 presentations:

    (a) at least 9 result in sales.

    (b) between 14 and 18, inclusive, result in sales.

15. A machine pours beer into bottles. Experience has shown that the number of ounces poured is normally distributed with a mean of 16 ounces with a standard deviation of 1.5 ounces. Find the probabilities that the amount of beer the machine will pour into the next bottle will be:

    (a) more than 17 ounces.

    (b) between 12 and 14 ounces.

CHAPTER 10

SAMPLING AND SAMPLING DISTRIBUTIONS

This chapter gives an introduction to various sampling methods. The chapter also introduces the concept of sampling distribution, which tells us how quantities determined from samples may vary from sample to sample. Also there is a discussion of how such variations are measured.

CHAPTER OBJECTIVES: By the end of this chapter, you should be able to:

1. Find the number of different samples of a given size that can be selected from a finite population. (10.1, 10.2)

2. Find probabilities in sampling from a finite population. (10.3, 10.4, 10.6, 10.7)

3. List the possible samples that can be drawn from a specific finite population. (10.5, 10.7)

4. Select a random sample using a random number table. (10.8 - 10.11)

5. Verify the formula $1 \Big/ \binom{N}{n}$, used to determine probabilities in sampling from a finite population. (10.13, 10.14)

6. Verify that the probability that the specific element of the population will be contained in a random sample of size n is $\frac{n}{N}$. (10.15)

7. List the possible systematic samples that can be drawn from a finite population. (10.16, 10.17)

8. List the possible stratified samples that can be drawn from a finite population. (10.19)

9. Find the number of ways of selecting a stratified sample from a given population with given strata. (10.20, 10.21)

10. Verify the formula for proportional allocation. (10.22)

11. Determine the strata sizes that will produce a proportional allocation for a stratified sample. (10.23, 10.24)

12. List all possible cluster samples of a given size for a given finite population. (10.25)

13. Determine the strata sizes that will produce optimum allocation for a stratified sample. (10.26 - 10.28)

14. Construct a sampling distribution. (10.31, 10.34, 10.36, 10.37)

15. Calculate the mean and standard deviation of a sampling distribution of the mean. (10.33, 10.35)

16. In a finite population, find probabilities that a sample mean differs from a population mean by a given number. (10.32, 10.34)

17. Evaluate changes in the standard error of the mean for given changes in the sample size. (10.38)

18. Evaluate the finite correction factor. (10.39)

19. Find the probable error of the mean. (10.40)

20. Calculate probabilities involving the sample mean using the central limit theorem. (10.46 - 10.51)

21. Calculate probabilities involving the sample mean using Chebyshev's theorem. (10.46, 10.47)

22. Compare the reliability of the mean and median in estimating the mean of a given population. (10.53, 10.54)

KEY POINTS OF THE CHAPTER:

1. Sampling from a finite population <u>with replacement</u> is equivalent to sampling from an infinite population.

2. A sample is random if (i) in each draw all elements of the population have the same probability of being selected, and (ii) successive draws are independent.

3. A <u>sample design</u> is a definite plan, completely determined before any data are collected, for obtaining a sample from a given population.

4. (a) <u>Systematic sampling</u> is a sampling procedure in which we select every 10th item on a list, or 20th on a list, etc. An element of randomness is usually introduced into this kind of sampling by using random numbers to pick the item with which to start.

    (b) The danger of systematic sampling lies in the possible presence of hidden periodicities.

5. (a) <u>Stratified sampling</u> involves stratifying (or dividing) the population into a number of nonoverlapping subpopulations or strata, then taking a sample from each stratum. If the items selected from each stratum constitute a simple random sample, the entire procedure (stratified and simple random sampling) is called <u>stratified (simple) random sampling</u>.

    (b) A stratified sample will generally lead to a higher degree of precision than a simple random sample of the same size drawn from the whole population.

    (c) The goal of stratification is to form strata in such a way that there is some relationship between being in a particular stratum and the answers sought in the statistical study, and within separate strata there is as much <u>homogeneity</u> as possible. Such homogeneity will produce much less variability within the two groups than there is in the entire population.

6. Stratified Sampling Methods

    (a) <u>Proportional Allocation</u>. Selecting the sample so that the sizes of the individual samples are proportional to the sizes of the respective strata. That is, for strata of sizes

$N_1, N_2, \ldots, N_k$ with a sample of size n_1 from the first stratum, a sample of size n_2 from the second stratum,..., the allocation is proportional if

$$\frac{n_1}{N_1} = \frac{n_2}{N_2} = \cdots \frac{n_k}{N_k} \qquad \text{or if these ratios are very close to being equal.}$$

Sample sizes that produce a proportional allocation can be found by using

$$n_i = \frac{N_i}{N} \cdot n \qquad \text{for } i = 1, 2, \ldots, k$$

The mean of a population can be estimated by the formula

$$\bar{x}_w = \frac{N_1\bar{x}_1 + N_2\bar{x}_2 + \ldots + N_k\bar{x}_k}{N_1 + N_2 + \ldots + N_k}$$

This is a weighted mean of the individual x's and the weights are the sizes of the strata. When the allocation is proportional the N's can be replaced by n's and $\bar{x}_w$ is the mean of all the data combined. Thus, proportional allocation is said to be self-weighting.

(b) Optimum Allocation. Selecting the sample so that for a fixed sample size, the sample chosen will have the smallest possible standard error for the estimate of the population mean. This will be satisfied if

$$\frac{n_1}{N_1\sigma_1} = \frac{n_2}{N_2\sigma_2} = \cdots \frac{n_k}{N_k\sigma_k} \qquad \text{or if these ratios are as nearly equal as possible}$$

Sample sizes that produce an optimum allocation can be found by using

$$n_i = \frac{n \cdot N_i \sigma_i}{N_1\sigma_1 + N_2\sigma_2 + \ldots + N_k\sigma_k} \qquad \text{for } i = 1, 2, \ldots, k$$

7. Quota Sampling. A method of stratified sampling in which the size of the sample in each strata is decided by quotas having few, if any, restrictions on how they are to be filled. The resulting samples are judgment samples which do not lend themselves to any sort of formal statistical evaluation.

8. Cluster Sampling. The total population is divided into a number of relatively small subdivisions, and then some of these subdivisions, or clusters, are randomly selected for inclusion in the overall sample.

   If the clusters are geographical subdivisions, cluster sampling is also called area sampling.

9. The standard error of the mean $\sigma_{\bar{x}} = \frac{\sigma}{\sqrt{n}}$ measures the extent to which sample means can be expected to fluctuate, or vary, due to chance.

10. The standard error of the mean increases as the variability σ of the population increases.

11. The standard error of the mean decreases as the number of items in the samples increases.

12. The finite population correction factor $\sqrt{\dfrac{N-n}{N-1}}$ in the formula for $\sigma_{\bar{x}}$ is usually ignored if the sample size is less than 5% of the population.

13. Chebyshev's theorem states that when we use the mean of a random sample to estimate the mean of a population, we can assert with a probability of at least $1 - \dfrac{1}{k^2}$ that our error will be less than $k \cdot \sigma_{\bar{x}}$.

14. The central limit theorem states that if the sample size n is large, the theoretical sampling distribution of the mean can be approximated closely with a normal distribution.

15. The central limit theorem is important since it allows us to use the normal curve table to solve a wide variety of problems. It applies to infinite populations and to finite populations where the sample size constitutes a small portion of the population. The theorem is applicable if n is at least 30.

16. The central limit theorem can be used to estimate the probability of error when we use the mean of a random sample to estimate the mean of the population.

AVOIDING COMMON ERRORS:

1. To test whether a given allocation is proportional, we use

$$\frac{n_1}{N_1} = \frac{n_2}{N_2} = \ldots = \frac{n_k}{N_k}$$

To find sample sizes using proportional allocation, we use

$$n_i = \frac{N_i}{N} \quad \text{for } i = 1, 2, \ldots, k$$

2. To test whether a given allocation is optimum, we use

$$\frac{n_1}{N_1 \sigma_1} = \frac{n_2}{N_2 \sigma_2} = \ldots \frac{n_k}{N_k \sigma_k}$$

or if these ratios are approximately equal.

To find sample sizes using optimum allocation, we use

$$n_i = \frac{n N_i \sigma_i}{N_1 \sigma_1 + N_2 \sigma_2 + \ldots + N_k \sigma_k} \quad \text{for } i = 1, 2, \ldots, k$$

3. To calculate probabilities involving $\bar{x}$ using the central limit theorem, we convert to z-scores using

$$z = \frac{\bar{x}-\mu}{\sigma/\sqrt{n}} \quad \underline{not} \quad z = \frac{x-\mu}{\sigma}$$

4. The finite population correction factor $\sqrt{\frac{N-n}{n-1}}$ is included in the formula for $\sigma_{\bar{x}}$ only if $n \geq .05N$.

KEY SYMBOLS:

N = population size

n = sample size

σ = population standard deviation

$\sigma_{\bar{x}}$ = standard error of the mean

$\mu_{\bar{x}}$ = mean of the sampling distribution of means

KEY FORMULAS:

1. The number of distinct samples of size n which can be drawn from a finite population of size N

$$\binom{N}{n}$$

2. The probability that for each random sample of size n drawing one sample at a time from a finite population of size N

$$\frac{1}{\binom{N}{n}}$$

3. The finite population correction factor

$$\sqrt{\frac{N-n}{N-1}}$$

4. The standard error of the mean (finite population)

$$\sigma_{\bar{x}} = \frac{\sigma}{\sqrt{n}}\sqrt{\frac{N-n}{N-1}} \qquad \text{This formula is used if } n \geq .05N$$

5. The standard error of the mean (infinite population)

$$\sigma_{\bar{x}} = \frac{\sigma}{\sqrt{n}} \qquad \text{This formula is used if } n < .05N$$

6. The mean of a sampling distribution of means

$$\mu_{\bar{x}} = \mu \qquad \mu = \text{population mean}$$

7. Chebyshev's theorem

   $k\sigma_{\bar{x}}$ = the error in estimating the population mean μ by using $\bar{x}$. The probability is <u>at least</u> $1 - \frac{1}{k^2}$

8. The error in estimating population mean μ by using the sample mean $\bar{x}$.

   $$\bar{x} - \mu$$

9. <u>The formula which converts $\bar{x}$ to a z-score</u>

   $z = \dfrac{\bar{x}-\mu}{\sigma/\sqrt{n}}$

   or

   $z = \dfrac{\text{error in estimating } \mu}{\text{standard error}}$

   These formulas arise when we want to measure the probabili<u>t</u>y of error in estimating μ by using $\bar{x}$. (The central limit theorem needs to be applicable.)

10. <u>The standard error of the median</u>

    $1.25 \dfrac{\sigma}{\sqrt{n}}$

<u>MODIFIED TRUE/FALSE</u>: If the statement is true, write true. If false, change the underlined words to make the statement true.

_____ 1. A <u>simple random sample</u> from a finite population is a sample which is chosen in such a way that each possible sample has the same probability of being selected.

_____ 2. Sampling with replacement from a finite population <u>is</u>, in effect, sampling from an infinite population.

_____ 3. When sampling with replacement, the finite population correction factor <u>can be</u> omitted.

_____ 4. In order for $\sigma_{\bar{x}}$ to be as low as possible in stratified sampling, it is preferable that each of the strata have as little <u>homogeneity</u> as possible.

_____ 5. The method of allocation such that for a fixed sample size, the sample chosen will have the smallest possible standard error for the estimate of the population mean is called <u>optimum</u> allocation.

_____ 6. A judgment sample is <u>usually not</u> a random sample.

_____ 7. A sampling distribution of the mean is <u>always</u> a probability distribution whose values are sample means.

_____ 8. It is <u>impossible</u> to apply the central limit theorem if the population does not follow a normal distribution.

_____ 9. The variance of the sampling distribution <u>can be</u> equal to the variance of the population.

103

_____ 10. As the sample size increases, the standard error of the mean <u>increases</u>.

_____ 11. The central limit theorem applies in situations when n constitutes a <u>large</u> proportion of the population.

<u>MULTIPLE CHOICE</u>: Write the letter of the best answer in the given space.

_____ 1. If the population is divided into relatively small subdivisions and then some of these subdivisions are selected for inclusion in the overall sample, the method is called _____ sampling.

(a) stratified   (c) quota
(b) cluster   (d) systematic

_____ 2. The possible presence of hidden periodicities is a danger of _____ sampling.

(a) stratified   (c) simple random
(b) cluster   (d) systematic

_____ 3. When we calculate a z-score in an application of the central limit theorem we use the formula:

(a) $z = \frac{x-\mu}{\sigma}$ (c) $z = \frac{\overline{x}-\mu}{\sigma}$

(b) $z = \frac{\overline{x}-\mu}{\sigma/\sqrt{n}}$ (d) $z = \frac{x-\mu}{\sigma/\sqrt{n}}$

_____ 4. The standard error of the mean of a sample of 100 items from a population will be equal to _____ times the standard error of the mean of 25 items.

(a) $\frac{1}{4}$ (b) $\frac{1}{2}$ (c) 4   (d) 2

_____ 5. The value we use for the standard error of the mean when n is at least 5% of the population size is:

(a) $\frac{\sigma}{\sqrt{n}}\sqrt{\frac{N-n}{N-1}}$ (b) σ (c) $\frac{\sigma}{\sqrt{n}}$ (d) s

_____ 6. If the digits 0, 2, 4, 6, 8 represent heads and the digits 1, 3, 5, 7, 9 represent tails, then the random numbers 527, 648, 910, 485 represent what sequence of numbers of heads in four flips of three coins?

(a) 2, 1, 1, 3   (c) 2, 0, 2, 1
(b) 2, 2, 1, 3   (d) 1, 3, 1, 2

_____ 7. Suppose we obtain a sample mean of 80 from a sample of size 100 from an infinite population with $\sigma = 50$. Then the probability is .75 that the error in estimating the population mean using Chebyshev's theorem is:

(a) between 30 and 130   (c) between 74 and 86
(b) less than 6   (d) less than 10

_____ 8. Our sample size criterion for applying the central limit theorem if the population may not be normal is:

    (a) $n \geq 30$ (b) $n \geq .05N$ (c) $n < .05N$ (d) $n \geq 5$

_____ 9. The central limit theorem can be used to estimate the:

    (a) population mean from the sample mean
    (b) probability of error in using $\bar{x}$ to estimate μ
    (c) mean of the sampling distribution by using the population mean
    (d) standard error of the mean by using σ

_____ 10. An important goal of _____ sampling is that there is less variability within the resulting subgroups than in the entire population.

    (a) stratified   (c) quota
    (b) cluster   (d) systematic

_____ 11. A stratified sample is taken from a population of size $N = 2000$ which consists of two strata of $N_1 = 800$, $N_2 = 1200$, $n_1 = 20$, $n_2 = 40$, $\sigma_1 = 3$, $\sigma_2 = 5$. Then the method of allocation is:

    (a) proportional   (c) neither proportional nor optimum
    (b) optimum   (d) both proportional and optimum

_____ 12. If the mean of a random sample of size 400 is used to estimate the mean of an infinite population with a standard deviation of 60, the probability is .95 that the error is less than:

    (a) 1.96   (b) 117.6   (c) 3.92   (d) 5.88

_____ 13. If we want to change a standard error from 12 to 4 by changing the sample size, we need to multiply the original sample size by:

    (a) 3   (b) 9   (c) $\frac{1}{3}$ (d) $\frac{1}{9}$

COMPLETION: Complete the following sentences by filling in the given blanks.

1. We use the value $\frac{\sigma}{\sqrt{n}}$ for the standard error of the mean if the sample size is _____.

2. A random sample of size 36 is selected from a population of size 101 whose standard deviation is 5. The standard error of the mean is _____.

3. The allocation in stratified sampling will be proportional if $n_i =$ _____ for $i = 1, 2, \ldots, k$.

4. If the population is divided into 3 strata and $\frac{n_1}{N_1 \sigma_1} = \frac{n_2}{N_2 \sigma_2} = \frac{n_3}{N_3 \sigma_3}$, then the allocation is called _____.

5. The probability of selecting a random sample of size 3 from a population of size 30 is _____.

105

6. The central limit theorem is important, since it justifies the use of _____ in solving problems.

7. The distribution of the totality of all sample means is called _____.

8. The error in estimating the mean of a population by using a sample mean is expressed in symbols by _____.

9. If we sample with replacement from a finite population, our sample would be random if in each draw all elements of the population _____ and successive draws are _____.

10. The central limit theorem gives the probability that the _____ will be less than a given number when we use the mean of a sample to estimate the _____.

PROBLEMS:

1. How many different samples of size:

   (a) 2 can be selected from a population of size 15

   (b) 3 can be selected from a population of size 12

2. An investor considers investing in the stocks of the following companies: IBM, Honeywell, Mobil, Eastman Kodak, and Homestake Mining.

   (a) In how many ways can the investor select

      (i) 2 stocks to buy

      (ii) 3 stocks to buy

   (b) Find the probability of

      (i) selecting any particular sample of 2 stocks

      (ii) any particular one of the companies being included in a sample of 2 stocks

106

3. Random samples of size 2 are selected from the finite population which consists of the numbers 4, 7, 10, 13, 16, 19.

(a) Find the mean and standard deviation of this population.

(b) List the 15 possible random samples of size 2 that can be selected from the finite population and calculate their means.

(c) Use the results of part (b) to construct the sampling distribution of the mean for random samples of size 2 from the given finite population. Assign each possible sample a probability of $\frac{1}{15}$.

(d) Calculate the mean and variance of the probability distribution obtained in part (c) and verify the results by comparing them with the results obtained by using the appropriate formulas.

4. Suppose that in a group of six athletes, there are three jockeys whose heights are 60, 65, and 55 inches, and three basketball players whose heights are 80, 75, and 85 inches.

(a) List all possible random samples of size 2 which may be taken from this population. Calculate the means of these samples, and calculate $\sigma_{\bar{x}}$.

(b) List all possible stratified random samples of size 2 which may be taken by selecting one jockey and one basketball player. Calculate the means of these samples, and calculate $\sigma_{\bar{x}}$.

(c) Suppose that the six athletes are divided into clusters according to their sports, each cluster is assigned a probability of $\frac{1}{2}$, and a random sample of size 2 is taken from one of the randomly chosen clusters. List all possible samples, calculate their means, and calculate $\sigma_{\bar{x}}$.

(d) Compare and discuss the results obtained for $\sigma_{\bar{x}}$ in parts (a), (b), and (c).

5. Suppose we want to estimate the mean salary of seven people based on a sample of size 3. The salaries of the seven people in thousands of dollars are 25, 10, 19, 57, 53, 55, and 63, so that the population mean we want to estimate is $\mu = 36.5$. If the first three of these salaries are those of bank trainees and the other four are salaries of officers of the bank, find n_1 and n_2 if the allocation is:

(a) proportional

(b) optimum

6. With reference to Problem 5:

    (a) if the allocation is proportional, find

        (i) the number of possible samples

        (ii) $\sigma_{\bar{x}}$ (provided the selection within each stratum is random)

    (b) if the allocation is optimal, find:

        (i) the number of possible samples

        (ii) $\sigma_{\bar{x}}$ (provided the selection within each stratum is random)

7. A stratified sample of size n=300 is to be taken from a population of size N=30,000 which consists of four strata for which N_1=10,000, N_2=5000, N_3=8000, N_4=7000, σ_1=15, σ_2=25, σ_3=20, and σ_4=30. How large a sample must be taken from each stratum if the allocation is to be:

    (a) proportional?

    (b) optimum?

8. When we sample from an infinite population, what happens to the standard error of the mean if the sample size is:

    (a) increased from 64 to 400

(b) decreased from 225 to 100

9. From the population 4, 7, 10, 13, 16, 19 (see Problem 3):

(a) List the 36 possible samples of size 2 that can be drawn with replacement from the given population.

(b) Determine the means of the 36 samples obtained in part (a) and, assigning the samples a probability of $\frac{1}{36}$ each, construct the sampling distribution of the mean for random samples of size 2 from this infinite population.

(c) Calculate the mean and standard deviation of the probability distribution obtained in part (b), and compare them with the corresponding values expected according to the appropriate formulas.

10. The mean number of errors in a random sample of 100 accounts to be audited is used to estimate the mean of the population of accounts having a standard deviation of $\sigma = 4$. What is the probability that the error will be less than .8:

(a) using Chebyshev's theorem?

(b) using the central limit theorem?

11. The mean of a random sample of size 49 is used to estimate the mean of a very large population, consisting of the lifetimes of certain stereo components which have a standard deviation of $\sigma = 35$ hours. What is the probability that our estimate will be in error by:

(a) less than 8 hours?

(b) less than 6 hours?

12. A new cure for the common cold has the side effect of producing dizziness in the user for an average of 40 minutes with a standard deviation of 12 minutes. In a random sample of 64 people who take the drug, find the probabilities that the average time that a user remains dizzy is:

(a) at least 38 minutes.

(b) between 41 and 45 minutes.

13. Give the standard error of the mean for the random variable in Problem 12.

14. Using the population of the numbers, 10, 38, 25, 18, 42, 15, construct the sampling distribution of the median for random samples of size n = 3 drawn without replacement from the given population.

15. The weights of ice cream in "one-scoop" cones by an employee of a certain ice cream store is known to have a mean of 4 ounces with a standard deviation of .6 ounces. What are the probabilities that in a random sample of 36 "one-scoop" cones the average weight is:

   (a) between 3.9 and 4.2 ounces?

   (b) at least 3.7 ounces?

CHAPTER 11

INFERENCES ABOUT MEANS

This chapter deals with different types of decision making in several situations:

    (1) finding confidence intervals for a population mean using large or small samples

    (2) finding the maximum error of estimating a population mean using large or small samples

    (3) finding the required sample size needed to produce an appropriate confidence interval

    (4) using Bayesian estimation of a population mean

    (5) testing hypotheses involving one population mean using large or small samples

    (6) testing hypotheses involving the difference between two population means using large or small samples

CHAPTER OBJECTIVES: By the end of this chapter, you should be able to:

1. Find the maximum error of estimate. (11.1, 11.4, 11.5, 11.6, 11.9)

2. Find a confidence interval for one mean for large samples. (11.2, 11.3, 11.7, 11.8, 11.10)

3. Given an interval, a sample mean, and standard deviation, find the appropriate level of confidence. (11.11, 11.12)

4. Using the finite correction factor, find

    (a) the maximum error of estimate

    (b) a large sample confidence interval   (11.13 - 11.16)

5. Find the required sample size. (11.19 - 11.23)

6. Find a confidence interval for one mean for small samples. (11.26, 11.29, 11.31, 11.33, 11.34, 11.36)

7. Find the maximum error of estimate in a small sample situation. (11.27, 11.28, 11.30, 11.32, 11.35)

8. Find the Bayesian estimate of a posterior mean. (11.38, 11.41a)

9. Find posterior and prior probabilities. (11.37, 11.39, 11.41b)

10. Find an alternative hypothesis given a decision-making situation. (11.42, 11.43)

11. Distinguish among Type I, Type II, and no error situations. (11.44 - 11.49)

12. Calculate probabilities of Type I and Type II errors. (11.50 - 11.57)

13. Set up appropriate hypotheses for a given situation. (11.64 - 11.66)

14. Decide on whether a one-sided or two-sided test is appropriate for a given situation. (11.67, 11.68)

15. Conduct an hypothesis test involving a large-sample mean. (11.70, 11.71, 11.73, 11.75, 11.77, 11.79, 11.80)

16. Find a tail probability corresponding to a given value of z. (11.74, 11.78, 11.80, 11.96)

17. Conduct an hypothesis test involving a small-sample mean. (11.82 - 11.91)

18. Conduct an hypothesis test involving a difference between large-sample means. (11.94 - 11.100)

19. Conduct an hypothesis test involving a difference between small-sample means. (11.103 - 11.108)

20. Conduct an hypothesis test involving paired data. (11.110, 11.111)

KEY POINTS OF THE CHAPTER:

1. A point estimate is a single number estimate of a population characteristic. For example, the sample mean $\bar{x}$ is a point estimate of the population mean μ.

2. The maximum error of estimate, denoted by E, is one-half the width of the corresponding confidence interval. The larger the sample size n, the smaller the maximum error of estimate.

3. A confidence interval is used to provide an interval for the population mean using the sample mean.

4. The large-sample confidence interval formula requires the use of z-scores. The small-sample confidence interval formula requires the use of the t distribution. The number of degrees of freedom needed to find $t_{\alpha/2}$ in the t distribution table is n-1.

5. If we increase (decrease) the confidence percentage, then we increase (decrease) the width of the interval.

6. Bayesian estimation. The prior feelings about the possible values of μ are expressed in the form of a prior distribution. This distribution has a mean μ_0 (called the prior mean) and a standard deviation σ_0 (called the prior standard deviation). The posterior mean μ can be obtained after the sample mean $\bar{x}$ is found. It provides a revised estimate of the population mean μ. Note that μ_1 is a weighted mean of $\bar{x}$ and μ_0 with weights $\frac{n}{\sigma^2}$ and $\frac{1}{\sigma_0^2}$.

7. The finite population correction factor must be used in certain formulas if the sample size is at least 5% of the population. (See Key Formula 11.)

8. Hypotheses for tests involving one population mean.

Example:

	Two-tailed test	One-tailed test (rejection region to left)	One-tailed test (rejection region to right
(null hypothesis)	$\mu = 50$	$\mu = 50$ or $\mu \geq 50$	$\mu = 50$ or $\mu \leq 50$
(alternative hypothesis)	$\mu \neq 50$	$\mu < 50$	$\mu > 50$

9. Hypotheses for tests involving the difference between two population means:

Example:

	Two-tailed test	One-tailed test (rejection region to left)	One-tailed test (rejection region to right)
(null hypothesis)	$\mu_1 - \mu_2 = \delta$	$\mu_1 - \mu_2 = \delta$ or $\mu_1 - \mu_2 \geq \delta$	$\mu_1 - \mu_2 = \delta$ or $\mu_1 - \mu_2 \leq \delta$
(alternative hypothesis)	$\mu_1 - \mu_2 \neq \delta$	$\mu_1 - \mu_2 < \delta$	$\mu_1 - \mu_2 > \delta$

10. Note above in (8) and (9) that the null hypothesis <u>always</u> contains the equal possibility, and that the alternative hypothesis <u>never</u> contains the equal possibility.

11. The location of the rejection region is always indicated by the alternative hypothesis. If the alternative hypothesis has an $\neq$ sign, the test is two-tailed and the rejection region is split into two equal parts in both directions. If the alternative hypothesis has a < sign, the test is one-tailed with the rejection region to the left; if it has a > sign, the test is one-tailed with the rejection region to the right.

12. The hypothesis testing procedure always assumes at the beginning that the null hypothesis is true. The test is performed to determine if there is sufficient evidence to refute the assumption.

13. The significance level, denoted by α, is always specified at the beginning of an hypothesis test. The value of α is the area of the rejection region for the null hypothesis.

14. A <u>Type I error</u> occurs if a true null hypothesis is rejected. The probability of making a Type I error is equal to α.

15. A <u>Type II error</u> occurs if a false null hypothesis is accepted. The probability of making a Type II error is designated by the symbol β.

16. A <u>p-value</u> is the probability of obtaining a particular sample value or more extreme value if the null hypothesis is true.

Example:

In a two-tailed test if the obtained z=1.00, the p-value equals the total area to the right of z=1.00 and to the left of z=-1.00, that is, the p-value equals 2(.5000 - .3413) = .3174.

In a one-tailed test--rejection region to the right--if the obtained z=1.00, the p-value equals .5000 - .3413 = .1587.

AVOIDING COMMON ERRORS:

1. When a question asks for the maximum error of estimate E, do not find a confidence interval. If a minimum sample size is required, do not attempt to find a confidence interval. Be sure to answer the question being asked and not confuse a confidence interval, maximum error, or sample size question with each other.

2. The <u>sample size formula</u> requires a z value that must be found from the given confidence percentage. Note that the given percentage itself is <u>not used</u> in the sample size formula.

3. <u>Stating hypotheses in an hypothesis test</u>. The equal possibility ($=$, $\leq$, or $\geq$) must always appear in the null hypothesis. The possibilities for the alternative hypotheses are $\neq$, $>$, or $<$.

4. <u>Large and small samples</u>. When finding a confidence interval or maximum error of estimate or testing an hypothesis involving one or two means the sample sizes in the problem must be noted since the formulas are different depending on the sample sizes involved. When one mean is involved; if $n \geq 30$, we use the z table and the large sample formula: if $n < 30$, we use the t table and the small sample formula (degrees of freedom is n-1). For the difference between means: if $n_1 \geq 30$, $n_2 \geq 30$, we use the z table and the large sample formula; if $n_1 < 30$ and $n_2 < 30$, we use the t table and the small sample formula (degrees of freedom is n_1+n_2-2).

KEY SYMBOLS:

E = maximum error of estimate μ_1 = posterior mean

n = sample size σ_1 = posterior standard deviation

$\bar{x}$ = sample mean α = total area of rejection region in an hypothesis test, also

μ = population mean

μ_0 = **prior mean** α = probability of making a Type I error

σ_0 = prior standard deviation β = probability of making a Type II error

KEY FORMULAS:

1. Maximum error of estimate

$$E = z_{\alpha/2} \cdot \frac{\sigma}{\sqrt{n}}$$

2. Sample size

$$n = \left[\frac{z_{\alpha/2} \cdot \sigma}{E} \right]^2$$

3. Large-sample confidence interval for μ ($n \geq 30$)

$$\bar{x} - z_{\alpha/2} \cdot \frac{\sigma}{\sqrt{n}} < \mu < \bar{x} + z_{\alpha/2} \cdot \frac{\sigma}{\sqrt{n}}$$

4. Small-sample confidence interval for μ $(n < 30)$

$$\bar{x} - t_{\alpha/2} \cdot \frac{s}{\sqrt{n}} < \mu < \bar{x} + t_{\alpha/2} \cdot \frac{s}{\sqrt{n}}$$

5. Maximum error of estimate (small sample)

$$E = t_{\alpha/2} \cdot \frac{s}{\sqrt{n}}$$

6. Posterior mean and standard deviation

$$\mu_1 = \frac{\dfrac{n}{\sigma^2} \cdot \bar{x} + \dfrac{1}{\sigma_o^2} \cdot \mu_o}{\dfrac{n}{\sigma^2} + \dfrac{1}{\sigma_o^2}}$$

$$\frac{1}{\sigma_1^2} = \frac{n}{\sigma^2} + \frac{1}{\sigma_o^2}$$

7. Statistic for large-sample test concerning one mean $(n \geq 30)$

$$z = \frac{\bar{x} - \mu_o}{\sigma/\sqrt{n}}$$

8. Statistic for small-sample test concerning one mean $(n < 30)$

$$t = \frac{\bar{x} - \mu_o}{s/\sqrt{n}} \qquad \text{degrees of freedom} = n - 1$$

9. Statistic for large-sample test concerning difference between two means $(n_1 \geq 30, \; n_2 \geq 30)$

$$z = \frac{(\bar{x}_1 - \bar{x}_2) - \delta}{\sqrt{\dfrac{\sigma_1^2}{n_1} + \dfrac{\sigma_2^2}{n_2}}}$$

10. Statistic for small-sample test concerning difference between two means $(n_1 < 30, \; n_2 < 30)$

degrees of freedom $= n_1 + n_2 - 2$

$$t = \frac{\bar{x}_1 - \bar{x}_2 - \delta}{\sqrt{\dfrac{(n_1-1)s_1^2 + (n_2-1)s_2^2}{n_1 + n_2 - 2} \cdot \left(\dfrac{1}{n_1} + \dfrac{1}{n_2}\right)}}$$

11. Finite correction factor formula applications

 If the sample size comprises at least 5% of the population, then the following formulas apply:

 (a) maximum error of estimate (large sample)

$$E = z_{\alpha/2} \frac{\sigma}{\sqrt{n}} \sqrt{\frac{N - n}{N - 1}}$$

 (b) confidence interval (large sample)

$$\overline{x} - z_{\alpha/2} \frac{\sigma}{\sqrt{n}} \sqrt{\frac{N - n}{N - 1}} < \mu < \overline{x} + z_{\alpha/2} \frac{\sigma}{\sqrt{n}} \sqrt{\frac{N - n}{N - 1}}$$

MODIFIED TRUE/FALSE: If the statement is true, write true. If false, change the underlined words to make the statement true.

_____ 1. In the hypothesis tests for large and small sample means and differences between means, the left hand term in the numerator is always a population value.

_____ 2. An hypothesis test is always an attempt to make a decision about a sample value.

_____ 3. The alternative hypothesis can never contain an equal sign.

_____ 4. If we increase the confidence level, then we decrease the width of the interval.

_____ 5. The larger the sample size n, the smaller the maximum error of estimate.

_____ 6. A confidence interval found by using the sample mean as an estimate is an attempt to provide an interval for the population mean.

_____ 7. The level of significance should always be specified before a significance test is performed.

_____ 8. Increasing the sample size increases the probability of making a Type I error.

_____ 9. If we reject a true hypothesis, then we are committing a Type II error.

_____ 10. The given confidence level is substituted into the formula used to obtain the required sample size.

MULTIPLE CHOICE: Write the letter of the best answer in the given space.

____ 1. In a hypothesis test, α indicates:

 (a) the area of the rejection region for the null hypothesis
 (b) the probability of a Type II error
 (c) whether the test is one-tailed or two-tailed
 (d) the probability of accepting the null hypothesis

_____ 2. In conducting an hypothesis test, the procedure always assumes that:

(a) the alternative hypothesis is true
(b) the alternative hypothesis is false
(c) the null hypothesis is true
(d) the null hypothesis is false

_____ 3. If the null and alternative hypotheses are: $H_O: \mu = 80$

$H_A: \mu > 80$

then the area of rejection for the null hypothesis is:

(a) to the left
(b) to the right
(c) split into two parts in both directions
(d) cannot be determined from the given information

_____ 4. When a null hypothesis cannot be rejected, we conclude that:

(a) the null hypothesis is true
(b) the null hypothesis may be true
(c) the alternative hypothesis is true
(d) the alternative hypothesis may be true

_____ 5. In a large-sample hypothesis test with an alternative hypothesis of $\mu > 60$, the p-value equals:

(a) α (c) the critical value of z
(b) β (d) the area to the right of the
                                         obtained z value

_____ 6. A null hypothesis will be rejected if:

(a) $\alpha = .05$ and p-value = .15
(b) $\alpha = .05$ and p-value = .03
(c) $\alpha = .01$ and p-value = .03
(d) the obtained value of z is closer to the null hypothesis mean than the critical value

_____ 7. In an hypothesis test that a population mean is at least 50, it is a Type I error to conclude that the mean is:

(a) at least 50 when it is not
(b) at least 50 when it is
(c) less than 50 when it is not
(d) less than 50 when it is

_____ 8. The location of the rejection region for the null hypothesis is determined by:

(a) the sign in the null hypothesis
(b) the sign in the alternative hypothesis
(c) the size of α
(d) the sample size n

_____ 9. If $\alpha = .05$ in a two-tailed large-sample hypothesis test for a population mean, then:

(a) 1.96 is a critical value   (c) 1.65 is a p-value
(b) 1.96 is a p-value   (d) 1.65 is a critical value

___ 10. Which of the following is a possible null hypothesis for a two-tailed hypothesis test?

   (a) $\bar{x} = 30$ (c) $\mu > 30$
   (b) $\mu \neq 30$ (d) $\mu = 30$

COMPLETION: Complete the following sentences by filling in the given blanks.

1. In a one-tailed test that a population mean is at least 50, the alternative hypothesis can be written in symbols as _____.

2. The probability of a Type I error is equal to _____.

3. The population value that $\bar{x}_1 - \bar{x}_2$ estimates is _____.

4. The failure to reject a false hypothesis is called a _____ error.

5. The finite population correction factor $\sqrt{\frac{N-n}{N-1}}$ should be applied to the formula for E (the maximum error) when _____.

6. Two other places that the null hypothesis mean applies in the hypothesis testing procedure are _____ and _____.

7. A small-sample confidence interval formula for a population mean differs from the corresponding large-sample formula in that the small-sample formula contains _____.

8. A sample size of 14 is used to find a confidence interval. The number of degrees of freedom needed is _____.

9. The value of z that separates the acceptance region from the rejection region is called _____.

10. In a test that a difference of two population means is equal to 5, the alternative hypothesis can be written in symbols as _____.

PROBLEMS:

1. A manager of a cafeteria wants to estimate the average time customers wait before being served. A random sample of 49 customers has an average waiting time of 8.4 minutes with a standard deviation of 3.5 minutes.

   (a) With 90% confidence, what can the manager conclude about the possible size of his error in using 8.4 minutes to estimate the true average waiting time?

   (b) Find a 90% confidence interval for the true average customer waiting time.

(c)   Repeat part (a) using a 98% confidence interval.

(d)   Repeat part (b) using a 98% confidence interval.

2.   Suppose the number of customers sampled in Problem 1 is n = 16
     with the same mean and standard deviation, $\bar{x}$ = 8.4 and s = 3.5.
     Answer the same questions as those in Problem 1.

     (a)

     (b)

     (c)

     (d)

3.   An employment agency wants to estimate the average number of people
     who will respond to one of their ads. If σ = 40 people, how large
     a sample is needed to be able to assert with probability .95 that
     the estimate will be off by at most 10 people?

4.   An automobile rustproofing company claims that their methods
     protect cars for 60 months. This hypothesis is tested against the
     alternative that the protection lasts for less than 60 months.
     A random sample of 100 cars produces an average protection time
     of 57 months with a standard deviation of 15 months.

     (a)   State the hypothesis in symbols.

     (b)   Test the hypothesis using the 5% significance level.

     (c)   Find the value of $\bar{x}$ necessary to reject the null hypothesis.

121

5. Two supermarket owners each claim that more customers enter their store than enter the other's store. A survey was taken and it was found that in 60 days an average of 810 people per day entered the first store with a standard deviation of 40 people. A corresponding survey found that in 80 days an average of 800 people per day entered the second store with a standard deviation of 30 people.

   (a) State the hypotheses if this is a two-tailed test.

   (b) Conduct the two-tailed test with $\alpha = .05$.

   (c) Test the hypothesis that $\mu_1 - \mu_2 = 5$ against a two-tailed alternative.

6. For the situation in Problem 4:

   (a) Explain under what condition

      (i) a Type I error would be committed

      (ii) a Type II error would be committed

   (b) Suppose that α was not given and that the null hypothesis is rejected if $\bar{x} < 58$ months and otherwise it is accepted. Find the probability of a Type I error.

7. An automobile manufacturer has claimed that his car averages at least 30 m.p.g. on the highway. A random sample of 16 such cars finds an average gas mileage of 25 m.p.g. with a standard deviation of 8 m.p.g.

   (a) State the hypotheses symbolically for the one-tailed test.

   (b) Conduct the hypothesis test if $\alpha = .01$.

8. A security analyst feels that the prior distribution of the average annual earnings per share of stock in a certain industry has a mean $\mu_o = \$4.50$ and a standard deviation $\sigma_o = \$.40$. He also knows that for any one company in the industry, earnings have varied from year to year with a standard deviation $\sigma = \$1.80$. If a particular company in the industry has average earnings during the past six years of $7.40 per share:

    (a) Find a Bayesian estimate of its true average earnings per share.

    (b) What is the posterior probability that the company's true average annual earnings per share are between $5 and $6?

9. A bank would like to evaluate whether there is a difference in the effectiveness in the methods they use to teach their management trainees. For 10 employees that are taught by method 1 the average score on an evaluation examination was 86 with a standard deviation of 6. For 12 employees taught by method 2 the average score was 81 with a standard deviation of 4.

    (a) State the hypotheses for the two-tailed test in symbols.

    (b) Conduct the hypothesis test using $\alpha = .05$.

10. A housing developer suspects that housing prices in a geographical area are higher than the national average.

    (a) If the developer decides to build a housing community only if a survey of housing prices in the area confirms his suspicions, what hypothesis and alternative should he set up?

    (b) If the developer decides to build the community if the survey of housing prices does not produce an average significantly lower than the national average, what hypothesis and alternative should he set up?

    (c) Suppose the average national home price is $64,000 with a standard deviation of $5,000, and the developer decides to build the community only if in a random sample of 50 newly sold houses the average price is more than $66,000:

(i) what is the probability that the developer builds the community when the prices in the area are only average?

(ii) what is the probability of the developer not building the community if the area price average is $67,000?

11. (a) We would like to estimate the average amount of time that all students at a certain college spent studying during Spring Weekend. We would like to be 90% confident that our estimate is within .5 hours of the actual population average. Find the minimum number of students that need to be sampled if it is known that the maximum and minimum amounts of hours were done by students who studied for 15 hours and 0 hours, respectively.

(b) Using values from part (a), find a 90% confidence interval for the average study time of all students at the college if the sample average was 3.5 hours.

12. The manufacturers of a deodorant claim that the mean drying time of their product is at most 15 minutes. A sample consisting of 16 cans of the product was used to test the manufacturer's claim. The experiment yielded a mean drying time of 18 minutes with a standard deviation of 6 minutes. Test the claim at the 5% significance level.

13. A college food service wanted to determine whether male students consumed <u>more</u> pizza during a given week than female students. A sample of 60 male students found an average consumption of 48 ounces with a standard deviation of 30 ounces. A sample of 80 female students finds an average consumption of 25 ounces with a standard deviation of 20 ounces. Test the appropriate hypothesis at the 1% significance level.

14. If hypotheses are H_0: μ = 50

   H_A: $\mu \neq 50$

with a sample size of 36 and s = 4, find the critical value of x necessary to reject H_0 for α = .02.

15. A motor vehicle bureau claims that the mean time it takes an arriving applicant to obtain a new registration is 30 minutes. If as suspected that this figure is too low, what null and alternative hypotheses should be used to put this to the test?

CHAPTER 12

INFERENCES ABOUT STANDARD DEVIATIONS

This chapter deals with:

(1) confidence intervals for the standard deviation of one population
(2) hypothesis tests for the standard deviation of one population
(3) hypothesis tests for the standard deviations of two populations

CHAPTER OBJECTIVES: By the end of this chapter, you should be able to:

1. Construct a confidence interval of σ. (12.1 - 12.5, 12.7, 12.8, 12.10 - 12.14)

2. Construct a confidence interval for σ^2. (12.6, 12.9)

3. Estimate the true standard deviation using the $\frac{\text{Range}}{d}$ formula. (12.15 - 12.17)

4. Test a null hypothesis that σ or σ^2 has a given value against a one-tailed or two-tailed alternative. (12.18 - 12.26)

5. Test a null hypothesis that the standard deviations of two populations are equal. (12.27 - 12.31)

KEY POINTS OF THE CHAPTER:

1. The sample standard deviation s provides an estimate of the population standard deviation σ.

2. The Chi-Square Distribution.

(i) The chi-square statistic $\chi^2 = \frac{(n-1)s^2}{\sigma^2}$ has a distribution called the chi-square distribution.

(ii) The mean of a chi-square distribution is n-1.

(iii) The number of degrees of freedom of a chi-square distribution is n-1.

(iv) The values of $\chi^2_{\alpha/2}$ and $\chi^2_{1-\alpha/2}$ are different since the chi-square distribution is not symmetrical.

3. Finding a small sample confidence interval for σ or σ^2. For a 95% confidence interval, this requires looking in Table III for $\chi^2_{.975}$ and $\chi^2_{1-.025}$. In general, finding a small sample (1-α) confidence interval for σ or σ^2 requires looking in Table III for $\chi^2_{\alpha/2}$ and $\chi^2_{1-\alpha/2}$.

4. Finding a large sample confidence interval for σ or σ^2. This requires the normal distribution table. This is true since: for large samples (n$\geq$30) the sampling distribution of s can be approximated by a normal distribution with mean σ and standard deviation $\frac{\sigma}{\sqrt{2n}}$.

5. When testing the null hypothesis $\sigma = \sigma_0$ that a population standard deviation σ equals a given constant σ_0:

   (a) the value σ_0 is the assumed value of the population standard deviation when the null hypothesis is true. The sample standard deviation s is an estimate of σ.

   (b) <u>Test involves a small sample--use χ^2</u>

      (i) For the one-tailed alternative hypothesis $\sigma < \sigma_0$ we reject the null hypothesis $\sigma = \sigma_0$ for values of χ^2 falling into the <u>left-hand</u> tail of the sampling distribution.

      (ii) For the one-tailed alternative hypothesis $\sigma > \sigma_0$ we reject the null hypothesis for values of χ^2 falling into the <u>right-hand</u> tail of the sampling distribution.

      (iii) For the two-tailed alternative hypothesis $\sigma \neq \sigma_0$ we reject the null hypothesis $\sigma = \sigma_0$ for values of χ^2 falling in either tail of the sampling distribution. For the given α value, the two critical values are $\chi^2_{\alpha/2}$ and $\chi^2_{1-\alpha/2}$. For example, if $\alpha = .01$, the critical values from Table III are $\chi^2_{.005}$ and $\chi^2_{.995}$.

   (c) <u>Tests involving a large sample--use $z = \dfrac{s - \sigma_0}{\sigma / \sqrt{2n}}$</u>

We have then three possible alternative hypotheses:

      (i) $\sigma < \sigma_0$: then we reject in <u>left-hand</u> tail for $z < -z_\alpha$.

      (ii) $\sigma > \sigma_0$: then we reject in <u>right-hand</u> tail for $z > z_\alpha$.

      (iii) $\sigma \neq \sigma_0$: then we reject in either tail for $z > z_{\alpha/2}$ or $z < -z_{\alpha/2}$.

6. <u>To test for the equality of two standard deviations</u>

   (a) the null hypothesis is $\sigma_1 = \sigma_2$
the alternative hypothesis is $\sigma_1 \neq \sigma_2$

   (b) the F ratio is $F = \dfrac{s_1^2}{s_2^2}$ or $F = \dfrac{s_2^2}{s_1^2}$ whichever is larger

   (c) Assuming that the populations from which the samples came have approximately the shape of normal distributions, the sampling distribution of an F ratio is called the F distribution.

   (d) In testing the null hypothesis $\sigma_1 = \sigma_2$, we reject the null hypothesis if $F > F_{\alpha/2}$.

      <u>Example:</u> If $\alpha = .10$, we reject the null hypothesis if (the obtained value) F is greater than $F_{.05}$.

(e) To use the F table we must first find F, which is the larger

of $\dfrac{s_1^2}{s_2^2}$ and $\dfrac{s_2^2}{s_1^2}$. Then, if $F = \dfrac{s_2^2}{s_1^2}$, we must determine F from the

F table by using n_2-1 for the degrees of freedom for the

numerator, and n_1-1 for the degrees of freedom for the

denominator. If $F = \dfrac{s_1^2}{s_2^2}$, then the numerator and denominator

degrees of freedom are n_1-1 and n_2-1 respectively.

AVOIDING COMMON ERRORS:

1. A small-sample confidence interval for σ^2 (the population variance)
    involves the chi-square distribution. A large-sample confidence
    interval for σ (the population standard deviation) involves the
    normal distribution.

2. The null hypothesis $\sigma = \sigma_o$ is not to be confused with the null
    hypothesis $\sigma_1 = \sigma_2$.

    (a) $\sigma = \sigma_o$ deals with the standard deviation of one population

         compared to a specific value. Testing the hypothesis involves
         a chi-square distribution formula if the data is based on a
         small sample, or the normal distribution (z) if the data is
         based on a large sample.

    (b) $\sigma_1 = \sigma_2$ deals with the comparison of the standard deviations of

         two populations. Testing this hypothesis involves the F

         distribution.

3. A calculated F is the larger of $\dfrac{s_1^2}{s_2^2}$ and $\dfrac{s_2^2}{s_1^2}$. Then the numerator

    and denominator degrees of freedom involved are n_1-1 and n_2-1

    respectively, if $F = \dfrac{s_1^2}{s_2^2}$; or n_2-1 and n_1-1 respectively,

    if $F = \dfrac{s_2^2}{s_1^2}$.

4. The tabled value of $F_{.05}$ involves an $\alpha=.10$.

    The tabled value of $F_{.01}$ involves an $\alpha=.02$.

KEY FORMULAS:

1. Chi-square statistic

$$\chi^2 = \frac{(n-1)s^2}{\sigma^2}$$

2. Small-sample confidence interval for σ^2

$$\frac{(n-1)s^2}{\chi^2_{\alpha/2}} < \sigma^2 < \frac{(n-1)s^2}{\chi^2_{1-\alpha/2}}$$

3. Large-sample confidence interval for σ

$$\frac{s}{1 + \dfrac{z_{\alpha/2}}{\sqrt{2n}}} < \sigma < \frac{s}{1 - \dfrac{z_{\alpha/2}}{\sqrt{2n}}}$$

4. Tests of hypotheses involving a population standard deviation

   (a) one-tailed test--rejection region to the right

   Hypotheses $\sigma = \sigma_0$
   $\sigma > \sigma_0$

   Reject null hypothesis if:

Small Sample	Large Sample
$\chi^2 = \dfrac{(n-1)s^2}{\sigma_0^2} > \chi^2_{\alpha}$	$z = \dfrac{s - \sigma_0}{\sigma_0/\sqrt{2n}} > z_{\alpha}$

   (b) one-tailed test--rejection region to the left

   Hypotheses $\sigma = \sigma_0$
   $\sigma < \sigma_0$

   Reject null hypothesis if:

Small Sample	Large Sample
$\chi^2 = \dfrac{(n-1)s^2}{\sigma_0} < \chi^2_{\alpha}$	$z = \dfrac{s - \sigma_0}{\sigma_0/\sqrt{2n}} < -z_{\alpha}$

   (c) two-tailed test--rejection region in both directions

   Hypotheses $\sigma = \sigma_0$
   $\sigma \neq \sigma_0$

   Reject null hypothesis if:

Small Sample	Large Sample
$\chi^2 = \dfrac{(n-1)s^2}{\sigma_0} < \chi^2_{\alpha/2}$	$z = \dfrac{s - \sigma_0}{\sigma_0/\sqrt{2n}} > z_{\alpha/2}$
or	or
$\chi^2 = \dfrac{(n-1)^2}{\sigma_0} > \chi^2_{1-\alpha/2}$	$z = \dfrac{s - \sigma_0}{\sigma_0/\sqrt{2n}} < -z_{\alpha/2}$

5. Tests of hypotheses involving the equality of two population standard deviations

Hypotheses $\sigma_1 = \sigma_2$

$\qquad\qquad \sigma_1 \neq \sigma_2$

Use $F = \dfrac{s_1^2}{s_2^2}$ or $\dfrac{s_2^2}{s_1^2}$, whichever is larger.

For a given α, reject the null hypothesis if $F > F_{\alpha/2}$.

6. Estimate of σ if population is approximately normal

$\sigma = \dfrac{\text{Range}}{d}$

n	2	3	4	5	6	7	8	9	10	11	12
d	1.13	1.69	2.06	2.33	2.55	2.70	2.85	2.97	3.08	3.17	3.26

MODIFIED TRUE/FALSE: If the statement is true, write true. If false, change the underlined words to make the statement true.

_____ 1. Finding a large-sample confidence interval for σ requires the use of the normal distribution, whereas finding a small-sample confidence interval for σ requires the use of the t distribution.

_____ 2. In testing the null hypothesis that a population standard deviation equals a specified constant, the value σ_0 is the hypothesized standard deviation.

_____ 3. The procedure used to evaluate the null hypothesis $\sigma_1 = \sigma_2$ is the same as the procedure used to evaluate the null hypothesis $\sigma = \sigma_0$ where σ_0 is a constant.

_____ 4. The F ratio can be used to evaluate the null hypothesis that the population standard deviation equals a given constant.

_____ 5. It is always true that the higher the value of χ^2 the more likely the null hypothesis that $\sigma = 28$ will be rejected.

_____ 6. A hypothesis test involving one population standard deviation always involves the calculation of

$\chi^2 = \dfrac{(n-1)s^2}{\sigma^2}$.

_____ 7. The value of the standard deviation σ_0 is sometimes obtained from a sample.

_____ 8. If $\dfrac{s_1^2}{s_2^2}$ has a value very close to 0, then the null

hypothesis of equal population standard deviations cannot be rejected.

_____ 9. An F ratio is the ratio of two <u>population standard deviations</u>.

_____ 10. In order to test the hypothesis that a population σ is a specified constant, it is <u>always</u> necessary to know the mean of the sample.

MULTIPLE CHOICE: Write the letter of the best answer in the given space.

____ 1. The symbol χ^2 has which of the following properties?

(a) It equals χ_α^2 (c) Has n-1 degrees of freedom

(b) The area to its right equals α (d) The area to its left equals $\alpha/2$

____ 2. To find a 90% confidence interval for the standard deviation from a small sample, we use the values:

(a) $\chi^2_{.90}$ and $\chi^2_{.10}$ (c) $\chi^2_{.975}$ and $\chi^2_{.025}$

(b) $\chi^2_{.95}$ and $\chi^2_{.05}$ (d) only $\chi^2_{.90}$

____ 3. If a significance level of .01 is used in testing the null hypothesis that $\sigma=.30$ against the alternative hypothesis that $\sigma>.30$, based on a random sample of size n=15, then the relevant tabled value is:

(a) $\chi^2_{.01}$ (c) $\chi^2_{.005}$

(b) $\chi^2_{.99}$ (d) $z_{.01}$

____ 4. To test the hypothesis that two population standard deviations are equal, we use which of the following distributions?

(a) F   (c) normal
(b) chi-square   (d) t

____ 5. If the hypothesis $\sigma=.20$ is tested against the hypothesis that $\sigma\neq.20$, with $\alpha=.05$, based on a random sample of size n=18, then the appropriate tabled value(s) is (are):

(a) $\chi^2_{.05}$ only   (c) $\chi^2_{.10}$ only

(b) $\chi^2_{.025}$ and $\chi^2_{.975}$ (d) $\chi^2_{.025}$ only

____ 6. A computed χ^2 value that is larger than the $\chi^2_{\alpha/2}$ value

allows us to reject the null hypothesis that _____ based on a _____.

(a) $\sigma=\sigma_o$, small sample   (c) $\sigma_1=\sigma_2$, small sample

(b) $\sigma=\sigma_o$, large sample   (d) $\sigma_1=\sigma_2$, large sample

_____ 7. The hypothesis that two population standard deviations are equal can be rejected at the 10% significance level if:

(a) $F > F_{.10}$

(c) $F > F_{.20}$

(b) $F > F_{.05}$

(d) $F < F_{.05}$

_____ 8. The more that the sample standard deviation s differs from the hypothesized value σ_0, the more likely that the null hypothesis:

(a) $\sigma_1 = \sigma_2$ can be rejected

(c) $\sigma = \sigma_0$ can be rejected

(b) $\sigma_1 = \sigma_2$ cannot be rejected

(d) $\sigma = \sigma_0$ cannot be rejected

_____ 9. In an effort to evaluate the hypothesis that $\sigma_1 = \sigma_2$, the sample variances $s_1^2 = 18$ and $s_2^2 = 54$ were obtained, based on sample sizes of $n_1 = 15$ and $n_2 = 10$ respectively. The numerator and denominator degrees of freedom are, respectively:

(a) 14 and 9

(c) 10 and 15

(b) 15 and 10

(d) 9 and 14

_____ 10. If $\alpha = .10$, the null hypothesis in Question 9 should be:

(a) rejected since F=3

(c) rejected since F=.33

(b) not rejected since F=3

(d) not rejected since F=.33

COMPLETION: Complete the following sentences by filling in the given blanks.

1. A sample estimate of σ is symbolized by _____ .

2. The mean of a chi-square distribution is equal to _____ .

3. The possible values that a chi-square distribution can assume are _____ .

4. If $s_1^2 = 30$ and $s_2^2 = 20$, then the F ratio we use is _____ .

5. In testing the null hypothesis that a population standard deviation equals a specified constant based on a small sample, the test statistic that is used is _____ .

6. In tests concerning the equality of two population variances, the test statistic is _____ .

7. In order to convert a small-sample confidence interval for the variance to a confidence interval for the standard deviation we must _____ .

8. An 80% confidence interval for σ obtained from a small sample will require the numbers _____ and _____ obtained from Table III.

9. When finding a confidence interval for σ^2, based on a small sample, the number of degrees of freedom for the chi-square distribution is _____ .

10. In testing for the equality of two standard deviations using the F statistic if $\alpha=.02$, the F table value that must be exceeded to reject the null hypothesis is given by the symbol _____ .

PROBLEMS:

1. Find the necessary values from the appropriate tables that are needed to answer the following questions:

   (a) Find a 90% confidence interval for σ^2 based on a sample of size n=15.

   (b) Find a 90% confidence interval for σ based on a sample of size n=60.

   (c) Test the null hypothesis that $\sigma^2=40$ against the alternative hypothesis that $\sigma^2 \neq 40$ at $\alpha=.01$ using a sample of size n=13.

   (d) Test the null hypothesis that $\sigma=40$ against the alternative hypothesis that $\sigma=40$ at $\alpha=.01$ using a sample of size n=80.

2. A random sample of 11 copies of a particular mechanical component has a mean length of 5 inches with a standard deviation of .60.

   (a) Find a 95% confidence interval for the population variance.

   (b) Find a 90% confidence interval for the population variance.

133

(c) Find a 95% confidence interval for the population standard
     deviation.

3. Repeat Problem 2 for a sample size of n=50.

    (a)

    (b)

    (c)

4. A vending machine company wants to limit the variation in the
    number of ounces of soda that their machine dispenses into each
    cup. Use the .01 level of significance to test the null hypothesis
    $\sigma=.12$ ounces against the alternative hypothesis $\sigma>.12$ ounces based
    on a random sample of size n=15 cups for which s=.18.

5. Suppose the sample size in Problem 4 is increased to 50 cups and
    the obtained sample standard deviation is .15 ounces. Test the
    same hypothesis at $\alpha=.01$.

6. The monthly sales of a shoe store during the past 10 months were
    $7500, $6250, $8000, $4000, $5800, $9500, $8200, $7200, $8400,
    $4800.   If the population of monthly sales is normally distributed,
    estimate the population standard deviation σ using the table below.

n	2	3	4	5	6	7	8	9	10	11	12
d	1.13	1.69	2.06	2.33	2.55	2.70	2.85	2.97	3.08	3.17	3.26

134

7. A man who needs an operation would like to evaluate the variation in survival rates in different hospitals for his type of operation. He hypothesizes that the standard deviation of survival rates at all hospitals is .08. Test this hypothesis against the alternative hypothesis if a random sample of 12 hospitals produces a standard deviation of .11. Use $\alpha = .10$.

8. Calculate the F ratio for each set of data and compare it to the appropriate tabled value. Make a decision concerning the null hypothesis of equal population standard deviations.

   (a) $s_1 = 5$ $n_1 = 13$

          $s_2 = 9$ $n_2 = 10$ $\alpha = .10$

   (b) $s_1 = 15$ $n_1 = 16$

          $s_2 = 7$ $n_2 = 10$ $\alpha = .02$

9. An owner of a chain of supermarkets claims that there is greater price competition among supermarkets than among small "convenience" food stores. A sample of ground beef prices in 13 supermarkets and 10 convenience stores gives standard deviations of $.15 and $.10 respectively. Evaluate the claim at the 10% significance level.

10. In a random sample of 9 gasoline stations in New York City, the prices per gallon of unleaded gas have a standard deviation of $.08 per gallon. In a random sample of 14 gasoline stations in Chicago, the prices per gallon have a standard deviation of $.03 per gallon. Use the 10% significance level to test the null hypothesis that the price per gallon of gasoline is equally variable in the two cities.

135

11. Give an important reason why a test concerning the equality of the standard deviations of two populations might be useful.

12. When might we be interested in testing a null hypothesis that a population standard deviation equals a specified constant?

13. To test the equality of two population standard deviations, σ_1 and σ_2, why must we choose <u>the larger of two</u> F ratios?

CHAPTER 13

INFERENCES ABOUT PROPORTIONS

The principal topics of this chapter are:

(1) confidence intervals and tests involving one population proportion
(2) tests concerning two population proportions
(3) tests concerning more than two population proportions
(4) tests involving data tallied in two-way classifications
(5) tests evaluating the degree to which the observed distribution agrees with a given distribution

CHAPTER OBJECTIVES: By the end of this chapter, you should be able to:

1. Construct a confidence interval for a population proportion. (13.2, 13.4, 13.6, 13.8, 13.11, 13.13, 13.14)

2. Find the maximum size of the error when a sample proportion is used as a point estimate of a population proportion. (13.3, 13.5, 13.7, 13.9, 13.12, 13.14)

3. Determine the minimum sample size needed for a sample proportion to have a given maximum error in estimating the population proportion for a given degree of confidence. (13.18 - 13.25)

4. Conduct an hypothesis test for a population proportion based on a small sample. (13.30 - 13.37)

5. Conduct an hypothesis test for a population proportion based on a large sample. (13.38 - 13.44)

6. Conduct an hypothesis test for the difference of two population proportions. (13.45 - 13.53)

7. State hypotheses for an $r \times c$ table. (13.58 - 13.60)

8. Test if there is a relationship between two variables in an $r \times c$ table using the chi-square statistic.   (13.61 - 13.67)

9. Calculate the contingency coefficient for a contingency table. (13.68)

10. Conduct an hypothesis test for the difference among k proportions using the chi-square statistic. (13.69 - 13.77)

11. Conduct a goodness-of-fit test using the chi-square statistic. (13.81 - 13.89)

KEY POINTS OF THE CHAPTER:

1. The sample proportion is given by $\frac{x}{n}$ where x is the number of successes in n trials. This sample proportion is an estimate of p, the population proportion.

2. In order to use all the formulas in the chapter that involve the value z (i.e., formulas that involve the normal distribution), we must have both $np > 5$ and $n(1-p) > 5$.

3. The quantity $\sqrt{\dfrac{p(1-p)}{n}}$ is called the standard error of the proportion.

4. The maximum error of estimate, E, equals $\frac{1}{2}$ of the width of a confidence interval.

5. When $n \leq 20$, hypothesis tests concerning proportions can be based on the binomial probability table. (Table V)

   Example: (two-tailed test) $p=.40$ against $p \neq .40$ at $\alpha=.05$ with $n=10$.

   Divide α by 2 to obtain .025 and look in Table V for $n=10$, the $p=.40$ column.

   Since the .006 in the $p=.40$ column is less than .025, we reject the null hypothesis if $x=0$. Similarly, since the sum of the values .011, .002, and .000 on the upper tail is less than .025, we reject the null hypothesis if $x=8,9,$ or 10. The null hypothesis is not rejected if the obtained x value is $1,2,3,4,5,6,7$. The corresponding rejection and acceptance regions for the one-tailed tests if $\alpha=.05$ are also given.

| | | alternative hypothesis | |
| | two-tailed | one-tailed | one-tailed |
x	p≠.40	p<.40	p>.40
0	*⌈.006	*⌈.006	⌈.006
1	⌈.040	⌊.040	.040
2	.121	⌈.121	.121
3	.215	.215	.215
4	**⌈.251	**⌈.251	**⌈.251
5	.201	.201	.201
6	.112	.112	⌊.112
7	⌊.043	.043	⌈.043
8	⌈.011	.011	.011
9	*⌈.002	.002	*⌈.002
10	⌊.000	.000	⌊000

6. The difference between sample proportions $\dfrac{x_1}{n_1} - \dfrac{x_2}{n_2}$ is an estimate of p_1-p_2, the difference between population proportions.

7. The standard error of the difference between two proportions is given by

$$\sqrt{\dfrac{p_1(1-p_1)}{n_1} + \dfrac{p_2(1-p_2)}{n_2}}$$

8. Comparison of statements of hypotheses for proportions

   Test of one proportion

	two-tailed	one-tailed	
(null)	p=.40	p=.40	p=.40
(alternative)	p≠.40	p<.40 or	p>.40

   Tests of difference between two proportions

	two-tailed	one-tailed	
(null)	$p_1-p_2=0$	$p_1-p_2=0$	$p_1-p_2=0$
(alternative)	$p_1-p_2 \neq 0$	$p_1-p_2<0$ or	$p_1-p_2>0$

   Tests of several proportions (2 x C table)

(null)	$p_1=p_2=p_3=p_4$
(alternative)	p_1,p_2,p_3,p_4 are not all equal

   *rejection   **acceptance region

9. χ^2 tests

   (a) When the χ^2 statistic is used to test a null hypothesis (e.g., differences among proportions, independence in a contingency table, goodness-of-fit), the null hypothesis should be accepted if the differences between the observed frequencies and the expected frequencies are small (or rejected if large).

   (b) The number of degrees of freedom for the chi-square distribution:

       (i)   differences among proportions
       (ii) independence in a contingency table $\Big]$ $(r-1)(c-1)$
       (iii) goodness-of-fit } $k - m - 1$

   (c) If any of the expected frequencies in a contingency table is less than 5, the chi-square distribution is applicable only if we combine some of the samples in such a way that none of the e's is less than 5.

   (d) For an $r \times k$ table, we use the χ^2 statistic to test the following hypothesis:

       (i) (null hypothesis) one variable is <u>independent</u> of the other; (alternative hypothesis) one variable <u>depends</u> on the other; or <u>equivalently</u>:
       (ii) (null hypothesis) there is <u>no relationship</u> between the two variables; (alternative hypothesis) there <u>is a relationship</u> between the two variables

10. Tests of independence between two variables are conducted on an $r \times c$ table. There are two types of such tables:

    (a) the column totals are fixed, the row totals are left to chance

    (b) both the column and row totals are left to chance. This second type of $r \times c$ table is called a <u>contingency table</u>.

11. (a) The <u>goodness-of-fit</u> test is used to determine if a set of data fits the pattern of a given distribution (e.g., binomial, Poisson, normal)

    (b) The closer the observed values fit the expected frequencies (the smaller the χ^2 value) the more likely the data fits the given distribution, i.e., the more likely the null hypothesis is true. The larger the χ^2 value the more likely we would reject the null hypothesis that the data fits the hypothesized distribution.

AVOIDING COMMON ERRORS:

1. <u>Sample size formula</u>. The given confidence percentage should not be substituted into the formula; but, rather, the z value that corresponded to the confidence percentage (e.g., to find the z value in determining the sample size for a 95% confidence interval, use z=1.96).

2. Difference between proportions hypothesis test. Use $p_1 - p_2$ in

    the statement of the hypotheses, not p, or $\dfrac{x_1}{n_1} - \dfrac{x_2}{n_2}$.

3. One population proportion hypothesis test. Use p in stating the
    hypothesis, not $p_1 - p_2$, or $\dfrac{x}{n}$.

4. Goodness-of-fit test. The null hypothesis in a goodness-of-fit
    test is that the observations are values of a random variable
    having a given distribution.

KEY FORMULAS:

1. Large-Sample Confidence Interval for p

$$\frac{x}{n} - z_{\alpha/2}\sqrt{\frac{\frac{x}{n}(1-\frac{x}{n})}{n}} < p < \frac{x}{n} + z_{\alpha/2}\sqrt{\frac{\frac{x}{n}(1-\frac{x}{n})}{n}}$$

2. Maximum Error of Estimate

$$E = z_{\alpha/2}\sqrt{\frac{\frac{x}{n}(1-\frac{x}{n})}{n}}$$

    This is the most useful formula for
    estimating the maximum error of estimate
    for a given confidence percentage, sample

    proportion $\dfrac{x}{n}$, and sample size n

3. Sample Size

$$n = p(1-p)\left[\frac{z_{\alpha/2}}{E}\right]^2$$

    This formula is used to obtain the
    minimum sample size when p is given.
    The obtained n value must always be
    rounded upward to the nearest whole
    number.

4. Sample Size When p Is Not Given

$$n = \frac{1}{4}\left[\frac{z_{\alpha/2}}{E}\right]^2$$

5. Statistic for Large-Sample Test Concerning Proportions

$$z = \frac{x - np_0}{\sqrt{np_0(1-p_0)}}$$

Standard Error of a Proportion

$$\sqrt{\frac{p(1-p)}{n}}$$

6. Statistic for Test Concerning Difference Between Two Proportions

$$z = \frac{\dfrac{x_1}{n_1} - \dfrac{x_2}{n_2}}{\sqrt{p(1-p)(\frac{1}{n_1} + \frac{1}{n_2})}} \quad \text{with } p = \frac{x_1 + x_2}{n_1 + n_2}$$

7. Estimate of Common Population Proportion

$$\frac{x_1 + x_2 + \ldots + x_k}{n_1 + n_2 + \ldots + n_k}$$

8. Statistic for Test Concerning

   (a) Differences Among Proportions

   $$\chi^2 = \sum \frac{(o-e)^2}{e}$$

   (b) Independence in a Contingency Table

   $$\chi^2 = \sum \frac{(o-e)^2}{e} \quad \text{(same formula as in (a))}$$

   (c) Goodness-of-Fit

   $$\chi^2 = \sum \frac{(o-e)^2}{e} \quad \text{(same formula as in (a))}$$

9. Contingency Coefficient

   $$C = \sqrt{\frac{\chi^2}{\chi^2 + n}} \qquad n = \text{total frequency for the table}$$

   maximum value of $C = \sqrt{\frac{k-1}{k}}$

MODIFIED TRUE/FALSE: If the statement is true, write true. If false, change the underlined words to make the statement true.

_____ 1. In determining the necessary sample size for a 95% confidence interval, the value .95% must be substituted into the formula for $z_{\alpha/2}$.

_____ 2. The chi-square test can be used to determine if there is a significant difference between two sample proportions.

_____ 3. In order to use the maximum error of estimate formula involving the sample value $\frac{x}{n}$, n must be large enough to justify the normal curve approximation to the binomial distribution.

_____ 4. To decide whether or not observed differences among 3 sample proportions can be attributed to chance requires the use of the normal distribution table.

_____ 5. The value of α has a definite effect on the number of degrees of freedom used to determine χ^2.

_____ 6. The null hypothesis in a goodness-of-fit test is that the distribution of the sample does not fit the theoretical distribution.

_____ 7. For a contingency table, the expected frequency values are based on the assumption that the <u>null hypothesis is true</u>.

_____ 8. The null hypothesis in a chi-square test of independence is that there is <u>no relationship</u> between the two variables.

_____ 9. The χ^2 statistic should <u>never</u> be applied to contingency tables as long as some of the expected frequencies are less than 5.

_____ 10. The formula $n = \dfrac{p(1-p)z^2_{\alpha/2}}{E^2}$ is often used to determine a <u>confidence interval</u> for a population proportion.

<u>MULTIPLE CHOICE</u>: Write the letter of the best answer in the given space.

____ 1. It is claimed that at most 70% of all local businesses last more than 1 year. The null hypothesis p=.70 is tested against the alternative p>.70 at α=.05 for a sample size of n=11. Suppose 8 of the businesses lasted more than 1 year. Which of the following decisions should be made regarding the null hypothesis?

(a) Reject, since 11>8   (c) Reject, since 8>4
(b) Do not reject,   (d) Do not reject, since 8>4
    since 11>8

____ 2. It is claimed that 40% of all shoppers at a shopping mall enter a particular one of its department stores. A random sample of 14 shoppers at the mall was selected. If the null hypothesis p=.40 is tested against the alternative that p<.40, the null hypothesis will be rejected at α=.01 if _____ of the 14 shoppers enter the store.

(a) at least 2   (c) at least 11
(b) at most 1   (d) at most 10

____ 3. The null hypothesis that two processes produce the same proportion of defectives can be written:

(a) p=0   (c) $p_1-p_2=0$

(b) $\dfrac{x_1}{n_1} - \dfrac{x_2}{n_2} = 0$ (d) $\dfrac{x}{n} = 0$

____ 4. A placement office at a large university claims that approximately 70% of the school's graduates will obtain jobs in their major field upon graduation. The administration feels that the percentage is larger than 70%. From a random sample of 100 recent graduates it was found that 75 had obtained jobs in their field. The hypotheses are:

(a) H_O: $p_1-p_2=.70$ (c) H_O: $p<.70$
    H_A: $p_1-p_2>.70$ H_A: $p\geq.70$

(b) H_O: $p=.70$ (d) H_O: $p=.70$
    H_A: $p>.70$ H_A: $p\neq.70$

_____ 5. If the observed frequencies are exactly equal to the expected frequencies in a chi-square test, the value of χ^2 is:

(a) close to 1
(b) a large positive value

(c) 0
(d) a very small positive value

_____ 6. A small computed χ^2 value for a contingency table reveals which of the following concerning the two variables?

(a) a strong relationship between them
(b) one is dependent on the other
(c) the observed frequencies greatly differ from the expected frequencies
(d) one is independent of the other

_____ 7. In a study to determine if a college student's year in college is independent of his or her major, a sample of 200 students was found to contain 40 juniors and 50 accounting majors. Then, the expected frequency of junior accounting majors is:

(a) 10
(b) 20

(c) 25
(d) 15

_____ 8. To test the null hypothesis that a population proportion is p=.40 using a sample size of n=12, we used the _____ distribution.

(a) t
(b) normal

(c) binomial
(d) chi-square

_____ 9. Which of the following conclusions is reasonable for a test of independence at α=.05 if $\chi^2_{.05}$ = 18.31?

(a) If χ^2 = 17.50, then dependent
(b) If χ^2 = 19.15, then independent
(c) If χ^2 = 18.95, then dependent
(d) If χ^2 = 18.60, then independent

_____ 10. For a contingency table, which of the following is true?

(a) numbers of rows and columns are equal
(b) each cell has frequency $\geq$ 5.
(c) column and row totals left to chance
(d) cannot be used to test for the equality of two populations

COMPLETION: Complete the following statements by filling in the given blanks.

1. The symbol $\frac{x}{n}$ represents a sample estimate of _____.

2. The standard error of the proportion is given by _____.

3. If n=400, an hypothesis test may be conducted to test a population proportion using the normal curve if p is between _____ and _____.

4. For a particular error value and confidence level, the maximum value that the sample size formula can assume occurs when p equals _____ .

5. The chi-square statistic for a 7 × 4 contingency table will have _____ degrees of freedom.

6. The sample value $\dfrac{x_1}{n_1} - \dfrac{x_2}{n_2}$ is an estimate of the population value

_____ .

7. When conducting a chi-square test for goodness-of-fit, the number of degrees of freedom is given by _____ .

8. The most useful formula for determining the maximum error of estimate is given by _____ .

9. To determine if a set of data fits the pattern of the binomial distribution, the test for _____ is used.

10. The larger the statistic in a goodness-of-fit test, the _____ likely the data fits the hypothesized distribution.

PROBLEMS:

1. (a) An office worker claims that at most 30% of the phone calls he makes are the nonbusiness type. Test the null hypothesis that p=.30 against a one-tailed alternative if a random sample of 13 of his calls reveals 8 nonbusiness calls. Use α =.05.

(b) Repeat part (a) using α=.01

(c) Conduct a two-tailed test of p=.30 at α=.05.

2. A cereal company is marketing a new breakfast food. In a random sample of 250 people who have tried the product, 175 people said that they would buy it again. What can we state with 99% confidence about the maximum size of our error if we use the sample proportion $\dfrac{175}{250}$ = .70 as an estimate of the actual population proportion of people who will buy the product a second time?

3. A drug company wants to know whether the probability is really .20 that one of their products will produce side effects. In a random sample of 150 consumers of the product, 42 were victims of side effects.

   (a) Conduct the two-tailed test. Use $\alpha = .01$. (State the hypotheses and draw the appropriate graph.)

   (b) Conduct a one-tailed test where the alternative is that the probability is greater than .20. Use $\alpha = .01$.

4. A suntan lotion manufacturer wants to estimate the proportion of people who will get a tan by using their product. In a sample of 80 people, 50 were tanned by the product. Find a 98% confidence interval for the population proportion of people who will receive a tan from the lotion.

5. A university placement office wants to estimate the percentage of graduates that obtain jobs within one month of graduation. They want to be 98% confident in their result and be within 5% of the true percentage.

   (a) Find the necessary sample size for this experiment.

   (b) Using your answer to (a) for the sample size, find a 98% confidence interval if 30% of the sample received jobs within one month of graduation.

6. (a) A television station wants to determine if there is a difference in the proportions of people who watched two of their programs. In random samples of 60 and 80 people, 25 and 40 people watched the first and second programs respectively. Using a 5% significance level, conduct the test.

(b) In part (a) suppose the station wants to know if less people watched the first program than the second. Use the same sample results and conduct the one-tailed test at α=.05.

7. A manufacturer has test-marketed a new men's cologne. Simple random samples of male students at a university were asked to try the product for four weeks, and then were asked the question: "Would you purchase the product?" The results are shown in the following table:

	sophomores	juniors	seniors	
will not purchase	13	12	25	50
will purchase	87	88	275	450
	100	100	300	500

Would you conclude the respondents' preferences are independent of year in college? Conduct the test at α=.05.

8. A sample of 210 people was telephoned. The number of rings that have <u>fully</u> elapsed before each person answered the phone are recorded below:

number of rings	number of people
0	19
1	44
2	68
3	48
4	18
5	7
6	6
	210

At the .05 level of significance, does it appear that the data may be looked upon as a random sample from a binomial population with p=.4 and n=6? Conduct the goodness-of-fit test.

9. A student wants to take a statistics course with a teacher who is a very easy grader. There are 3 teachers scheduled to teach the course next semester. The student manages to obtain a random sample of grades given by the 3 teachers this past year.

	Professor			
Grade	#1	#2	#3	
A	10	12	28	50
B	15	30	25	70
C	35	30	15	80
	60	72	68	200

146

Using the 1% level of significance, test the hypothesis that a student's grade was independent of the student's teacher.

10. (a) Calculate the contingency coefficient for the data in Problem 9.

    (b) What is the maximum value of C for a 4 × 4 contingency table?

11. A company is marketing a laser disk recorder. A survey of 80 randomly selected male students at a college reveals that 45 would be interested in buying such a recorder. A corresponding survey of 120 female students reveals that 75 want to buy it. Test the hypothesis that there is no difference between the males and the females on this issue. Use the 5% significance level.

12. Ninety out of 120 house-husbands prefer detergent A. If the 80 house-husbands represent a random sample from a population of all potential purchases, estimate the fraction of total house-husbands favoring detergent A by constructing a 98% confidence interval.

13. In Problem 12, if 34 use the sample proportion $\frac{90}{120}$ = .75 as an estimate of the true percentage of house-husbands who prefer detergent A , with what confidence can we assert that our error does not exceed 5%?

14. An auditor is assigned to investigate the probability of a bank's accounts having errors. If she has reason to believe that the probability is anywhere between .15 and .40, how large a sample will she need to be 99% confident that the estimated percentage of accounts containing errors is within .02 of the true percentage?

15. An automobile repair service asks 170 customers with annual incomes under $20,000, 180 customers with annual incomes from $20,000 to $50,000 and 150 customers with annual incomes over $50,000 whether they rated the repair service as outstanding, above average, average, below average, or poor. What hypotheses do we want to test if we are going to perform a chi-square analysis of the resulting 5 x 3 table?

CHAPTER 14

ANALYSIS OF VARIANCE

This chapter considers the problem of deciding whether observed differences among <u>more than two</u> sample means can be attributed to chance, or whether there are real differences among the means of the population samples.

<u>CHAPTER OBJECTIVES</u>: By the end of this chapter, you should be able to:

1. Test whether there is a significant difference among several means using a one-way analysis of variance:

    (a) when the number of elements in each sample is the same. (14.1 - 14.5), (14.10 - 14.14, 14.28)

    (b) when the number of elements in the samples may differ. (14.15 - 14.17)

2. Perform a two-way analysis of variance in a complete block experiment. (14.24 - 14.28)

3. Perform a two-way analysis of variance for a two-factor experiment. (14.29, 14.30)

4. <u>List</u> all the necessary tests that comprise a complete factorial <u>experiment</u>. (14.31a, 14.33)

5. <u>Count the number</u> of tests that comprise a complete factorial <u>experiment</u>. (14.31b, 14.32)

6. Complete a given Latin square. (14.34, 14.37)

7. Analyze a given Latin square. (14.35, 14.36)

8. Finish a balanced incomplete block design. (14.38, 14.39)

<u>KEY POINTS OF THE CHAPTER</u>:

1. The subject of this chapter is "analysis of variance." This is a method that involves evaluating the differences among more than two means by comparing two variances (MS(Tr) and MSE). That is, the title of the subject does <u>not</u> refer to the goal (comparing means), but, rather, to the method of achieving that goal.

2. When using the F table in a one-way ANOVA we need to know

    numerator df = k-1   (treatment degrees of freedom)
    denominator df = k(n-1)   (error degrees of freedom)

3. The treatment sum of squares SS(Tr) measures the variation between samples.

4. In a one-way ANOVA, the error sum of squares (SSE) measures the variation within samples.

5. A blocking variable is an extraneous variable--one of no special interest--which is used primarily to reduce the error sum of squares.

6. Two types of experiments which involve a two-way ANOVA are:

    (a) a complete block experiment in which there are two variables, one variable of material concern, the other a blocking variable.

    (b) a two-factor experiment in which there are two variables, both of material concern.

7. When using the F table in a two-way ANOVA we need to know:

    numerator df = k-1 ——————→ (treatment degrees of freedom)
    denominator df = (k-1)(n-1) ←——→ (error degrees of freedom)

8. (a) If the null hypothesis in a one-way ANOVA is true, then the variation among samples is close to the variation within samples.

    (b) If the null hypothesis in a one-way ANOVA is false, then the variation among samples is significantly larger than the variation within samples.

9. It is possible to conduct a one-way ANOVA when the sample sizes differ. (See Key Formula 7.)

10. Latin Square Design

    (a) A Latin square is a square array of letters A, B, C, D,... which is such that each letter occurs once and only once in each row and in each column.

    (b) This is an incomplete design in which there must be 3 factors indicated by: (1) the rows, (2) the columns, and (3) the letters.

    (c) All 3 factors must have the same number of levels. For example, if there are 4 levels for the main treatment indicated by the letters A, B, C, D, then each of the row and column factors must have 4 levels so that the square must be 4 by 4.

11. An Incomplete Block Design is a design in which it is impossible to have each treatment in each block. If each treatment appears together with each other treatment once within the same block, the design is referred to as a balanced incomplete block design.

AVOIDING COMMON ERRORS

1. A two-factor experiment requires the testing and evaluation of two null hypotheses. That is, two different obtained F values are each compared to possibly different tabled F values.

2. The error degrees of freedom for a two-way ANOVA (complete-block experiment or two-factor experiment) are equal to

$$(k-1)(n-1)$$

This is different from the error degrees of freedom for a one-way ANOVA which is equal to

$$n(k-1)$$

3. In this chapter, note the following definition of symbols:

k = number of treatments

n = number of observations in the sample (if equal sample sizes)

4. To construct an incomplete block design (see Problems 13.24 and 13.25 in the text), it is helpful to first make a list of all <u>pairs</u> of observations. Then, in constructing the list of blocks each pair of observations can be crossed off as it appears in the block.

KEY SYMBOLS:

1. SST=total sum of squares

2. SS(Tr)=treatment sum of squares

3. MS(Tr)=treatment mean square

4. SSE=error sum of squares

5. MSE=error mean square

6. x_{ij}=a sample observation

7. $T_{..}$total of all observations in all samples

8. $T_{i.}$=total of all observations in the ith treatment

9. n_i=number of observations in the ith treatment if sample sizes are unequal

10. N=total number of observations in all samples when there are unequal sample sizes

KEY FORMULAS:

1. F ratio

$$F = \frac{\text{variation among means}}{\text{variation within samples}} = \frac{MS(Tr)}{MSE}$$

2. Total Sum of Squares

$$SST = \sum_{i=1}^{k} \sum_{j=1}^{n} (x_{ij} - x..)^2$$

3. Identity for a One-Way ANOVA

$$SST = n \sum_{1=1}^{k} (\bar{x}_i - \bar{x}..)^2 + \sum_{1=1}^{k} \sum_{j=1}^{n} (x_{ij} - \bar{x}_i)^2$$

4. Treatment Mean Square

$$MS(Tr) = \frac{SS(Tr)}{k-1}$$

5. <u>Error Mean Square</u>

$$MSE = \frac{SSE}{k(n-1)}$$

6. <u>One-Way ANOVA</u>

   <u>Computing Formula for Sums of Squares</u> (equal sample sizes)

   (a) $SST = \sum_{i=1}^{k} \sum_{j=1}^{n} x_{ij}^2 - \frac{1}{kn} \cdot T_{..}^2$ Total df = nk-1

   (b) $SS(Tr) = \frac{1}{n} \cdot \sum_{i=1}^{k} T_{i.}^2 - \frac{1}{kn} \cdot T_{..}^2$ df for treatments = k-1
                                                                df for error = k(n-1)

   (c) $SSE = SST - SS(Tr)$

7. <u>One-Way ANOVA</u>

   <u>Computing Formulas for Sums of Squares</u> (unequal sample sizes)

   (a) $SST = \sum_{i=1}^{k} \sum_{j=1}^{n} x_{ij}^2 - \frac{1}{N} \cdot T_{..}^2$ total df = N-1

   (b) $SS(Tr) = \sum_{i=1}^{k} \frac{T_{i.}^2}{n_i} - \frac{1}{N} \cdot T_{..}^2$ df for treatments = k-1
                                                                df for error = N-k

   (c) $SSE = SST - SS(Tr)$

8. <u>Computing Formula for Block Sum of Squares</u>

$$SSB = \frac{1}{k} \cdot \sum_{j=1}^{n} T_{.j}^2 - \frac{1}{kn} \cdot T_{..}^2$$

9. <u>Error Sum of Squares - Two-Way ANOVA</u>

   (a) <u>Complete-Block Experiment</u>

   $SSE = SST - SS(Tr) - SSB$

   (b) <u>Two-Factor Experiment</u>

   $SSE = SST - SSA - SSB$

<u>MODIFIED TRUE/FALSE</u>: If the statement is true, write true. If false, change the underlined words to make the statement true.

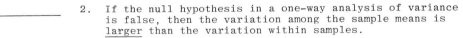

        1. Analysis of variance is a method by which we can decide whether or not observed differences among more than two sample <u>variances</u> can be attributed to chance.

        2. If the null hypothesis in a one-way analysis of variance is false, then the variation among the sample means is <u>larger</u> than the variation within samples.

        3. The treatment sum of squares measures the variation <u>within</u> samples.

_____ 4. The formula for SST in a two-factor experiment is <u>the same as</u> the one for a complete-block experiment.

_____ 5. In a one-way analysis of variance, the null hypothesis is rejected if the obtained F value is <u>greater than</u> the tabled F value.

_____ 6. The treatment sum of squares is symbolized by <u>SST</u>.

_____ 7. A Latin Square experiment <u>is</u> an example of a complete factorial experiment.

_____ 8. The method of analysis of variance <u>is not</u> applicable for data in which sample sizes are not all equal.

_____ 9. A two-way ANOVA <u>sometimes</u> involves a blocking factor.

_____ 10. In a two-way ANOVA, the degrees of freedom for treatment is calculated in <u>the same</u> way as that for a one-way ANOVA.

_____ 11. In a Latin Square experiment, it is <u>impossible</u> for one factor to have 3 levels and another <u>to have 4</u> levels.

MULTIPLE CHOICE: Write the letter of the best answer in the given space.

_____ 1. In testing the null hypotheses $\mu_1 = \mu_2 = \mu_3 = \mu_4$, the computed F value is found by calculating:

(a) $\dfrac{MST}{MSE}$ (c) $\dfrac{MS(Tr)}{MST}$

(b) $\dfrac{MSE}{MS(Tr)}$ (d) $\dfrac{MS(Tr)}{MSE}$

_____ 2. In a complete-block design:

(a) SST = SS(Tr) + SSE   (c) SST = SSB + SSE
(b) SST = SS(Tr) + SSB   (d) SST = SS(Tr) + SSB
    +SSE

_____ 3. The degrees of freedom for error in a two-way ANOVA equals:

(a) k(n-1)   (c) (k-1)n
(b) (k-1)(n-1)   (d) k-1

_____ 4. The degrees of freedom for blocks in a complete-block design equals:

(a) k(n-1)   (c) k-1
(b) (k-1)(n-1)   (d) n-1

_____ 5. In a one-factor ANOVA having 3 treatment levels with 5 observations in each sample, the between samples degrees of freedom is equal to:

(a) 2   (c) 12
(b) 4   (d) 10

6. A blocking factor is:

(a) the treatment factor in a one-way ANOVA
(b) a treatment factor in a two-way ANOVA
(c) a factor which causes variations that are included in SSE
(d) an extraneous variable which causes variations not included in SSE

7. In a one-factor ANOVA having 3 treatment levels with 5 observations in each sample, the within-samples degrees of freedom equals:

(a) 2   (c) 12
(b) 4   (d) 10

8. It is not true that the F ratio for a one-way ANOVA:

(a) can be less than one   (c) measures $\dfrac{SS(Tr)}{SSE}$

(b) must be at least zero   (d) involves two kinds of degrees of freedom

9. If the null hypothesis in a one-way ANOVA is true, the between-samples variation is probably _____ the within-samples variation.

(a) close to
(b) significantly larger than
(c) significantly smaller than
(d) significantly different from (more or less)

10. An experimental design in which the number of rows must equal the number of columns is provided by the:

(a) Latin square experiment   (c) complete factorial experiment
(b) incomplete block design   (d) two-way analysis of variance

11. If each kind of treatment appears with each other kind of treatment once within the same block, the design is referred to as the _____ design.

(a) Latin square   (c) randomized block
(b) complete factorial   (d) balanced incomplete block

12. The ratio which evaluates the significance of an extraneous variable in an analysis of variance is:

(a) $\dfrac{MST}{MSE}$ (c) $\dfrac{MS(Tr)}{MST}$

(b) $\dfrac{MS(Tr)}{MSE}$ (d) $\dfrac{MSB}{MSE}$

COMPLETION: Complete the following sentences by filling in the given blanks.

1. In an F ratio for a one-way ANOVA, the numerator degrees of freedom is _____.

2. In an F ratio for a one-way ANOVA, the denominator degrees of freedom is _____.

3. The _____ sum of squares measures the variation within samples.

4. A two-way analysis of variance applied to an experiment in which we want to test both factors is called a _____.

5. In a one-way ANOVA, in terms of other sums of squares, SSE = _____.

6. A two-way ANOVA in which only one variable is of material concern, consists of one treatment factor and one _____.

7. The _____ sum of squares measures the variation between samples.

8. In a complete-block design, the sum of squares for blocks measures the variation _____ samples.

9. In a complete-block design, in terms of sums of squares, SSE = ____.

10. In a two-factor ANOVA, in terms of sums of squares, SST = _____.

11. When each kind of treatment appears together with each other kind of treatment once within the same block, the design is referred to as _____.

12. In a Latin square experiment, there are always _____ factors.

13. A complete factorial experiment with 4 factors having 3, 5, 4, and 2 levels, respectively, requires _____ observations.

PROBLEMS:

1. Find

    (a) $F_{.05}$ if df for treatments is 4
          df for error is 12

    (b) $F_{.05}$ for 4 treatments, 3 elements per sample

    (c) $F_{.01}$ if df for treatments is 4
          df for error is 12

    (d) $F_{.01}$ for 4 treatments, 3 elements per sample

2. The analysis of variance table below represents part of the calculations for testing the null hypothesis $\mu_1=\mu_2=\mu_3=\mu_4=\mu_5$.

   Complete the table and test the null hypothesis at $\alpha=.01$.

Source of Variaton	Degrees of Freedom	Sum of Squares	Mean Square	F
Treatments		80		
Error				
Total	16	100		

3. The analysis of variance table below for a complete-block experiment represents part of the calculations for testing the null hypothesis $\mu_1=\mu_2=\mu_3$, in which the samples have 6 observations each. If SST=50, SSB=5, and SSE=35, fill in the ANOVA table and test the null hypothesis at $\alpha=.01$.

Source of Variation	Degrees of Freedom	Sum of Squares	Mean Square	F
Treatments				
Block				
Error				
Total				

4. A job performance evaluator is concerned with how workers' performance ratings are affected by their skill level and their attitude. He obtained the following data:

		Attitude			
		Poor	Fair	Good	Excellent
Skill Level	Low	60	62	70	68
	Medium	65	63	65	70
	High	70	75	72	73

   (a) Construct the ANOVA table.

   (b) Test the two hypotheses at $\alpha=.05$

5. A complete-block design is being used to test the null hypothesis that mean responses are identical under 4 treatments, with 3 levels used for the blocking factor. The following data are obtained:

   SS(Tr) = 60
   SSB = 90
   SST = 200

(a) Construct the ANOVA table.

(b) Should the null hypothesis of identical population means be rejected at the $\alpha = .05$ significance level?

6. A complete-block experiment is used to test the null hypothesis that 3 teaching methods produce no difference in mean achievement score. The blocking variable consists of 4 ability levels. The following data is obtained:

		Method		
		1	2	3
	very low	85	80	82
ability	low	80	83	85
level	average	90	84	78
	high	92	80	84

(a) Construct the ANOVA table.

(b) The null hypothesis of equal population means is tested at $\alpha = .05$. Should it be rejected?

7. A two-factor ANOVA is being used to evaluate two null hypotheses. The first factor has 5 levels and the second has 4 levels. The following data are obtained:

SSA = 60
SSB = 40
SST = 124

(a) Construct the ANOVA table.

(b) The two null hypotheses of equal means are tested at $\alpha = .05$. What are the conclusions?

8. A new all-purpose cleaner is placed in 4 different locations in a
    supermarket. We would like to evaluate whether there is a
    significant difference in the number of cans sold with regard
    to location. The sample data below gives the number of cans sold
    in randomly selected supermarkets during a one-week period.

                            Locations

            1   2   3   4
           20   12   25   20
           15   14   28   22
           25   10   30   24

    (a) Complete the one-way ANOVA table.

    (b) Test whether there is a significant difference in sales of
         the all-purpose cleaner with regard to location. Use $\alpha = .01$.

9. Repeat Problem 8 using $\alpha = .01$ for the following sample data:

                            Locations

            1   2   3   4
           20   12   25   20
           15   14   28   22
           25   10   24
           30   18

10. An educational researcher wants to compare four different teaching
    methods A, B, C, D which she wants to try on freshmen (F) and
    juniors (J) who have three different ability levels: low (L),
    medium (M), and high (H). List the 24 tests she must perform so
    that each teaching method is used once with each combination of
    grade level and ability level.

11. A marketing researcher wants to evaluate the success (based on resulting sales) of 3 different marketing strategies (I, II, III) employing 3 different media (radio, television, and newspapers) in 3 different cities: Chicago, New York, and Los Angeles.

	CHICAGO	NY	LA
Radio	I 48	II 95	III 70
Television	III 68	I 94	II 69
Newspapers	II 49	III 96	I 95

Analyze this Latin Square, using the .05 level of significance for each test.

12. Suppose we want to compare the abilities of nine different trainees in a management development program. The trainees are assigned so that three of them at a time work under one of four different supervisors. The different supervisors provide the blocking variable and the nine trainees are denoted by R, S, T, U, V, W, X, Y, Z:

1.	I	S T U	8.	III	U V W
2.	I	V Y	9.	III	T X Y
3.	I	$\overline{Z}$ W X	10.	IV	T _ Z
4.	II	X S V	11.	IV	R $\overline{U}$ X
5.	II	W _ T	12.	IV	_ _ _
6.	II	Z $\overline{U}$ Y			
7.	III	S Z R			

Replace the six spaces with the appropriate letters so that each trainee works with each other trainee once with only one supervisor, so that the arrangement is a balanced incomplete block design.

13. Under what circumstances would a Latin square design be used in an experiment?

14. What is a complete block experiment?

15. Under what circumstances would a complete block design be a desirable design for an experiment?

CHAPTER 15

REGRESSION

This chapter deals with the problem of predicting the average value of one variable in terms of the known value of another variable (or the known values of other variables).

CHAPTER OBJECTIVES: By the end of this chapter, you should be able to:

1. Solve the normal equations to find the equation of a least-squares line. (15.3a)

2. Solve for a and b directly using the "solutions of normal equations." (15.3b, 15.6a, 15.7, 15.8a, 15.10, 15.14a)

3. Make predictions using the least-squares line. (15.4, 15.6b, 15.8b, 15.11, 15.14b)

4. Find the least-squares regression in line when the given x and y variables are interchanged. (15.15)

5. Test a null hypothesis involving the regression coefficient β. (15.19 - 15.22)

6. State a null hypothesis in words. (15.23)

7. Test a null hypothesis involving the regression intercept. (15.23, 15.24)

8. Construct a confidence interval for β. (15.25 - 15.27)

9. Construct a confidence interval for α. (15.28 - 15.30)

10. Find a confidence interval for the mean of y when $x = x_o$. (15.31 - 15.33)

11. Find a confidence interval for a single future observation (limits of prediction). (15.34, 15.35)

12. Make predictions using a multiple regression equation. (15.38b, 15.39b, 15.40b)

13. Fit a least-squares multiple regression equation. (15.38 - 15.41)

14. Fit an exponential curve to given data. (15.42 - 15.44)

15. Fit a power function to given data. (15.45, 15.46)

16. Fit a parabola to given data. (15.47 - 15.50)

KEY POINTS OF THE CHAPTER:

1. Least-squares regression for one independent variable using a straight line involves deriving a mathematical equation of the line and using it to predict the value of one variable from a given value of another.

2. The equation of the line which we fit to our data is such that the sum of the squares of the vertical deviations of the points from the line is a minimum.

3. (a) The standard error of estimate gives the extent of the dispersion of the data points around the regression line.

   (b) There are two equivalent formulas for the standard error of estimate: one is based on the definition, the other is the short-cut formula which is used more often.

4. To conduct hypothesis tests involving α or β , use the t formula (see Key Formula 7) which allows us to determine whether the sample a or b is sufficient to reject the hypothesis.

5. Confidence intervals for α or β may be obtained by using a or b respectively, as sample estimates in the t formula (see Key Formula 8).

6. A confidence interval for μ_{y/x_o}, the true (population) value of y given $x = x_o$ may be obtained using the t table and Key Formula 9.

7. A confidence interval for a future individual observation may be obtained using the t table and Key Formula 10.

8. (a) When we find the least-squares regression equation involving two or more independent variables, we are dealing with multiple regression.

   (b) To determine the multiple regression equation when there are two independent variables, we must solve the normal equations (see Key Formula 11).

9. When data depart widely from linearity, we must consider fitting some curve other than a straight line. Some other possible curves are (1) a parabola, (2) an exponential curve, or (3) a power curve.

10. If paired data are plotted on semi-log paper (with equal subdivisions for x and a logarithmic scale for y), this indicates that an exponential curve will provide a good fit.

11. If points representing paired data fall close to a straight line when plotted on log-log paper (with logarithmic scales for both x and y), this indicates that a power function will provide a good fit.

AVOIDING COMMON ERRORS:

1. The symbol $\mu_{y/x}$ should not be confused with the symbol μ_{y/x_o}. The $\mu_{y/x}$ is the true mean of y for a given value of x (or the predicted values of the population regression line). The μ_{y/x_o} is the true mean of y given x_o, a particular value of x.

2. When using the t table to find confidence intervals or conduct hypothesis tests involving regression with one independent variable the number of degrees of freedom is n-2, not n-1.

3. The equation of the exponential regression equation should not be confused with that of a power regression equation. For the exponential equation, the independent variable x is the exponent. For the power equation, the independent variable x is the base.

<u>KEY SYMBOLS</u>:

$\hat{y}$ (1)   the predicted values obtained from the sample least-squares regression line

(2)   a sample estimate of $\mu_{y/x}$ (the y-intercept of the population regression line)

a   (1)   the y-intercept of the sample least-squares regression line

(2)   a sample estimate of α (the y-intercept of the population regression line)

b   (1)   the slope of the sample least-squares regression line

(2)   a sample estimate of β (the slope of the population regression line)

$\mu_{y/x}$ (1)   the true mean of y for a given value of x

(2)   the predicted values of the population regression line

α the y-intercept of the true (population) regression line

β the slope of the true (population) regression line

s_e the standard error of estimate

$\Sigma(y-\hat{y})^2$ the sum of squares of the vertical deviations from the points to the line. It is the numerator in the definition formula for the standard error of estimate.

n-2   the number of degrees of freedom used to obtain values from the t table. Such values are found when conducting hypothesis tests or finding confidence intervals in regression problems involving one independent variable.

μ_{y/x_0} the true mean of y given x_0

b_0 the intercept in the multiple regression equation

b_1, b_2 the coefficients of the independent variables in the multiple regression equation with two independent variables

n   the number of data points in a regression situation

<u>KEY FORMULAS</u>:

1. <u>Least-squares regression equation</u>

$\hat{y} = a + bx$

where   a = y-intercept
        b = slope

This is the equation of the line for which the sum of the squares of the distances from the original points to the line is as small as possible

163

2. Sum of Squares

$$S_{xx} = \sum x^2 - \frac{1}{n}(\sum x)^2$$

$$S_{yy} = \sum y^2 - \frac{1}{n}(\sum y)^2$$

These formulas are needed for the regression equations below.

$$S_{xy} = \sum xy - \frac{1}{n}(\sum x)(\sum y)$$

3. Normal equations

$$\Sigma y = na + b(\Sigma x)$$

$$\Sigma xy = a(\Sigma x) + b(\Sigma x^2)$$

From these equations, we can find the a and b in the least-squares regression equation above.

4. Solutions of normal equations

$$b = \frac{S_{xy}}{S_{xx}}$$

$$a = \frac{\sum y - b(\sum x)}{n}$$

From these equations, we can solve for the a and b in the least-squares regression equation more directly than by using the normal equations.

5. Equation of the true regression line

$$\mu_{y/x} = \alpha + \beta x$$

where $\mu_{y/x}$ = the true mean of y for a given value of x

α = y-intercept of true regression line

β = slope of true regression line

$\mu_{y/x}$, α, β are each population values

$\hat{y}$ is a sample estimate of $\mu_{y/x}$

a is a sample estimate of α

b is a sample estimate of β

6. Standard error of estimate (definition formula)

$$s_e = \sqrt{\frac{\Sigma(y-\hat{y})^2}{n-2}}$$

Standard error of estimate (short-cut formula)

$$s_e = \sqrt{\frac{S_{yy} - bS_{xy}}{n-2}}$$

s_e gives a measure of the dispersion, or error of the given data points around the regression line. Note that all deviations are measured vertically from the points to the line.

164

7. Statistics for inferences about regression coefficients

$$t = \frac{a - \alpha}{s_e \sqrt{\dfrac{1}{n} + \dfrac{\bar{x}^2}{S_{xx}}}}$$

This formula is applied in hypothesis tests concerning α.

$$t = \frac{b - \beta}{s_e / \sqrt{S_{xx}}}$$

This formula is applied in hypothesis tests concerning β.

8. Confidence limits for regression coefficients

$$a \pm t_{\alpha/2} \cdot s_e \sqrt{\frac{1}{n} + \frac{\bar{x}^2}{S_{xx}}}$$

This formula gives a confidence interval for α, the y-intercept of the population regression line.

$$b \pm t_{\alpha/2} \cdot \frac{s_e}{\sqrt{S_{xx}}}$$

This formula gives a confidence interval for β, the slope of the population regression line.

9. Confidence interval for mean of y when $x = x_0$

$$(a + bx_0) \pm t_{\alpha/2} \cdot s_e \sqrt{\frac{1}{n} + \frac{(x_0 - \bar{x})^2}{S_{xx}}}$$

This formula gives a confidence interval for μ_{y/x_0}, the true mean of y given x_0.

10. Limits of prediction

$$(a + bx_0) \pm t_{\alpha/2} \cdot s_e \sqrt{1 + \frac{1}{n} + \frac{(x_0 - \bar{x})^2}{S_{xx}}}$$

This formula gives a confidence interval for a single future observation when $x = x_0$.

11. <u>Least-squares multiple regression equation for two independent variables</u>

$$\hat{y} = b_o + b_1 x_1 + b_2 x_2$$

12. <u>Normal equations (two independent variables)</u>

$$\Sigma y = n \cdot b_o + b_1(\Sigma x_1) + b_2(\Sigma x_2)$$

$$\Sigma x_1 y = b_o(\Sigma x_1) + b_1(\Sigma x_1^2) + b_2(\Sigma x_1 x_2)$$

$$\Sigma x_2 y + b_o(\Sigma x_2) + b_1(\Sigma x_1 x_2) + b_2(\Sigma x_2^2)$$

From these equations, we can find the b_o, b_1, and b_2 in the least-squares regression equation above.

13. <u>Exponential regression equation</u>

$$\hat{y} = ab^x$$

This is the equation of the exponential curve for which the sum of the squares of the distances from the original points to the curve is as small as possible.

14. <u>Normal equations for fitting exponential curve</u>

$$\Sigma \log y = n(\log a) + (\log b)(\Sigma x)$$

$$\Sigma x(\log y) = (\log a)(\Sigma x) + (\log b)(\Sigma x^2)$$

From these equations, we can find the a and b in the least-squares regression equation in 13 above.

15. <u>Parabolic regression equation</u>

$$\hat{y} = a + bx + cx^2$$

This is the equation of the parabola for which the sum of the squares of the distances from the original points to the curve is as small as possible.

16. **Normal equations fitting parabola**

$$\Sigma y = na + b(\Sigma x) + c(\Sigma x^2)$$

$$\Sigma xy = a(\Sigma x) + b(\Sigma x^2) + c(\Sigma x^3)$$

$$\Sigma x^2 y = a(\Sigma x^2) + b(\Sigma x^3) + c(\Sigma x^4)$$

From these equations, we can find the a, b, and c in the regression equation in 14.

17. **Power regression equation**

$$\hat{y} = a \cdot x^b$$

This is a power function for which the sum of the squares of the distances from the original points to the curve is as small as possible.

18. **Normal equations for fitting power function**

$$\Sigma \log y = n(\log a) + b(\Sigma \log x)$$

$$\Sigma (\log x)(\log y) = (\log a)(\Sigma \log x) + b(\Sigma \log^2 x)$$

From these equations, we can find the a and b in the regression equation in 16 above.

MODIFIED TRUE/FALSE: If the statement is true, write true. If false, change the underlined words to make the statement true.

_____ 1. The estimated regression line is the line that minimizes the sum of the <u>absolute values</u> of the distances from the given points to the line.

_____ 2. The symbol $\hat{y}$ gives the true mean of y for a given value of $x = x_o$.

_____ 3. The <u>standard deviation</u> measures the dispersion of the y values about the estimated least-squares line.

_____ 4. A confidence interval for a future individual value is <u>wider</u> than a confidence interval for a mean of y when $x = x_o$.

_____ 5. In regression analysis, the variable that we are trying to predict is called the <u>independent</u> variable.

_____ 6. Multiple regression involves at least two <u>dependent</u> variables.

_____ 7. In general, the <u>larger</u> the standard error of estimate the better the least-squares regression line.

_____ 8. The estimated and true regression lines are <u>always</u> the same.

_____ 9. If the slope of the true regression line is zero, then the slope of the sample regression line <u>may be</u> different from zero.

_____ 10. If paired data plotted on log-log paper fall close to a straight line, we would expect <u>a parabola</u> to provide a good fit for the data.

167

MULTIPLE CHOICE: Write the letter of the best answer in the given space.

____ 1. The slope of the true regression line is given by:

(a) α (b) β (c) a   (d) b

____ 2. In regression analysis, the quantity that gives the amount by which y changes for a unit change in x is called the:

(a) y-intercept   (c) standard error of estimate
(b) slope   (d) standard deviation

____ 3. The symbol used to indicate the y values of points on a least-squares line is:

(a) b   (c) $\hat{y}$

(b) $\bar{y}$ (d) y

____ 4. The normal equations are obtained from minimizing:

(a) $\Sigma(y-\hat{y})^2$ (c) $\Sigma(y-\hat{y})$
(b) $\Sigma(y-\bar{y})^2$ (d) $\Sigma(\bar{y}-\hat{y})$

____ 5. The symbol a in the least-squares equation is a sample estimate of:

(a) α (c) $\mu_{y/x}$

(b) β (d) s_e

____ 6. If we are testing the hypothesis that $\beta=0$ against the alternative that $\beta \neq 0$ when there are 12 data points and $\alpha = .05$, the correct t value to be used is:

(a) 1.812   (c) 2.228
(b) 1.796   (d) 2.201

____ 7. The symbol b in the least-squares equation is a sample estimate of:

(a) α (c) $\mu_{y/x}$

(b) β (d) s_e

____ 8. Given the regression equation $\hat{y}=3+7x$, the most central value in a confidence interval for x=4 is:

(a) 4   (c) 7
(b) 31   (d) 3

____ 9. The symbol that represents the true regression line is:

(a) $\hat{y}$ (c) β
(b) μ_{y/x_o} (d) $\mu_{y/x}$

168

___ 10. The width of a confidence interval for μ_{y/x_o} will be increased if:

(a) x_o is moved closer to $\bar{x}$ (c) n is increased

(b) s_e is decreased   (d) t is increased

COMPLETION: Complete the following sentences by filling in the given blanks.

1. When we make inferences about the regression coefficients α and β, the number of degrees of freedom that is required to use the t table is _____.

2. The term which measures the dispersion of the y values about the estimated least-squares line is called _____.

3. In linear regression analysis, we assume that for each value of x the variable to be predicted has a mean of _____.

4. The symbols used for the estimated regression coefficients when there is one independent variable are _____ and _____.

5. In a test of the null hypothesis that $\beta=10$ against the alternative hypothesis that $\beta>10$, the null hypothesis will be rejected if the obtained t value is _____ the tabled t value.

6. When we use observed data to derive a mathematical equation and use it to predict the value of one variable from a given value of another, the procedure is known as _____.

7. The symbol for the mean of y when $x=x_o$ is _____.

8. In a two-tailed hypothesis test that $\beta=0$, the tabled t values are -2.262 and 2.262. If the obtained t value is 1.83, the null hypothesis _____ rejected.

9. A multiple regression equation with three independent variables has the form _____.

10. If paired data plotted on semi-log paper fall close to a straight line, then we would expect a (an) _____ to provide a good fit for the data.

PROBLEMS:

1. The advertising expense and profit of a company for each of five years is given below:

advertising expense (in thousands) x	profit (in thousands) y
2	15
7	50
10	110
15	220
20	200

(a) Solve the normal equations to find the equation of the least-squares line which will allow us to predict profit from advertising expense.

(b) Check your values of a and b using the "solutions of normal equations."

(c) If advertising expense is to be $9000 for a particular year, predict the profit for that year.

2. For the data in Problem 1, find:

    (a) s_e

    (b) a 95% confidence interval for μ_{y/x_o} for $x_o = 9$ (advertising expense of $9000)

    (c) a 95% confidence interval for a single future observation

3. (a) For the data in Problem 1, find the least-squares line that predicts advertising expense from the profit.

(b) Predict advertising expense for a profit of $40,000.

4. A personnel manager wants to predict the salary of a systems analyst
    based on number of years experience. A random sample of 12 systems
    analysts produces the following results:

X years' experience	Y salary (thousands)
5.5	19.9
9.0	25.5
4.0	23.9
8.0	24.0
9.5	22.5
3.0	20.5
7.0	21.0
1.5	17.7
8.5	30.0
7.5	25.0
9.5	21.0
6.0	18.6

(a) Find the least-squares line which predicts salary based on
     years of experience.

(b) Predict the salary of a systems analyst with 5 years'
     experience.

5. For the data in Problem 4:

    (a) Test the hypothesis that $\alpha = 0$ against the alternative that $\alpha \neq 0$. First, state the hypothesis in words. Use the .05 significance level.

    (b) Find a 95% confidence interval for α.

6. For the data in Problem 4:

    (a) Test the hypothesis that $\beta = 0$ against the alternative that $\beta > 0$. First, state the hypothesis in words. Use the .05 significance level.

    (b) Construct a 98% confidence interval for β.

7. For the data in Problem 4:

    (a) Find a 95% confidence interval for the mean of y when x=6.0.

(b) Find a 95% confidence interval for a single future observation if x=6.0.

8. Given the following annual profit figures (in thousands of dollars) for a company:

Year	Profit
1	500
2	700
3	1000
4	1800
5	3000

Fit an exponential trend to this data.

9. Fit a power curve to the data in Problem 8.

10. The following data give the demand of a product (in hundreds of units) for five different price levels (in dollars):

Price	12	10	8	6	4
Demand	80	100	120	110	90

Fit a parabola to this data.

173

11. (a) The data below gives the number of 18-25 year olds (for the given years) whose families earn between $15-$25,000 per year (X) and the number of U.S. college students for the given year (Y). Find the least-squares regression equation which predicts Y from X.

Year	X (in millions)	Y (in millions)
1971	3.90	8.09
1972	4.02	8.31
1973	4.05	8.18
1974	4.16	8.83
1975	4.25	9.70
1976	4.20	9.95
1977	4.25	10.22
1978	4.26	9.84

(b) Find the standard error of estimate.

(c) Predict Y if X=4.00.

174

12. Suppose an additional variable (X_2), the number of families with total income between $15,000 and $25,000, is added to the data of Problem 11:

Year	X_2 (in millions)
1971	4.09
1972	5.00
1973	4.84
1974	4.30
1975	5.08
1976	7.83
1977	7.29
1978	6.86

(a) Using the data and the information in Problem 11, find the least-squares multiple regression equation which predicts Y from X_1 and X_2.

(b) For 4 million 18-25 year olds whose families are in the $15-$25,000 income bracket and 7 million families whose income is $15-$25,000, predict the number of U.S. college students.

13. A study is supposed to examine the relationship between the amount spent on advertising a new product (x) and consumer awareness of the product (y) based on the proportion of people who have heard of it. Suppose a sample shows the following data for four different products.

x Advertising Expense (in \$1,000s)	y Consumer Awareness (percent)
800	90
180	20
100	10
200	50

(a) Find the equation of the least-squares line that will allow use to predict consumer awareness from the advertising expense.

(b) Calculate the standard error of estimate.

14. Can the equation found in Problem 13(a) be used for an advertising expense of 60 thousand dollars? Why or why not?

15. (a) Using a 95% confidence level, construct an interval estimate of the mean consumer awareness of a single product, assuming that 700,000 dollars is spent for its promotion.

(b) Using a 5% significance level, test the hypothesis that advertising expenditure has no impact on consumer awareness.

CHAPTER 16

CORRELATION

This chapter deals with the problem of evaluating how well a least-squares line fits given paired data.

CHAPTER OBJECTIVES: By the end of this chapter, you should be able to:

1. Calculate a correlation coefficient. (16.1, 16.2, 16.5, 16.6, 16.9, 16.13, 16.14, 16.19)

2. Calculate the percentage of total variation accounted for by a variable. (16.3, 16.7, 16.9)

3. State whether two given variables are likely to produce a positive, negative, or no correlation. (16.11, 16.12)

4. Test a null hypothesis involving ρ using a large or small sample. (16.20 - 16.31)

5. Construct a confidence interval for ρ. (16.32, 16.33)

6. Calculate the multiple correlation coefficient. 16.34 - 16.36, 16.38)

7. Calculate the partial correlation coefficient. (16.39, 16.40)

KEY POINTS OF THE CHAPTER:

1. The coefficient of determination, symbolized by r^2, gives the proportion of total variation that is explained by the regression line. The possible values for r^2 are given by the inequality: $0 \leq r^2 \leq 1$.

2. (a) The product-moment coefficient of correlation, symbolized by r, is equal to ± the square root of the coefficient of determination. The plus sign is used when the relationship between the variable is direct (when b is positive). The minus sign is used when the relationship is inverse (when b is negative). The possible values for r are given by the inequality: $-1 \leq r \leq 1$.

    (b) The sample correlation coefficient r is a sample estimate of the population coefficient ρ.

    (c) The correlation coefficient is zero if the regression line is horizontal.

3. The computing formula for the correlation coefficient can be used to find r without reference to regression.

4. Null hypotheses involving inferences about ρ can be evaluated using a z score obtained by using the Fisher Z transformation.

5. A multiple correlation coefficient gives us a way of evaluating whether two variables x_1 and x_2, together, account for a higher percentage of the total variation in y than does either x_1 or x_2 alone.

6. The partial correlation coefficient $r_{12.3}$ measures the relationship between x_1 and x_2 after the effects of x_3 are eliminated.

AVOIDING COMMON ERRORS:

1. Do not confuse z with Z. The z is a normal curve variable. The Z is used to obtain z in testing a null hypothesis involving ρ.

2. Finding a confidence interval for ρ requires first finding a confidence interval for μ_Z.

KEY SYMBOLS:

1. r = Pearsonian correlation coefficient or product-moment correlation coefficient

2. r^2 = proportion of variation in y attributed to the relationship with x

3. $\Sigma(y-\hat{y})^2$ = the variation from the regression line

4. $\Sigma(y-\bar{y})^2$ = the total variation from the mean

5. $\dfrac{\Sigma(y-\hat{y})^2}{\Sigma(y-\bar{y})^2}$ = the proportion of total variation which is unexplained

6. Z = Fisher's Z--used to test hypotheses involving ρ

KEY FORMULAS:

1. The product-moment correlation coefficient

$$r = \pm \sqrt{1 - \frac{\Sigma(y-\hat{y})^2}{\Sigma(y-\bar{y})^2}}$$

2. Computing formula for correlation coefficient

$$r = \frac{S_{xy}}{\sqrt{S_{xx} \cdot S_{yy}}}$$

3. Formulas for testing hypotheses involving ρ

$$\mu_Z = \frac{1}{2} \ln \frac{1+\rho}{1-\rho}, \quad \sigma_Z = \frac{1}{\sqrt{n-3}}$$

$$z = \frac{Z-\mu_Z}{\sigma_Z} \quad \text{or} \quad z = (Z-\mu_Z)\sqrt{n-3}$$

4. Confidence interval for μ_Z

$$Z - \frac{z_{\alpha/2}}{\sqrt{n-3}} < \mu_Z < Z + \frac{z_{\alpha/2}}{\sqrt{n-3}}$$

5. Formula relating r to b (the slope of the regression line)*

$$r = b \frac{s_x}{s_y}$$

s_x = the standard deviation of the x's

s_y = the standard deviation of the y's

6. Multiple correlation coefficient

$$\sqrt{\frac{\Sigma(\hat{y}-\bar{y})^2}{\Sigma(y-\bar{y})^2}}$$

7. Partial correlation coefficient

$$r_{12.3} = \frac{r_{12}-r_{13} \cdot r_{23}}{\sqrt{1-r_{13}^2} \; \sqrt{1-r_{23}^2}}$$

MODIFIED TRUE/FALSE: If the statement is true, write true. If false, change the underlined words to make the statement true.

_____ 1. The correlation coefficient r must have a value between 0 and 1.

_____ 2. If r has a value of .60, then 60% of the variation in y can be explained by the variation in x.

_____ 3. In order to find the correlation coefficient, the estimated least-squares regression line is always found first.

_____ 4. It is never possible for $\Sigma(y-\hat{y})^2$ to exceed $\Sigma(y-\bar{y})^2$.

_____ 5. A high correlation between two variables will not prove that one variable causes the other to occur.

_____ 6. The hypothesis of no correlation between two variables can always be rejected if r is greater than zero.

_____ 7. The value of z is a natural logarithm.

_____ 8. Testing an hypothesis of no correlation based on a sample value of r always involves the calculation of a z-score.

_____ 9. The slope of the regression line is sometimes equal to the correlation coefficient.

_____ 10. If the correlation between x and y is not zero, then the variability about the estimated regression line will be less than the total variability in y.

* This formula is not in the textbook.

MULTIPLE CHOICE: Write the letter of the best answer in the given space.

____ 1. A statistic that measures the relationship between variables while eliminating the effects of other variables is called the:

(a) correlation coefficient
(b) regression coefficient
(c) standard error of estimate
(d) partial correlation coefficient

____ 2. Which of the following pairs of statements cannot both be true?

(a) $\hat{y}$ = 3 - 5x and r = .20
(b) $\hat{y}$ = 8 + 2x and r = .40
(c) $\hat{y}$ = -6 - 8x and r = -.40
(d) $\hat{y}$ = -9 + 10x and r = +.60

____ 3. The sum $\Sigma(\hat{y}-\bar{y})^2$ is called the _____ sum of squares.

(a) regression   (c) least
(b) total   (d) residual

____ 4. The sum $\Sigma(\hat{y}-\bar{y})^2$ is called the _____ sum of squares.

(a) regression   (c) least
(b) total   (d) residual

____ 5. In regression analysis, the quantity that gives the amount by which y changes for a unit change in x is called the:

(a) partial correlation coefficient
(b) slope of the regression line
(c) y-intercept of the regression line
(d) correlation coefficient

____ 6. If a perfect curvilinear relationship exists between two variables, but no linear relationship exists, then:

(a) r = 1   (c) r = +1
(b) r = 0   (d) r cannot be determined from the given information

____ 7. In linear regression, when will r = b?

(a) always
(b) if the standard error of estimate is very small
(c) if the standard deviation of the x's equals the standard deviation of the y's
(d) if s_x = 0

____ 8. If the true correlation coefficient ρ equals zero, then:

(a) r = 0   (c) α = 0
(b) β = 0   (d) b = 0

____ 9. The correlation coefficient is equal to:

(a) the total variation
(b) the unexplained variation
(c) one minus the proportion of unexplained variation
(d) the square root of the explained variation

_____ 10. If the hypothesis that $\rho = 0$ is rejected, then:

    (a) s_e must be zero   (c) the regression slope may be close to zero

    (b) r^2 must be close to one   (d) there is a strong relationship between x and y

COMPLETION: Complete the following sentences by filling in the given blanks.

1. If the slope of the regression line is negative, then the relationship between the independent and dependent variable is called _____ .

2. The value r^2 can assume any value between _____ .

3. The sample coefficient r is an estimate of _____ .

4. If large values of the independent variable are associated with large values of the dependent variable, then the relationship is _____ .

5. If the multiple correlation coefficient is .80, then the proportion of total variation in y that can be attributed to the x's is _____ .

6. The equation $\hat{y} = 3 + 4x_1 + 5x_2$ is considered to be a better predictor of y than the equation $\hat{y} = 7 + 2x_1$, if the multiple correlation coefficient is _____ the correlation coefficient involving x_1 and y.

7. If a regression line is horizontal, then the correlation between the two variables is _____ .

8. If all data points lie on the regression line, then the standard error of estimate is _____ .

9. If all data points lie on a regression line having a nonzero slope, then r^2 equals _____ .

10. The proportion of total variation which is unexplained can be denoted in symbols by _____ .

PROBLEMS:

1. The mathematics S.A.T. scores and college grade point averages of 8 students are given below:

Math S.A.T. score x	College Grade Point Average y
600	3.20
550	3.00
500	3.00
650	3.50
625	2.80
480	2.60
700	3.60
580	3.10

(a) Calculate the correlation coefficient r.

(b) What is the proportion of total variation in y that is accounted for by x?

2. For the data in Problem 1, test the null hypothesis of no relationship between the two variables at $\alpha=.05$. First, state the hypothesis in symbols.

3. For the data in Problem 1, calculate a 95% confidence interval for ρ.

4. In a multiple regression problem, the **regression** sum of squares is $\Sigma(\hat{y}-\bar{y})^2 = 12,000$ and the total sum of squares is $\Sigma(y-\bar{y})^2 = 20,000$. Find the value of the multiple correlation coefficient.

5. Below is a list of countries with their 1979 "excess monetary growth"* along with their mid 1980 inflation rate.

Country	1979 excess monetary growth (percent) x	mid 1980 inflation rate (percent) y
Switzerland	10	4
Austria	7	6
Germany	2	6
Japan	7	8
Canada	14	9
Israel	97	131
Ethiopia	7	7
Argentina	164	113
Brazil	60	81
Chile	56	39

(a) Calculate the correlation coefficient.

(b) What is the proportion of the total variation in inflation rate that is explained by excess monetary growth?

* Excess monetary growth is the extent to which money supply growth exceeds the growth of constant dollar GNP; specifically, the ratio of 1979 M2 to 1978 M2 is divided by the ratio of 1979 real GNP to 1978 real GNP.

6. For the data in Problem 5, test the null hypothesis that $\rho = .3$ at $\alpha = .01$. First, state the hypotheses in words and in symbols.

7. For the data in Problem 5, calculate a 99% confidence interval for ρ.

8. The table below gives the number of housing starts and the unemployment rates for a sequence of quarters:

	Quarter	Housing starts (millions)	Unemployment rate (percent)
1978	I	1.72	6.2
	II	2.36	5.9
	III	2.20	6.0
	IV	2.05	6.0
1979	I	1.96	6.2
	II	1.98	6.5
	III	2.02	6.6
	IV	2.12	6.6

(a) Calculate the correlation coefficient.

(b) What is the proportion of total variation in unemployment rates that is explained by the number of housing starts?

9. For the data in Problem 8, test the null hypothesis that $\rho = -.1$ at $\alpha = .05$. First, state the hypotheses in symbols.

10. For the data in Chapter 15, Problem 12 (Study Guide), find the multiple correlation coefficient.

11. A financial economist wants to evaluate how interest rates affect the inflation rate. Here are some results on yearly prime interest rates (x) and inflation rates (y) for the 13 years 1965 through 1977.

$$\Sigma \ xy = 500 \qquad \Sigma \ y = 78 \qquad \Sigma \ x^2 = 450$$

$$\Sigma \ y^2 = 600 \qquad \Sigma \ x = 65$$

(a) Calculate the sample coefficient of determination and correlation coefficient.

(b) Give the proportion of variation explained by the regression line.

12. For the data in Problem 11, test the null hypothesis of no correlation against a two-tailed alternative at the .01 significance level.

13. For two sets of data, x and y, $r = .75$. Suppose each value of x is measured in feet. If each x value is converted to inches by multiplying by 12, what is the new value of r?

14. Suppose, instead, a constant is <u>added to</u> each value of x. What is the new r value?

15. The variables circulation (x_1) and advertising income (x_2) are used to predict the annual profit of a daily newspaper (y). A multiple correlation coefficient of .65 is obtained. For predicting annual profit on the basis of advertising income alone, a value of $r = .78$ is found. Comment on these results.

CHAPTER 17

NONPARAMETRIC TESTS

This chapter considers the following topics in nonparametric statistics:

(1) the sign test for one sample or two dependent samples
(2) the U test for two independent samples
(3) the signed-rank test for one sample or two dependent samples
(4) the Kruskal-Wallis test for analysis of variance
(5) the number of runs test for randomness
(6) the rank-correlation coefficient to measure the association between two variables.

CHAPTER OBJECTIVES: By the end of this chapter, you should be able to:

1. Apply the one-sample sign test to small-sample data by using Table V. (17.1 - 17.4)

2. Apply a paired-sample sign test to small-sample data by using Table V. (17.5 - 17.7)

3. Apply the one-sample sign test to large-sample data using the normal approximation to the binomial distribution. (17.8 - 17.10)

4. Apply a paired-sample sign test to large-sample data using the normal approximation to the binomial distribution. (17.11, 17.12)

5. For a given alternative hypothesis, identify the T statistic on which the decision is based. (17.13 - 17.16)

6. Test an hypothesis using a one-sample signed-rank test. (17.17 - 17.20, 17.24)

7. Compare two populations using a signed-rank test. (17.21 - 17.23, 17.25, 17.26)

8. Compare two populations using the small-sample U test. (17.27 - 17.38)

9. Compare two populations using the large-sample U test. (17.39 - 17.44)

10. Compare more than two populations using the H (Kruskal-Wallis) test. (17.45 - 17.50)

11. Test for randomness from runs involving two letters. (17.51 - 17.59)

12. Test for randomness from runs above and below a median. (17.60 - 17.64)

13. Calculate a rank correlation coefficient. (17.65, 17.66, 17.68, 17.69, 17.72, 17.73)

14. Test a rank-correlation coefficient for significance. (17.67 - 17.71)

KEY POINTS OF THE CHAPTER:

1. Parameters methods are statistical methods which require
   assumptions about the distribution of the population.

2. Nonparametric methods are statistical methods which require less
   stringent assumptions about the population distribution than
   parametric methods.

3. The sign test

   (a) The one-sample sign test is a nonparametric method of
       conducting an hypothesis test involving one population mean.
       (The null hypothesis is $\mu = \mu_o$.)

   (b) The paired-sample sign test is a nonparametric method of
       conducting an hypothesis test involving a comparison of two
       populations where each element in one sample relates to a
       particular element in the other sample.

   (c) In a one-sample sign test or a paired-sample sign test, the
       null hypothesis can be written as $p = \frac{1}{2}$. The sign test
       applied to one small sample or to paired data when the sample
       sizes are small requires the use of the binomial
       distribution (Table V).

4. The Wilcoxon signed-rank test is another nonparametric method
   used to analyze paired data.

5. The U test (or the Mann-Whitney test or the Wilcoxon test) is a
   nonparametric method of conducting an hypothesis test for comparing
   two independent population means. (The null hypothesis is $\mu_1 = \mu_2$.)
   The test involves rank sums.

6. The Kruskal-Wallis test (or H test) is a nonparametric alternative
   to the one-way analysis of variance. Thus, this test involves
   evaluating differences among more than two populations. The null
   hypothesis in an application of the H test is that all of the
   population means are equal. The H test involves an application of
   the chi-square distribution. This χ^2 approximation can only be
   used if all samples have at least 5 items. The test involves
   rank sums and must be two-tailed.

7. The number of runs test for randomness is a nonparametric test
   for evaluating the randomness of sequences of letters or numbers.
   If the sequence involves numbers, runs above and below the median
   are considered. The test must be two-tailed and requires the use
   of the u table.

8. The rank-correlation coefficient r_s can be used to test the
   hypothesis of no correlation without the assumptions underlying r.

9. Testing the significance of values of r_s requires the normal
   distribution.

10. Ties

   (a) The sign test for one-sample

   All sample values that equal the hypothesized value should be ignored; then the end value is reduced accordingly.

   (b) The sign test for paired-sample data

   All pairs whose values are equal are eliminated from consideration so that the n value is reduced accordingly.

   (c) The Mann-Whitney test (U test or Wilcoxon test)

   Ties within samples are ignored. For ties between samples tied observations are assigned the mean of the ranks which they jointly occupy.

   Example:

	A	A	B	A	A	B
Data	30	35	35	40	40	45
Ranks	1	2.5	2.5	4	5	6

   Since the 35's produce a tie between samples A and B, we average $\frac{2+3}{2}$ = 2.5 to obtain each rank. The 40's produce a tie within sample A so the ranks continue as usual.

   (d) Wilcoxon signed-rank test

   Tied values are eliminated from consideration. The n value is reduced accordingly.

11. Null hypotheses involved in nonparametric tests

	Nonparametric Test	Null Hypothesis
(a)	one-sample sign test	$\mu = \mu_o$ translates to $p = \frac{1}{2}$
(b)	paired-sample sign test	$\mu_1 = \mu_2$ translates to $p = \frac{1}{2}$ Each element of sample from population 1 is related to a particular element of sample from population 2.
(c)	Mann-Whitney (U test)	$\mu_1 = \mu_2$ where independent random samples come from identical populations.
(d)	Wilcoxon signed-rank test	$\mu = \frac{1}{2}$ translates to $p = \frac{1}{2}$ (one-sample case) $\mu_1 = \mu_2$ translates to $p = \frac{1}{2}$ (paired-sample case)
(e)	Kruskal-Wallis test (H test)	$\mu_1 = \mu_2 = \mu_3 = \ldots = \mu_k$ k (more than 2) independent random samples come from identical populations.

Nonparametric Test	Null Hypothesis
(f) Number of Runs test	
(i) runs of letters	(i) data is random--the number of runs is <u>not</u> too few or too many
(ii) runs of numbers	(ii) data is random--the number of runs below and above the median is <u>not</u> too few or too many
(g) Rank-Correlation Coefficient	$r_s = 0$ tests whether there is a relationship between the two variables.

AVOIDING COMMON ERRORS:

1. The paired-sample sign test and the 2 population signed-rank test are not used in the same problems as the U test. Both tests involve comparing two populations; however, for the U test to be applicable there must be no relationship between elements of one sample and any elements of the other sample.

2. In the number of runs test for randomness, the null hypothesis is that the sequence is random. An extremely high or low number of runs is required to reject the null hypothesis.

3. Tests involving rank sums (U test and H test) require adjustments for ties.

4. Note that Table VII is applied for the U test; Table VIII for the number of runs test (small sample). There is no connection between the U in the U test and the u in the number of runs test.

KEY SYMBOLS:

μ_0 = hypothesized value of μ in the one-sample sign test

W_1 or W_2 = sum of the ranks of one of the samples in application of the U test

T^+ = the sum of the ranks corresponding to positive differences in the signed-rank test

n_i = number of items in the ith sample in application of H test

R_i = sum of ranks assigned to the n_i values of the ith sample in application of the H test

u = number of runs in the test for randomness

r_s = the rank-correlation coefficient

KEY FORMULAS:

1. One-sample sign test (large sample)

$$z = \frac{x - np_o}{\sqrt{np_o(1-p_o)}}$$

2. Paired-sample sign test (large sample)

$$z = \frac{x - np_o}{\sqrt{np_o(1-p_o)}}$$

3. Mann-Whitney Test (or U Test)

   (a) Small sample $(n_1 \leq 8$ or $n_2 \leq 8)$

$$U_1 = W_1 - \frac{n_1(n_1 + 1)}{2}$$

$$U_2 = W_2 - \frac{n_2(n_2 + 1)}{2}$$

   U = the smaller of U_1 and U_2

   (b) Large sample $(n_1 > 8$ and $n_2 > 8)$

$$z = \frac{U_1 - \mu_{U_1}}{\sigma_{U_1}} \qquad \text{where} \quad \mu_{U_1} = \frac{n_1 n_2}{2}$$

$$\sigma_{U_1} = \sqrt{\frac{n_1 n_2(n_1 + n_2 + 1)}{12}}$$

4. Mean and standard deviation of T^+ statistic

$$\mu_{T^+} = \frac{n(n+1)}{4}$$

$$\sigma_{T^+} = \sqrt{\frac{n(n+1)(2n+1)}{24}}$$

5. Statistic for large-sample signed rank test

$$z = \frac{T^+ - \mu_{T^+}}{\sigma_{T^+}}$$

6. Number of Runs Test for Randomness

$$z = \frac{U - \mu_u}{\sigma_u} \quad \text{where} \quad \mu_u = \frac{2n_1 n_2}{n_1 + n_2} + 1 \qquad \sigma_u = \sqrt{\frac{2n_1 n_2(2n_1 n_2 - n_1 - n_2)}{(n_1 + n_2)^2(n_1 + n_2 - 1)}}$$

191

7. Kruskal-Wallis test (or H test)

$$H = \frac{12}{n(n+1)} \sum_{i=1}^{k} \frac{R_i^2}{n_i} - 3(n+1)$$

8. Rank Correlation Coefficient

$$r_s = 1 - \frac{6(\Sigma d^2)}{n(n^2-1)}$$

9. Statistic for testing significance of r_s

$$z = \frac{r_s - 0}{\frac{1}{\sqrt{n-1}}} = r_s \sqrt{n-1}$$

MODIFIED TRUE/FALSE: If the statement is true, write true. If false, change the underlined words to make the statement true.

_____ 1. An advantage of nonparametric tests is that they require <u>less stringent assumptions</u> than parametric tests.

_____ 2. The use of the H test <u>requires</u> the assumption that they have roughly the shape of a normal distribution.

_____ 3. If there were an extremely large or small number of runs in the data, then we would be more likely to believe that the data <u>is</u> random.

_____ 4. The application of the U test <u>requires</u> that the two independent samples have the <u>same sample size</u>.

_____ 5. The χ^2 approximation should only be used in the H test if each sample has more than <u>five</u> items.

_____ 6. In the <u>Kruskal-Wallis</u> test, all terms involving ties are eliminated from consideration.

_____ 7. In the U test the statistic U is always the <u>larger</u> of U_1 and U_2.

_____ 8. In a test of randomness if the null hypothesis is true, then the number of runs we would expect to obtain (i.e., the mean number of runs) is given by σ_u.

_____ 9. When evaluating differences among more than two populations, the appropriate nonparametric test is the <u>Kruskal-Wallis</u> test.

_____ 10. Nonparametric methods are usually <u>less efficient</u> than parametric methods.

MULTIPLE CHOICE: Write the letter of the best answer in the given space.

_____ 1. When we are comparing two populations and our two samples are
           such that each element of one sample relates to a particular
           element of the other sample, an appropriate nonparametric test
           would be the:

           (a) one-sample sign test   (c) Wilcoxon test (rank sums)
           (b) signed-rank test   (d) U test

_____ 2. The nonparametric alternative to the two-sample t test for the
           difference between two independent means is the:

           (a) one-sample sign test   (c) U test
           (b) paired-sample sign test   (d) Kruskal-Wallis test

_____ 3. The nonparametric alternative to the one-way analysis of
           variance is the:

           (a) U test   (c) Wilcoxon test (rank sums)
           (b) paired-sample sign test   (d) H test

_____ 4. The Kruskal-Wallis test involves an application of the:

           (a) normal distribution   (c) binomial distribution
           (b) chi-square distribution   (d) t distribution

_____ 5. The sign test applied to small samples of paired data requires
           the use of the:

           (a) binomial distribution   (c) t distribution
           (b) normal distribution   (d) chi-square distribution

_____ 6. Suppose that the U test is to be applied to the following
           sequence:

                 60.1   70.1   70.1   80.1   80.1   85
                  B   A   A   B   A   B

           The correct rankings in order are:

           (a) 1 2 3 4 5 6   (c) 1   2   3   4.5   4.5   6
           (b) 1 2.5 2.5 4 5 6   (d) 1   2.5 2.5 4.5 4.5 5

_____ 7. The sign test is used with n=9 to test the null hypothesis that
           the new method and the old method produce equally high scores
           against the alternative hypothesis that the new method
           produces higher scores than the old. If we obtain 8 plus
           signs in subtracting (new score - old score), then with
           α=.05, the null hypothesis should:

           (a) be rejected since 6<7   (c) be rejected since 7<8
           (b) not be rejected   (d) not be rejected since 7<8
                since 6<7

_____ 8. The Mann-Whitney test is the same as the:

           (a) one-sample sign test   (c) Kruskal-Wallis test
           (b) U test   (d) paired-sample sign test

___ 9. Which of the following tests must be two-tailed?

    (a) U test   (c) number of runs test
    (b) one-sample sign test   (d) paired-sample sign test

___ 10. If the U test is applied in a test whose alternative hypothesis is $\mu_1 \neq \mu_2$ with $n_1=7$, $n_2=7$, $\alpha=.05$, the null hypothesis can be rejected if:

    (a) $W_1 \geq 70$ and $W_2 \geq 70$ (c) $U_1 > 8$ or $U_2 > 8$

    (b) $U_1 \leq 8$ or $U_2 \leq 8$ (d) $W_1 \leq 70$ or $W_2 \leq 70$

COMPLETION: Complete the following sentences by filling in the given blanks.

1. In a one-sample sign test, the null hypothesis can be written as _____ or _____ .

2. The H test is another name for the _____ test.

3. The normal approximation to the binomial distribution can be used in an application of the sign test if n is at least _____ .

4. The runs test is a test for _____ .

5. For a ranked sample of size n, the sum of the ranks is _____ .

6. The null hypothesis in the runs test is that the sequence of observations is _____ .

7. Two examples of rank sum tests are _____ and _____ .

8. In a U test, the large sample statistic can be applied if n_1 _____ and n_2 _____ .

9. In the U test, U_1 and U_2 take on values between _____ and _____ , and their sum always equals_____ .

10. In applying the number of runs test to the sequence 15, 10, 13, 20, 28, 30, 11, 17, 9, the value of u is _____

11. A nonparametric measure of the association between two variables is called the _____ .

PROBLEMS:

1. The following random sample gives the numbers of dollars spent by 12 individuals at a supermarket: $17.50, $5.75, $12.20, $24.10, $21.35, $19.05, $16.60, $32.00, $15.80, $14.70, $16.00, $13.90. Use an appropriate nonparametric test with $\alpha=.05$ to test the null hypothesis that people spend an average of $15.00 at the supermarket against the alternative that the average is greater than $15.00.

2. Independent random samples of 9 male and 7 female students at a college showed the following weekly food expenses in dollars:

Men: 20, 21, 25, 28, 30, 28, 23, 24, 26
Women: 25, 18, 17, 23, 20, 24, 22

Test the null hypothesis that the men and women have the same average food expenses against the alternative hypothesis that they do not have the same average food expenses. Use $\alpha = .05$.

3. The following are the monthly sales (in thousands of dollars) of two department stores, A and B, for the months January through December, 1979: 10 and 9, 7 and 4, 8 and 5, 7 and 6, 11 and 10, 15 and 16, 15 and 13, 12 and 13, 9 and 8, 18 and 17, 19 and 13, 21 and 20. Use the small sample sign test with $\alpha = .05$ to test the null hypothesis that on the average the two department stores have equal sales against the alternative that on the average

(a) department store A has more sales

(b) there is a difference in sales between the two stores.

4. Repeat Problem 3 using the large sample sign test. How do your answers compare?

5. Students were observed as they arrived at a college dance. The following is the order in which men and women arrived at the dance. M M M W M M W W M M W W W M M M M W M W W W M M M M

Test the sequence for randomness at the .05 significance level.

6. A test was conducted to compare the miles per gallon obtained by three subcompact automobiles. The following data (in miles per gallon) were obtained from 6 tankfuls of the same gasoline. Use a nonparametric test to evaluate whether or not there are significant differences in gasoline economy among the automobiles. Use $\alpha = .05$.

    I: 24, 22, 23, 25, 22, 21
    II: 23, 22, 26, 24, 27, 25
    III: 30, 28, 26, 27, 26, 24

7. Random samples of 15 Model I cars and 13 Model II cars were obtained and we recorded the number of miles (in thousands) that each lasted from new until the car was "junked":

    Model I: 70, 60, 80, 75, 81, 73, 80, 90, 82, 93, 89, 95, 91, 88, 90
    Model II: 88, 80, 95, 105, 90, 99, 93, 88, 95, 102, 98, 95, 91

    Test the null hypothesis that the two models have the same average life expectancy against the alternative hypothesis that they do not have the same average life expectancy. Use $\alpha = .01$.

8. Repeat Problem 7 with the change that the alternative hypothesis is that Model II has a greater life expectancy than Model I.

9. An aptitude test is given to trainees in a high-tech firm. Here are the grades on the test in the order that the trainees completed the test:

    98, 92, 95, 85, 80, 78, 75, 83, 82, 95, 92, 87, 80, 65, 92, 93, 82, 98, 93, 72, 70

    Test whether the trainees finished the test in random order with regard to grades. Use $\alpha = .01$.

10. Suppose the 21 trainees in Problem 9 comprise a random sample from a large population of trainees at the company. Use the sign test with $\alpha = .05$ to test the null hypothesis that trainees average 80 on the aptitude test against the alternative hypothesis that the average is higher than 80.

11. The mathematics S.A.T. scores and college grade point averages of 8 students are given below:

Student	x Math S.A.T. Score	y College G.P.A.
1	600	3.20
2	550	3.00
3	500	3.00
4	650	3.50
5	625	2.80
6	480	2.60
7	700	3.60
8	580	3.10

(a) Calculate the rank-correlation coefficient r_s.

(b) Test the null hypothesis of no correlation using r_s. Let $\alpha = .05$.

12. The following table shows the scores made on the verbal and mathematical components of an SAT by 15 high school seniors who plan to go to a certain college.

SUBJECT	VERBAL	MATHEMATICAL
1	450	375
2	375	350
3	535	550
4	420	580
5	365	350
6	680	695
7	520	480
8	527	550
9	442	430
10	384	390
11	611	661
12	519	535
13	671	660
14	510	525
15	420	410

Calculate the Spearman Rank-Correlation Coefficient for the test scores.

13. A consumer advocate is interested in testing whether the number of french fries in a portion in a particular college cafeteria is different from that of a particular restaurant. Random samples of 10 portions of french fries each are selected and fries counted. Conduct the test using $\alpha = .01$.

Cafeteria	Restaurant
12	14
8	7
15	10
10	8
18	16
13	13
16	15
12	11
18	16
20	15

14. A company that makes foot-long hot dogs requires that the median lengths of its hot dogs be 12 inches. A sample of 18 hot dogs produced by this company in order actually have lengths in inches:

    10, 11, 13, 13, 14, 12, 11, 9, 13, 12, 14, 13, 11, 13, 14, 10, 14, 15

    Does this data provide sufficient evidence to indicate a lack of randomness in the pattern of too short and too long hot dogs? Use $\alpha = .05$.

15. Suppose we want to test whether or not two samples come from the same population. If the assumptions of the standard test for the difference between two large sample means (given in Chapter 11) are satisfied, and we are to choose either that test or the U test, which one should we choose? Why?

CHAPTER 1
MODIFIED TRUE/FALSE
1. true
2. is not involved
3. Statistical inference
4. descriptive statistics
5. true
6. true

MULTIPLE CHOICE
1. c
2. d
3. a
4. d
5. d
6. a

COMPLETION
1. set up inequalities
2. form differences
3. set up inequalities
4. multiply or divide
5. "begging the question"
6. ordinal

PROBLEMS
1. (a) descriptive methods
   (b) descriptive methods
   (c) requires generalization
   (d) requires generalization

2. (a) ratio   (0 points indicates absence of points)
   (b) nominal   (the numbers serve only to label people)
   (c) ordinal   (can set up inequalities, but not differences)
   (d) ratio   (0 points indicates absence of points)

3. (a) Sample may contain a higher proportion of high income people than is in the population.
   (b) The question shows the bias of the question; it is "begging the question."

4. (a) descriptive methods. The truth of the statement can be seen from the data.
   (b) descriptive methods. The truth of the statement can be seen from the data.
   (c) requires a generalization. The conclusion may be true, but cannot be seen from the data.
   (d) requires a generalization. The statement may be true, but cannot be seen from the data.

5. (a) The sample of people is likely to contain a higher proportion of people against the law than exists in the population.
   (b) The students' views may be influenced by their failures.

6. (a) nominal (the numbers serve only to label people)
   (b) ratio   (0 dollars indicates absence of dollars)
   (c) nominal (the numbers serve only to distinguish one phone from another)
   (d) ordinal (can set up inequalities but not differences)

CHAPTER 2
MODIFIED TRUE/FALSE
1. raw data
2. true
3. never
4. true
5. impossible
6. An ogive
7. more
8. sometimes
9. true
10. 67.5-75.5

MULTIPLE CHOICE
1. a
2. c
3. a
4. d
5. b
6. c
7. d
8. b
9. d
10. d

COMPLETION
1. 6, 15
2. class mark
3. leaf
4. percentage
5. qualitative distribution
6. histogram
7. the lower and upper limits
8. range of values of a class
9. limits
10. quantitative

PROBLEMS
1.
class limits	class boundaries
100-149.99	99.995-149.995
150-199.99	149.995-199.995
200-249.99	199.995-249.995
250-299.99	249.995-299.995

class ranks	class intervals
124.995	50
174.995	50
224.995	50
274.995	50

2.
class limits	rel. frequencies
100-149.99	15/80 = 18.75%
150-199.99	10/80 = 12.5%
200-249.99	30/80 = 37.5%
250-299.99	25/80 = 31.25%

CHAPTER 2 (continued)

3. (a)

less than	cum. f
100	0
150	15
200	25
250	55
300	80

(b)

greater than	cum. f
99.99	80
149.99	65
199.99	55
249.99	25
299.99	0

(c)

or less	cum. f
99.99	0
149.99	15
199.99	25
249.99	55
299.99	80

4. (a)

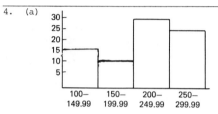

(b)

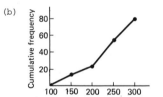

5. (a)

scores	frequency
41 - 50	2
51 - 60	3
61 - 70	7
71 - 80	17
81 - 90	20
91 - 100	11

(b)

scores	relative frequency
41 - 50	2/60
51 - 60	3/60
61 - 70	7/60
71 - 80	17/60
81 - 90	20/60
91 - 100	11/60

6. (a)

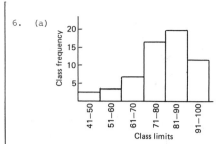

(b)

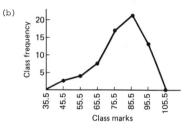

7. (a)

more than	cumulative frequency
40	60
50	58
60	55
70	48
80	31
90	11
100	0

(b)

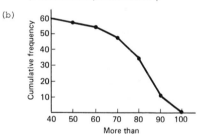

8. (a)

class marks	class boundaries	class limits
22	18-26	18.5-25.5
30	26-34	26.5-33.5
38	34-42	34.5-41.5
46	42-50	42.5-49.5

(b)

class boundaries	class limits	class marks
30.95-42.95	31.45-42.45	36.95
42.95-54.95	43.45-54.45	48.95
54.95-66.95	55.45-66.45	60.95
66.95-78.95	67.45-78.45	72.95

CHAPTER 2 (continued)
9. (a)

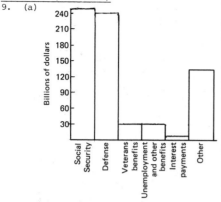

(b)

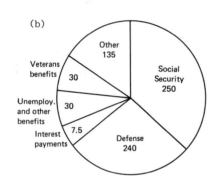

10. (a)

1**	25	71	75	82	82
2**	28	34	52	81	85
3**	05	07	10	12	

(b)

16*	5
17*	1 5
18*	2 2
19*	
20*	
21*	
22*	8
23*	4
24*	
25*	2
26*	
27*	
28*	1 5
29*	
30*	5 7
31*	0 2

11. There is no place for 50, and 75 can go either in the second or the third class.

12. It gives a misleading impression if we try to compare areas rather than the heights of rectangles. Since the third class has three times the width of the other classes, we can make the areas represent the class frequencies by dividing the height of the third rectangle by 3.

13. (a) 36, 32, 35, 37, 32

    (b) 472, 451, 436, 423, 495

    (c) 51.12, 51.34, 51.57, 51.25, 51.17

CHAPTER 3
MODIFIED TRUE/FALSE

1.	true	6.	median
2.	sometimes	7.	population
3.	less than	8.	sometimes
4.	true	9.	sometimes
5.	sum of the	10.	unchanged
	frequencies		

MULTIPLE CHOICE

1.	b	6.	a
2.	d	7.	c
3.	b	8.	a
4.	a	9.	b
5.	c	10.	c

COMPLETION
1. population
2. sometimes
3. the sum of the frequencies
4. sometimes
5. mode
6. -2
7. 0
8. rearrange, in numerical order
9. geometric mean
10. first quartile, third quartile

PROBLEMS
1. (a)

6*	6 8 4
7*	0 2 3 5
8*	0 6 0
9*	4 1

(b) $\bar{x} = \dfrac{\Sigma x}{n} = \dfrac{919}{12} = 76.58$

(c) $\dfrac{73 + 75}{2} = 74$

(d) 80

2. (a) $\tilde{x} = 70.5 + \frac{5}{8}(10)$

    $= 70.5 + 6.25 = 76.75$

    (b) $.75(30) = 22.5$

    $Q_3 = 80.5 + \frac{4.5}{10}(10)$

    $= 80.5 + 4.5 = 85$

3. (a)
11*	5	
12*	0	
13*	6	
14*	0	4
15*	5	
16*	0	
17*		
18*	2	
19*	0	
20*	0	

    (b) $\frac{144 + 155}{2} = 149.5$

4. Class marks

x	u	f	uf	$u^2 f$
32499.50	-2	233	-466	932
47499.50	-1	204	-204	204
62499.50	0	71	0	0
77499.50	1	18	18	18
92499.50	2	9	18	36
		535	-634	1190

    (a) $\bar{x} = x_0 + \frac{\Sigma uf}{n} \cdot c$

    $= 62499.50 + \frac{-634}{535}(15000)$

    $= 62499.50 - 17775.701$

    $= 44723.799$

    (b) $\tilde{x} = L + \frac{j}{f} \cdot c$

    $= 40000 + \frac{35}{204}(15000)$

    $= 40000 + 2573.5294$

    $= 42573.53$

5.
w no. of shares	x price per share	xw
100	5	500
200	4	800
400	2	800
		2100

    $x_w = \frac{\Sigma xw}{\Sigma w} = \frac{2100}{700} = \$3 \text{ per share}$

6. (a) $\Sigma x = 465$

    $\bar{x} = \frac{465}{16} = 29.0625$

    (b) median $= 29$

    (c) mode $= 32$

    (d) midrange $= \frac{13 + 38}{2} = 25.5$

7. (a) $.70(40) = 28$

    $D_7 = 160.5 + \frac{7}{9} = 176.06$

    (b) $.30(40) = 12$

    $P_{30} = 140.5 + \frac{1}{10}(20) = 142.25$

8. $\frac{1600}{1000} = 1.6, \frac{2000}{1600} = 1.25, \frac{2400}{2000} = 1.2,$

    $\frac{2640}{2400} = 1.1$

    g.m. $= \sqrt[4]{1.6(1.25)(1.2)(1.1)} = 1.275$

    $= 1.275 - 1 = .275 = 27.5\%$

9. harmonic mean $= \frac{n}{\Sigma 1/x}$

    $= \frac{3}{\frac{1}{20} + \frac{1}{15} + \frac{1}{30}} = \frac{3}{\frac{3}{60} + \frac{4}{60} + \frac{2}{60}} = \frac{3}{\frac{9}{60}} = \frac{3}{9} = \$20$

10. (a) $\sum_{i=1}^{15} x_1^2$ (b) $\sum_{i=3}^{6} 2y_i f_i$

11. (a) $x_2 y_2 + x_3 y_3 + x_4 y_4 + x_5 y_5$

    (b) $(y_1 - z_1) + (y_2 - z_2) + (y_3 - z_3)$

12. (a) $3(1) + 4(2) + 1(2) + 5(1) = \underline{18}$

    (b) $x_2^2 + x_3^2 + x_4^2 = 4^2 + 1^2 + 5^2 = \underline{42}$

13. (a) none (b) none

CHAPTER 4
MODIFIED TRUE/FALSE

1. range
2. positively
3. central location
4. true
5. positively skewed
6. true
7. standard deviation
8. sample
9. at least zero
10. true

CHAPTER 4 (continued)

MULTIPLE CHOICE

1.	d	6.	c
2.	a	7.	b
3.	a	8.	c
4.	b	9.	d
5.	a	10.	a

COMPLETION

1. mean
2. z-score
3. population standard deviation
4. sample
5. greatly affected by extreme values
6. empirical rule
7. coefficient of variation
8. zero
9. outliers
10. standard deviation

PROBLEMS

1. (a) range = 94 - 64 = 30

   (b) $s^2 = \dfrac{n(\Sigma x^2) - (\Sigma x)^2}{n(n-1)}$

   $= \dfrac{12(71427) - (919)^2}{12(11)}$

   $= 95.174$

   (c) $s = 9.75$

2. (a) $s^2 = c^2 \dfrac{n\Sigma u^2 f - (\Sigma uf)^2}{n(n-1)}$

   $= 10^2 \dfrac{30(40) - 0^2}{30(29)}$

   $= 100(1.379)$

   $s^2 = 137.90$

   (b) $s = 11.74$

3. (a) 115, 120, 136, 140, 144, 155, 160, 182, 190, 200

   lower hinge $= \dfrac{136 + 140}{2} = 138$

   upper hinge $= \dfrac{160 + 182}{2} = 171$

   (b)

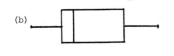

   110   130   150   170   190   210

   (c) $Q_1 = 138$ $Q_3 = 171$

   Interquartile Range $= Q_3 - Q_1$
   $= 171 - 138$
   $= 33$

4. (a) $s^2 = \dfrac{n(\Sigma x^2) - (\Sigma x)^2}{n(n-1)}$

   $= \dfrac{10(245,306) - (1542)^2}{10(9)}$

   $s^2 = 836.62$

   (b) Range = 200 - 115 = 85

5. (a) $s^2 = c^2 \dfrac{n(\Sigma u^2 f) - (\Sigma uf)^2}{n(n-1)}$

   $= 15000^2 \dfrac{535(1190) - (-634)^2}{535(534)}$

   $= 15000^2 \dfrac{234694}{285690}$

   $s^2 = 184,837,236.2$

   (b) $s = 13,595.49$

6. (a) $z = \dfrac{x - \bar{x}}{s}$

   (1) $z = \dfrac{6000 - 8000}{500}$

   $z = \dfrac{-2000}{500} = -4$

   (2) $z = \dfrac{6000 - 7500}{300}$

   $z = \dfrac{-1500}{300} = -5$

   Company 2

   (b) Chebyshev's theorem:

   $\bar{x} - ks = 7000$

   $8000 - k(500) = 7000$

   $-500k = -1000$

   $k = 2$

   $1 - \dfrac{1}{k^2} = 1 - \dfrac{1}{2^2}$

   $= \dfrac{3}{4}$

   $= 75\%$

   (c) $1 - \dfrac{1}{k^2} = \dfrac{35}{36}$

   $\dfrac{1}{k^2} = \dfrac{1}{36}$

   $k^2 = 36$

   $k = 6$

   $\bar{x} - ks$ $\bar{x} + ks$

   $8000 - 6(500)$ $8000 + 6(500)$

   5000 and 11000

   (d) $c.v. = \dfrac{s}{\bar{x}} \cdot 100$

   (1) $c.v. = \dfrac{500}{8000} \cdot 100 = 6.25$

   (2) $c.v. = \dfrac{300}{7500} \cdot 100 = 4$

CHAPTER 4 (continued)
7. (a) range = 38 - 13

(b) $\sigma = \sqrt{\dfrac{\Sigma(x - \bar{x})^2}{n}} = \sqrt{\dfrac{636.9375}{16}}$

$= \sqrt{39.8086}$

$= \underline{6.31}$

(c) SK $= \dfrac{3(\text{mean} - \text{median})}{\text{standard dev.}}$

$= \dfrac{3(.0625)}{6.31} = .03$

8. lower hinge = 27
    upper hinge = 32

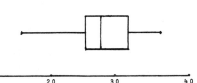

9. (a) Range = 260 - 15 = 245

(b) $s = \sqrt{\dfrac{9(29300) - (450)^2}{9(8)}}$

$= \sqrt{850}$

$= 29.15$

(c) Interquartile range = 60 - 30 = 30

10. (a) $z = \dfrac{8 - 14}{4} = -1.5$ junior

$z = \dfrac{18 - 24}{6} = -1$ senior

The senior

(b) $1 - \dfrac{1}{k^2} = \dfrac{8}{9}$

$\dfrac{1}{k^2} = \dfrac{1}{9}$

$k = 3$

$10 - 3(2)$ $10 + 3(2)$
$\underline{4 - 16}$

(c) $14 + 4k = 22$
$k = 2$

$1 - \dfrac{1}{2^2} = \dfrac{3}{4} = \underline{75\%}$

11. $\bar{x} - s$ $\bar{x} + s$
    24 - 6   24 + 6
       18 - 30

12. c.v. $= \dfrac{s}{\bar{x}}$

$\dfrac{2}{10} = 0.2$, $\dfrac{4}{14} = 0.29$, $\dfrac{6}{24} = 0.25$

Juniors have highest.

13. (a) 128 + 25 = 153
    (b) 160 + 25 = 185
    (c) 8.2
    (d) $(8.2)^2 = 67.27$

14. (a) It is less than half the range.
    (b) It is more than half the range.

CHAPTER 5
MODIFIED TRUE/FALSE

1. $\dfrac{11 \cdot 10 \cdot 9}{3 \cdot 2 \cdot 1}$ 7. Law of Large Nos.
2. different from   8. $\dfrac{8 \cdot 7 \cdot 6}{3 \cdot 2 \cdot 1}$
3. classical
4. not equal to   9. $10^4 - 1 = 9999$
5. true
6. true   10. $30 \cdot 29 \cdot 28 \cdot 27$

MULTIPLE CHOICE

1. b   6. a
2. b   7. c
3. c   8. b
4. c   9. d
5. a   10. c

COMPLETION

1. $\binom{11}{5}$ 6. 7!

7. $\dfrac{8!}{3!}$

2. $\dfrac{7 \cdot 6 \cdot 5}{3 \cdot 2 \cdot 1} = 35$

8. $8 \cdot 5 \cdot 6 \cdot 4 = 960$

3. $7 \cdot 6 \cdot 5 = 210$ 9. $\dfrac{7 \cdot 6 \cdot 5}{3 \cdot 2 \cdot 1} = 35$

4. $\binom{20}{7}$

10. $5 \cdot 8 \cdot 3 = 120$

5. $\dfrac{3}{13}$

PROBLEMS

1. (a)

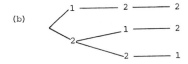

(b)

CHAPTER 5 (continued)

2. (a) $3 \cdot 3 \cdot 3 \cdot 3 \cdot 3 \cdot 3 \cdot 3 \cdot 3 = 3^8$

    (b) $8 \cdot 8 \cdot 8 = 8^3$

    (c) $4 \cdot 4 \cdot 4 \cdot 5 \cdot 5 \cdot 5 \cdot 5 \cdot 5 \cdot 5 = 4^3 \cdot 5^7$

3. (a) $6 \cdot 5 \cdot 4 = 120$

    (b) $6! = 720$

4. (a) $\binom{8}{3} = \frac{8 \cdot 7 \cdot 6}{3 \cdot 2 \cdot 1} = \underline{56}$

    (b) $\binom{6}{2} \cdot \binom{8}{3} = \frac{6 \cdot 5}{2 \cdot 1} \cdot \frac{8 \cdot 7 \cdot 6}{3 \cdot 2 \cdot 1} = 15 \cdot 56 = \underline{840}$

    (c) $\binom{14}{5} = \frac{14 \cdot 13 \cdot 12 \cdot 11 \cdot 10}{5 \cdot 4 \cdot 3 \cdot 2 \cdot 1} = \underline{2002}$

5. (a) $\binom{11}{3} = \frac{11 \cdot 10 \cdot 9}{3 \cdot 2 \cdot 1} = \underline{165}$

    (b) $\binom{11}{2} = \frac{11 \cdot 10}{2 \cdot 1} = \underline{55}$

6. (a) 5/6

    (b) 1/2

7. (a) $\frac{4}{52} \cdot \frac{3}{51}$

    (b) $\frac{13}{52} \cdot \frac{12}{51}$

    (c) $\frac{4}{52} \cdot \frac{4}{51}$

8. (a) $15 \cdot 14 \cdot 13 \cdot 12 \cdot 11 \cdot 10$

    (b) $\frac{15 \cdot 14 \cdot 13 \cdot 12 \cdot 11 \cdot 10}{6 \cdot 5 \cdot 4 \cdot 3 \cdot 2 \cdot 1}$

9. (a) $\frac{\binom{3}{2} \binom{13}{5}}{\binom{16}{7}} = \frac{3(1287)}{11440} = \underline{.3375}$

    (b) $\frac{\binom{3}{3} \binom{13}{4}}{\binom{16}{7}} = \frac{1(715)}{11440} = \underline{.0625}$

    (c) $\frac{\binom{3}{0} \binom{13}{7}}{\binom{16}{7}} = \frac{1716}{11440} = \underline{.15}$

10. (a) $\binom{9}{2} = \frac{9 \cdot 8}{2 \cdot 1} = \underline{36}$

    (b) $\binom{7}{3} = \frac{7 \cdot 6 \cdot 5}{3 \cdot 2 \cdot 1} = \underline{35}$

11. (a) $\frac{11!}{3!2!2!} = 1,663,200$ (There are 3 i's, 2 t's, 2 n's.)

    (b) $11! = 39,916,800$

12. (a) $5!5! \cdot 2 = 28,800$

    (b) $6! \cdot 5 = 3,600$

    (c) $6! \cdot 5 = 3,600$

13. $\binom{10}{4} = \frac{10 \cdot 9 \cdot 8 \cdot 7}{4 \cdot 3 \cdot 2 \cdot 1} = 210$

14. $_{11}P_4 = 11 \cdot 10 \cdot 9 \cdot 8 = 7,920$

15. (a) $\binom{8}{4} \cdot \binom{5}{2} = \frac{8 \cdot 7 \cdot 6 \cdot 5}{4 \cdot 3 \cdot 2 \cdot 1} \cdot \frac{5 \cdot 4}{2 \cdot 1} = 700$

    (b) $\binom{13}{6} = \frac{13 \cdot 12 \cdot 11 \cdot 10 \cdot 9 \cdot 8}{6 \cdot 5 \cdot 4 \cdot 3 \cdot 2 \cdot 1} = 1716$

CHAPTER 6
MODIFIED TRUE/FALSE

1. P(A/B)
2. at most
3. mutually exclusive
4. true
5. unequal
6. unequal
7. "and"
8. independent
9. mutually exclusive
10. true

MULTIPLE CHOICE

1. d
2. b
3. a
4. b
5. d
6. b
7. a
8. c
9. b
10. c

COMPLETION

1. 5 to 2
2. .40
3. .925
4. {2,4,6}
5. A∩B'
6. The student either buys a stereo or does not buy a personal computer.
7. .12
8. P(A/B)
9. 15/100
10. 40/60

PROBLEMS

1. (a) (i) The student graduates this year and his father does not buy him a car this year.

1. (a) (ii) The student graduates this year and his father buys him a car this year.

    (iii) The student will not graduate this year, and the student's father will buy him a car this year.

    (iv) The student will not graduate this year and his father will not buy him a car.

    (b) The student does not graduate this year.

    (c) The student's father will buy him a car this year.

    (d) Either or both. The student will graduate and his father will buy him a car this year.

2. (a) {12, 13, 14, 18}

    (b) {10, 12, 14, 16, 18}

    (c) {16}

    (d) {12, 14}

3. (a) $P(R') = 1 - P(R) = 1 - .62 = \underline{.38}$

    (b) $P(R \cup T) = P(R) + P(T) - P(R \cap T')$
    $= .62 + .75 - .43 = \underline{.94}$

    (c) $P(R) = P(R \cap T) + P(R \cap T')$
    $P(R \cap T') = P(R) - P(R \cap T)$
    $= .62 - .43 = \underline{.19}$

    (d) $P(R \cup T') = P(R) + P(T') - P(R \cap T')$
    $= .62 + .25 - .19 = \underline{.68}$

4. (a) probability that radio advertising is not successful

    (b) probability that either or both radio and TV advertising is successful

    (c) probability that the radio advertising is successful and TV advertising is not

    (d) probability that either or both of radio advertising is successful or TV advertising is not

5. (a) $\dfrac{8}{13} \cdot \dfrac{7}{12} = \dfrac{56}{156} = \underline{\dfrac{14}{39}}$

    (b) $\dfrac{5}{13} \cdot \dfrac{8}{12} = \dfrac{40}{156} = \underline{\dfrac{10}{39}}$

6. (a) $\dfrac{625}{1000}$ (d) $\dfrac{200}{700}$ (g) $\dfrac{500}{1000}$

    (b) $\dfrac{300}{1000}$ (e) $\dfrac{175}{375}$ (h) $\dfrac{125}{1000}$

    (c) $\dfrac{175}{300}$ (f) $\dfrac{500}{700}$ (i) $\dfrac{125}{1000}$

7. Probability of selecting a person:

    (a) who is male
    (b) whose favorite snack is not ice cream
    (c) who is not a male, given that his favorite snack is pizza
    (d) who is a female, given that her favorite snack is ice cream
    (e) whose favorite snack is pizza, given that the person is not a male
    (f) who is not a female, given that the person's favorite snack is not pizza
    (g) who is a female or a person whose favorite snack is pizza
    (h) who is a male and whose favorite snack is not ice cream
    (i) same as (h)

8. $P(R) = .04$, $P(C) = .5$, $P(R \cap C) = .25$

    (a) $P(C/R) = \dfrac{P(C \cap R)}{P(R)} = \dfrac{.25}{.40} = \dfrac{5}{8}$

    (b) $P(R/C) = \dfrac{P(R \cap C)}{P(C)} = \dfrac{.25}{.50} = \dfrac{1}{2}$

    (c) $P(R \cup C) = P(R) + P(C) = P(R \cap C)$
    $= .4 + .5 - .25 = \underline{.65}$

    (d) $P(R)P(C) = .4(.5) = .20$
    $P(R \cap C) = .25$
    $P(R \cap C) \neq P(R)P(C)$

    So R and C are not independent.

9. (a) $P(D') = 1 - P(D) = 1 - .34 = \underline{.66}$

    (b) $P(C \cap D) = \underline{0}$ (mutually exclusive)

    (c) $P(C \cup D) = P(C) + P(D)$
    $= .61 + .34 = \underline{.95}$

    (d) $P(C' \cup D') = P(C \cap D)'$
    $= 1 - P(C \cap D) = 1 - 0 = \underline{1}$

    (e) $P(C' \cap D') = P(C \cup D)'$
    $= 1 - P(C \cup D) = 1 - .95$
    $= \underline{.05}$

10. $P(T) = .60$, $P(C) = .50$, $P(C/T) = .70$

   (a) $P(T \cap C) = P(T)P(C/T) = .60(.70)$
                      $= \underline{.42}$

   (b) $P(T/C) = \dfrac{P(T \cap C)}{P(C)} = \dfrac{.42}{.50} = \underline{.84}$

   (c) $P(T \cup C) = P(T) + P(C) - P(T \cap C)$
                $= .60 + .50 - .42 = \underline{.68}$

   (d) $P(T \cup C)' = 1 - P(T \cup C)$
                 $= 1 - .68 = .32$

   (e) $P(C)P(T) = .50(.60) = .30$
       $P(C \cap T) = .42$
       $P(C \cap T) \neq P(C)P(T)$

   So C and T are not independent.

11. (a) $\dfrac{52}{91}$ (e) $\dfrac{38}{60}$

    (b) $\dfrac{6}{26}$ (f) $\dfrac{8}{30}$

    (c) $\dfrac{8}{91}$ (g) $\dfrac{28}{63}$

    (d) $\dfrac{17}{65}$ (h) $\dfrac{23}{91}$

12. $P(M) = 0.3$ $P(D) = 0.4$ $P(M/D) = 0.6$

   (a) $P(M \cup D) = P(M) + P(D) - P(M \cap D)$
               $= 0.3 + 0.4 - 0.4(0.6)$
               $= \underline{0.46}$

   (b) $P(D/M) = \dfrac{P(D \cap M)}{P(M)} = \dfrac{0.24}{0.30} = \underline{0.80}$

   (c) $P[(M \cup D)'] = 1 - P(M \cup D)$
                $= 1 - 0.46 = \underline{0.54}$

13. $P(M)P(D) = 0.4(0.3) = 0.12$
    $P(M \cap D) = 0.24$
    $0.12 \neq 0.24$ No
    $P(M)P(D) \neq P(M \cap D)$

14. (a) $P(A \cup C) = P(A) + P(C)$ (mutually
                              exclusive)
         $= 0.20 + 0.28 = \underline{0.48}$

   (b) $P[A \cup B \cup C)'] = 1 - P(A \cup B \cup C)$
               $= 1 - (0.20 + 0.25 + 0.28)$
               $= \underline{0.27}$

   (c) ii

15. (a) $P(X \cup Y) = P(X) + P(Y) - P(X \cap Y)$
                  $= P(X) + P(Y) - P(X)P(Y)$
                  $= 0.4 + 0.6 - 0.24$
                 [since independent]
                 $= \underline{0.76}$

   (b) i

CHAPTER 7
MODIFIED TRUE/FALSE

1.	true	6.	not equal to
2.	true	7.	expected profit under
3.	maximax		uncertainty
4.	true	8.	column
5.	true	9.	true
		10.	divided

MULTIPLE CHOICE

1.	d	6.	b
2.	c	7.	a
3.	b	8.	c
4.	c	9.	b
5.	a	10.	a

COMPLETION

1. maximax
2. minimum, maximum
3. negative
4. greatest, smallest
5. fair game
6. probabilities
7. highest, row
8. the expected profit with perfect info.
9. A3
10. A2

PROBLEMS

1. (a)

a	p
150	$\dfrac{1}{600}$
-1	$\dfrac{599}{600}$

    $E = 150\left(\dfrac{1}{600}\right) - 1\left(\dfrac{599}{600}\right)$
       $= -\dfrac{499}{600} = -.749$

   (b)

a	p	ap
2	6/25	12/25
3	11/25	33/25
4	8/25	32/25

    $E = \dfrac{12}{25} + \dfrac{33}{25} + \dfrac{32}{25} = \dfrac{77}{25}$

    $= \$3.08$

    $\$3.08 < \$3.50$ No

   (c)

a	p	ap
0	.15	0
2000	.20	400
5000	.35	1750
10000	.18	1800
12000	.12	1440

    $E = 0 + 400 + 1750 + 1800 + 1440$
       $= \underline{\$5390}$

2. (a)

a	p	ap
40000	.5	20000
25000	.5	12500

$$E = 20000 + 12500 = \$32500$$

(b)

a	p	ap
40000	2/3	$\dfrac{80000}{3}$
25000	1/3	$\dfrac{25000}{3}$

$$E = \frac{80000}{3} + \frac{25000}{3} = \frac{105000}{3} = \$35000$$

(favorite) E = $35000
(underdog) E = $5000

---

3. (a)

	new restaurant	established restaurant
economy improves	70000	40000
recession	-10000	8000

(b) $70000 \ (\frac{3}{4}) \quad 8000 \ (\frac{1}{4}) = \dfrac{218000}{4}$

$$= 54500$$

(c) $70000 \ (\frac{2}{3}) + 8000 \ (\frac{1}{3}) = \dfrac{148000}{3}$

$$= 49333.33$$

---

4. (a) $70000 \ (\frac{3}{4}) - 10000 \ (\frac{1}{4}) = \dfrac{200000}{4}$

$$= \$50,000$$

$40000 \ (\frac{3}{4}) + 8000 \ (\frac{1}{4}) = \dfrac{128000}{4}$

$$= \$32000$$

$54500 - $50000 = \underline{\$4500}

(b) $70000 \ (\frac{2}{3}) - 10000 \ (\frac{1}{3}) = \dfrac{130000}{3}$

$$= \$43333.33$$

$40000 \ (\frac{2}{3}) + 8000 \ (\frac{1}{3}) = \dfrac{88000}{3}$

$$= \$29333.33$$

$49333.33 - $43333.33 = \underline{\$6000}

---

5. (a) <u>230</u>, 220, 225, 210   A

(b) 245, <u>260</u>, 250, 255   B

---

6. (a)

		investment	no investment
balance sheet claim	true	15000	0
	false	-5000	0

(b) 15000(.20) + (-5000)(.80) = -$1000
    0(.20) + 0(.80) = 0
    $0 > -$1000 <u>make no investment</u>

(c) 15000(.30) + (-5000)(.70) = $1000
    $1000 > $0
    change decision to: <u>make the investment</u>

---

7. (a) $8.00 < $8.50 < $9.00
       so you would go to <u>C</u>

(b) $6.75 < $7.00 < $7.65
       so you would go to <u>B</u>

---

8. p = probability of exceeding quota

$$20000 + 8000p > 25000$$
$$8000p > 5000$$
$$p > 5/8$$

---

9. a = amount ticket is worth

$$E = a \cdot \frac{1}{3} + 0 \cdot \frac{2}{3} = a \cdot \frac{1}{3}$$

$$20 = a \cdot \frac{1}{3} \qquad a = \$60$$

---

10. (a) choose mode = 30

(b) choose median = 34

(c) choose mean = $\dfrac{368}{10} = 36.8$

---

11. It is a game in which the mathematical expectation of each player is zero.

---

12. In this kind of analysis, probabilities are assigned to the alternatives about which uncertainties exist. Then we choose whichever alternative promises the greatest expected profit or the smallest expected loss.

CHAPTER 8
MODIFIED TRUE/FALSE

1.	true	6.	true
2.	sometimes	7.	$\mu = np$
3.	true	8.	$\sigma^2 = np(1-p)$
4.	binomial	9.	trials
5.	binomial	10.	mean

MULTIPLE CHOICE

1.	a	6.	c
2.	c	7.	b
3.	a	8.	d
4.	b	9.	a
5.	a	10.	a

COMPLETION

1. from 1 through 20, .05, .1, 2, ...9, .95
2. There are n independent trials, two possible outcomes for each trial, the probability of success is the same from trial to trial.
3. 1
4. λ
5. more than 2
6. one success in one trial
7. at least
8. 2
9. a + b
10. mean, standard deviation

PROBLEMS

1. (a) No, sum of probabilities is $\neq$ 1.

   (b) Yes, sum of probabilities equals 1. Each probability is between 0 and 1, inclusive.

   (c) No, sum of probabilities is $\neq$ 1.

   (d) No, probability cannot be negative.

2. hypergeometric distribution
   a = 6, b = 12, n = 7

   (a) $f(2) + f(3) + f(4)$

   $$= \frac{\binom{6}{2}\binom{12}{5}}{\binom{18}{7}} + \frac{\binom{6}{3}\binom{12}{4}}{\binom{18}{7}} + \frac{\binom{6}{4}\binom{12}{3}}{\binom{18}{7}}$$

   $$= \frac{15(792)}{31824} + \frac{20(495)}{31824} + \frac{15(220)}{31824}$$

   $$= \frac{11880 + 9900 + 3300}{31824} = \frac{25080}{31824}$$

   $$= \underline{.79}$$

   (b) $f(3) = \frac{9900}{31824} = \underline{.31}$

3. (a) $\mu = \frac{na}{a+b} = \frac{7(6)}{18} = \frac{42}{18} = \frac{7}{3} = \underline{2.33}$

   (b)

x	p(x)	x^2	$x^2 p(x)$
0	.025	0	0
1	.174	1	.174
2	.373	4	1.492
3	.311	9	2.799
4	.104	16	1.664
5	.012	25	.300
6	.000	36	0
			6.429

3. (continued)

$$\sigma^2 = \Sigma x^2 p(x) - \mu^2$$
$$= 6.429 - (2.33)^2$$
$$= \underline{1.00}$$

   (c) $\sigma = \sqrt{1.00} = 1$

---

4. binomial distribution

   $\mu = 1000(.003) = 3$

   use Poisson approximation

   (a) $f(5) = \frac{3^5 e^{-3}}{5!} = \frac{243(.050)}{120} = \underline{.101}$

   (b) $1 - \{f(0) + f(1) + f(2)\}$

   $$= 1 - \left[\frac{3^0 e^{-3}}{0!} + \frac{3^1 e^{-3}}{1!} + \frac{3^2 e^{-3}}{2!}\right]$$

   $$= 1 - e^{-3}(1 + 3 + 4.5)$$

   $$= 1 - .050(8.5)$$

   $$= 1 - .425 = \underline{.575}$$

   (c) $f(0) + f(1) + f(2) + f(3) + f(4)$

   $$= .425 + f(3) + f(4)$$

   $$= .425 + \frac{3^3 e^{-3}}{3!} + \frac{3^4 e^{-3}}{4!}$$

   $$= .425 + \frac{27(.050)}{6} + \frac{81(.050)}{24}$$

   $$= .425 + .225 + .169 = \underline{.819}$$

   (d) $f(4) + f(5) + f(6)$

   $$= .169 + .101 + \frac{3^6 e^{-3}}{6!}$$

   $$= .270 + \frac{729(.050)}{720}$$

   $$= .270 + .051 = \underline{.321}$$

---

5. binomial distribution

   (a) $f(5) = \binom{12}{5}(.25)^5(.75)^7 = \underline{.103}$

   (b) $1 - \{f(0) + f(1) + f(2)\}$

   $$= 1 - \left[\binom{12}{0}(.25)^0(.75)^{12}\right.$$

   $$+ \binom{12}{1}(.25)^1(.75)^{11}$$

   $$\left. + \binom{12}{2}(.25)^2(.75)^{10}\right]$$

   $$= 1 - (.0317 + .1267 + .2323)$$

   $$= 1 - (.3907) = \underline{.609}$$

6. (a) $\mu = np = 12(.25) = \underline{3}$

   (b) $\sigma^2 = np(1-p) = 12(.25)(.75) = \underline{2.25}$

   (c) $\sigma = \sqrt{2.25} = \underline{1.5}$

CHAPTER 8 (continued)

7. binomial distribution
   use Table V   n = 10   p = .40

   (a) $f(5) = \underline{.201}$

   (b) $f(0) = \underline{.006}$

   (c) $1 - \{f(0) + f(1) + f(2)\}$
       $1 - (.006 + .040 + .121)$
       $1 - .167 = .833$

   (d) $f(0) + f(1) + f(2)$
       $= .006 + .040 + .121 = .167$

   (e) $f(2) + f(3) + f(4)$
       $= .121 + .215 + .251 = .587$

8. Multinomial distribution

   $\dfrac{12!}{5!4!3!}(.50)^5(.30)^4(.20)^3$

   $= 27720(.03125)(.0081)(.008) = \underline{.056}$

9. (a)
x	p(x)
0	.30
1	.20
2	.20
3	.15
4	.10
5	.05

   $\mu = \Sigma x p(x)$
   $= 0(.30) + 1(.20) + 2(.20)$
   $\quad + 3(.15) + 4(.10) + 5(.05)$
   $= .2 + .4 + .45 + .4 + .25$
   $= 1.7$

   (b) $\sigma^2 = \Sigma x^2 p(x) - \mu^2$
   $= 0^2(.30)^2 + 1^2(.20) + 2^2(.20)$
   $\quad + 3^2(.15) + 4^2(.10) + 5^2(.05)$
   $\quad - (1.7)^2$
   $= 0 + .2 + .8 + 1.35 + 1.6$
   $\quad + 1.25 - 2.89$
   $= 5.20 - 2.89 = \underline{2.31}$

   (c) $\sigma = \sqrt{2.31} = \underline{1.52}$

10. (a) $k = \dfrac{\mu - \bar{x}}{\sigma}$

    $k = \dfrac{80 - 68}{6} = \dfrac{12}{6} = 2$

    $1 - \dfrac{1}{k^2} = 1 - \dfrac{1}{2^2} = 1 - \dfrac{1}{4} = \dfrac{3}{4} = .75$

    $\underline{\text{at least 75\%}}$

    (b) $1 - \dfrac{1}{k^2} = \dfrac{35}{36}$

    $-\dfrac{1}{k^2} = -\dfrac{1}{36}$

10. (continued)

    $k^2 = 36$

    $k = 6$

    $80 - 6(6)$ to $80 + 6(6)$
    $\underline{\quad 44 \quad}$ to $\underline{\quad 116 \quad}$

11. binomial distribution
    use Table V with n = 10,   p = .6

    (a) $1 - [f(0) + f(1)]$
        $= 1 - [0 + .002] = \underline{.998}$

    (b) $f(6) = \underline{.251}$

    (c) $f(0) + f(1) + f(2)$
        $= 0 + .002 + .011 = \underline{0.013}$

12. binomial
    $\mu = np = 100(.02) = 2$
    use Poisson approximation

    (a) $1 - [f(0) + f(1) + f(2)]$

        $= 1 - \left[\dfrac{2^0 e^{-2}}{0!} + \dfrac{2^1 e^{-2}}{1!} + \dfrac{2^2 e^{-2}}{2!}\right]$

        $= 1 - .135[1 + 2 + 2]$

        $= 1 - .135(5) = 1 - .675 = \underline{.325}$

    (b) $f(0) + f(1) + f(2) = \underline{.675}$

    (c) $f(4) = \dfrac{2^4 e^{-2}}{4!} = \dfrac{16(.135)}{24} = \underline{.09}$

13. hypergeometric distribution

    (a) $f(0) = \dfrac{\binom{4}{0} \cdot \binom{6}{3}}{\binom{10}{3}} = \dfrac{20}{120} = \underline{\dfrac{1}{6}}$

    (b) $f(2) = \dfrac{\binom{4}{2} \cdot \binom{6}{1}}{\binom{10}{3}} = \dfrac{36}{120} = \underline{\dfrac{3}{10}}$

14. (a) $f(0) + f(1) + f(2) + f(3) + f(4)$

        $= 5\left(\dfrac{1}{5}\right) = 1$ $\underline{\text{Yes}}$

    (b) $f(1) + f(2) + f(3) = .25 + .40$
        $+ .30 = 0.95$

        $.95 \neq 1$ $\underline{\text{No}}$

CHAPTER 9
MODIFIED TRUE/FALSE

1. sometimes
2. binomial
3. left
4. population mean
5. true
6. positive
7. never
8. $z = \dfrac{x - \mu}{\sigma}$
9. true
10. the standard

MULTIPLE CHOICE

1. d	6. c
2. b	7. b
3. c	8. d
4. a	9. b
5. d	10. d

COMPLETION

1. 0
2. discrete, continuous;
   discrete, continuous
3. 1
4. 0, 1
5. 0
6. .6554
7. sample mean
8. $np > 5$, $n(1-p) > 5$
9. $-.84$
10. probability

PROBLEMS

1. (a) $2(\frac{3}{8}) = \frac{6}{8} = \underline{\frac{3}{4}}$

   (b) $\frac{1}{2}(\frac{3}{8}) + \frac{1}{2}(\frac{1}{8}) = \frac{4}{16} = \underline{\frac{1}{4}}$

   (c) $1(\frac{1}{8}) = \underline{\frac{1}{8}}$

2. (a) $.4032 - .1554 = \underline{.2478}$

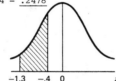

   (b) $.5 + .2486 = \underline{.7486}$

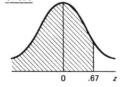

   (c) $.5 - .2054 = \underline{.2946}$

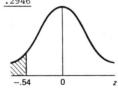

3. (a) $z = \frac{32 - 30}{5} = \frac{2}{5} = .4$

   $.5 + .1554 = \underline{.6554}$

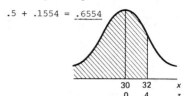

   (b) $z = \frac{31 - 30}{5} = .2$

   $z = \frac{35 - 30}{5} = 1$

   $.3413 - .0793 = \underline{.2620}$

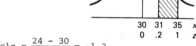

   (c) $z = \frac{24 - 30}{5} = -1.2$

   $z = \frac{28 - 30}{5} = -.4$

   $.3849 - .1554 = \underline{.2295}$

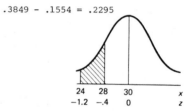

4. (a) $z_{.05} = \underline{1.65}$

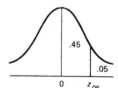

   (b) $z_{.45} = \underline{.13}$

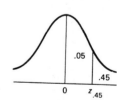

212

4. (c) $z_{.65} = \underline{-.39}$

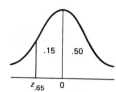

(d) $z_{.90} = \underline{-1.28}$

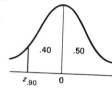

5. (a) (i) $z = \underline{1.96}$

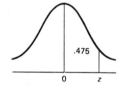

(ii) $z = \underline{-1.28}$

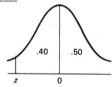

(iii) $z = \underline{-.99}$

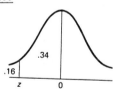

(b) (i) $z = \dfrac{x - \mu}{\sigma}$

$-1 = \dfrac{54 - 60}{\sigma} = \dfrac{-6}{\sigma}, \; \sigma = 6$

$z = \dfrac{64 - 60}{6} = .67$

$.5 - .2486 = \underline{.2514}$

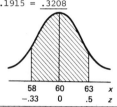

(ii) $z = \dfrac{58 - 60}{6} = -.33$

$z = \dfrac{63 - 60}{6} = .5$

$.1293 + .1915 = \underline{.3208}$

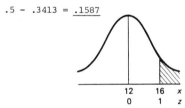

6. (a) $z = \dfrac{16 - 12}{4} = 1$

$.5 - .3413 = \underline{.1587}$

(b) $z = \dfrac{15 - 12}{4} = .75$

$z = \dfrac{18 - 12}{4} = 1.5$

$.4332 - .2734 = \underline{.1598}$

7. normal approximation
    $\mu = np = 80(.70) = 56$

    $\sigma = \sqrt{np(1-p)} = \sqrt{80(.7)(.3)} = 4.1$

    (a) $P(x \geq 60)$ use continuity
        correction
        $z = \dfrac{59.5 - 56}{4.1} = \dfrac{3.5}{4.1} = .85$

        $.5 - .3023 = \underline{.1977}$

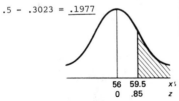

    (b) $P(x \leq 50)$ use continuity
        correction
        $z = \dfrac{50.5 - 56}{4.1} = \dfrac{-5.5}{4.1} = -1.34$

        $.5 - .4099 = .0901$

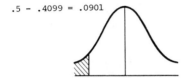

    (c) $P(55 \leq x \leq 59)$ use continuity
        correction
        $z = \dfrac{54.5 - 56}{4.1} = \dfrac{-1.5}{4.1} = -.37$

        $z = \dfrac{59.5 - 56}{4.1} = \dfrac{3.5}{4.1} = .85$

        $.1443 + .3023 = \underline{.4466}$

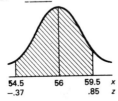

8. (a) $z = \dfrac{48 - 45}{6} = .5$

        $.5 + .1915 = \underline{.6915}$

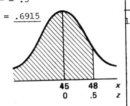

    (b) $z = \dfrac{39 - 45}{6} = -1$

        $z = \dfrac{43 - 45}{6} = -.33$

        $.3413 - .1293 = \underline{.2120}$

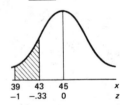

9. normal approximation
    $\mu = np = 90(.4) = 36$

    $\sigma = \sqrt{np(1-p)} \quad \sqrt{90(.4)(.6)} = 4.65$

    (a) $P(x < 32) = P(x \leq 31)$ use continuity
        correction
        $z = \dfrac{31.5 - 36}{4.65} = -.97$

        $.5 - .3340 = .1660$

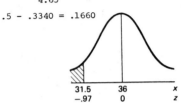

    (b) $P(38 \leq x \leq 42)$ use continuity
        correction
        $z = \dfrac{37.5 - 36}{4.65} = .32$

        $z = \dfrac{42.5 - 36}{4.65} = 1.40$

        $.4192 - .1255 = .2937$

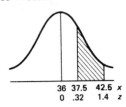

10. (a) $1 - e^{-\frac{30}{45}} = 1 - e^{-.67}$

        $1 - .512 = .488$

214

10. (b) $(1 - e^{-\frac{50}{45}}) - (1 - e^{-\frac{35}{45}})$

$= e^{-\frac{35}{45}} - e^{-\frac{50}{45}} = e^{-.78} - e^{-1.1}$

$= .458 - .333 = \underline{.125}$

11.

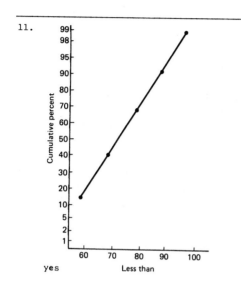

12. (a) .5000
      −.4332
      ──────
      .0668

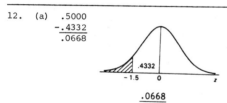

      $\underline{.0668}$

(b) .4032
    +.3413
    ──────
    .7445

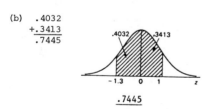

    $\underline{.7445}$

(c) .4772
    −.3413
    ──────
    .1359

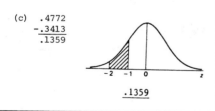

    $\underline{.1359}$

13. (a)

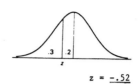

    $z = \underline{-.52}$

(b)

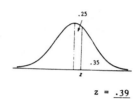

    $z = \underline{.39}$

14. binomial distribution
     $\mu = np = 60(.20) = 12 > 5$
     $n(1-p) = 60(.80) = 48 > 5$
     use normal approximation

     $\sigma = \sqrt{np(1-p)} = \sqrt{60(.2)(.8)} = 3.10$

(a) $z = \dfrac{8.5 - 12}{3.10} = -1.13$

    .5000
   +.3708
   ──────
    .8708

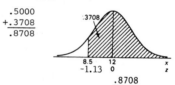

    $\underline{.8708}$

(b) $z = \dfrac{13.5 - 12}{3.10} = .48$

    $z = \dfrac{18.5 - 12}{3.10} = 2.10$

    .4821
   −.1844
   ──────
    .2977

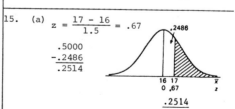

    $\underline{.2977}$

15. (a) $z = \dfrac{17 - 16}{1.5} = .67$

    .5000
   −.2486
   ──────
    .2514

    $\underline{.2514}$

215

CHAPTER 9 (continued)

15. (b) $z = \dfrac{14 - 16}{1.5} = -1.33$

  $z = \dfrac{12 - 16}{1.5} = -2.67$

  .4962
  $-$.4082
  .0880

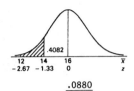

  .0880

CHAPTER 10

MODIFIED TRUE/FALSE

1. true   7. true
2. true   8. possible
3. true   9. cannot be
4. variation   10. decreases
5. true   11. small
6. true

MULTIPLE CHOICE

1. b   6. d   11. c
2. d   7. d   12. d
3. b   8. a   13. b
4. b   9. b
5. a   10. a

COMPLETION

1. less than .05 N

2. $\dfrac{5}{6}\sqrt{\dfrac{65}{100}} = \dfrac{1}{12}\sqrt{65}$

3. $\dfrac{N_i}{N}$

4. optimum

5. $\dfrac{1}{\binom{30}{3}} = \dfrac{1}{4060}$

6. the normal distribution

7. the sampling distribution of the mean

8. $\bar{x} - \mu$

9. have the same probability of being selected; independent

10. error, population mean

PROBLEMS

1. (a)   (b)
  $\binom{15}{2} = \dfrac{15 \cdot 14}{2 \cdot 1} = \underline{105}$ $\binom{12}{3} = \dfrac{12 \cdot 11 \cdot 10}{3 \cdot 2 \cdot 1} = \underline{220}$

---

2. (a) (i)   (ii)
  $\binom{5}{2} = \dfrac{5 \cdot 4}{2 \cdot 1} = \underline{10}$ $\binom{5}{3} = \binom{5}{2} = \underline{10}$

  (b) (i)   (ii)
  $\dfrac{1}{\binom{5}{2}} = \dfrac{1}{\underline{10}}$ $\dfrac{\binom{4}{1}}{\binom{5}{2}} = \dfrac{4}{10} = \dfrac{2}{5}$

---

3. (a)
  $\mu = \underline{11.5}$ $\sigma = \sqrt{\dfrac{\Sigma(x_i - \bar{x})^2}{N}} = \underline{5.12}$

  (b) 4,7   4,16   7,13   10,13   13,16
       4,10   4,19   7,16   10,16   13,19
       4,13   7,10   7,19   10,19   16,19

  (c)

$\bar{x}$	5.5	7	8.5	10	11.5	13	14.5	16	17.5
$p(\bar{x})$	$\frac{1}{15}$	$\frac{1}{15}$	$\frac{2}{15}$	$\frac{2}{15}$	$\frac{3}{15}$	$\frac{2}{15}$	$\frac{2}{15}$	$\frac{1}{15}$	$\frac{1}{15}$

  (d) $\mu_{\bar{x}} = \Sigma \bar{x} p(\bar{x})$

  $5.5(\tfrac{1}{15}) + 7(\tfrac{1}{15}) + \ldots + 17.5(\tfrac{1}{15})$

  $= \dfrac{172.5}{15} = \underline{11.5}$

  $\sigma_{\bar{x}} = (5.5-11.5)^2(\tfrac{1}{15}) + \ldots + (17.5-11.5)^2(\tfrac{1}{15})$

  $= \underline{3.24}$

  $\sigma_{\bar{x}} = \dfrac{\sigma}{\sqrt{n}}\sqrt{\dfrac{N-n}{N-1}} = \dfrac{5.12}{\sqrt{2}}\sqrt{\dfrac{6-2}{6-1}} = \underline{3.24}$

---

4. (a)

	$\bar{x}$		$\bar{x}$		$\bar{x}$
60,65	62.5	66,55	60	55,75	65
60,55	57.5	65,80	72.5	55,85	70
60,80	70	65,75	70	80,75	77.5
60,75	67.5	65,85	75	80,85	82.5
60,85	72.5	55,80	67.5	75,85	80

  $\sigma_{\bar{x}} = \sqrt{\dfrac{15(74200) - (1050)^2}{210}} = \sqrt{50}$

  $= 7.071$

  (b)

	$\bar{x}$		$\bar{x}$		$\bar{x}$
60,80	70	65,80	72.5	55,80	67.5
60,75	67.5	65,75	70	55,75	65
60,80	72.5	65,85	75	55,85	70

  $\sigma_{\bar{x}} = \sqrt{\dfrac{9(44175) - (630)^2}{9(8)}} = \sqrt{9.375}$

  $= \underline{3.062}$

(c)

	$\bar{x}$			$\bar{x}$
60,65	62.5		80,75	77.5
60,55	57.5		80,85	82.5
65,55	60		75,85	80

$$\sigma_{\bar{x}} = \sqrt{\frac{6(30025) - (420)^2}{30}} = \sqrt{125}$$

$$= 11.18$$

(d)

The stratified sample gives the lowest $\sigma_{\bar{x}}$. The cluster sample gives the largest $\sigma_{\bar{x}}$.

5. (a)
$$n_2 = \frac{N_2}{N} \cdot n = \frac{4}{7} \cdot 3 \approx 2$$

(b) Calculate $\sigma_1 = 7.55$, $\sigma_2 = 4.32$

$$n_1 = \frac{3(3)(7.55)}{3(7.55)+4(4.32)} = \frac{67.95}{39.93} \approx 2$$

$$n_2 = \frac{3(4)(4.32)}{39.93} = \frac{51.84}{39.93} \approx 1$$

6. (a)

(i) $\binom{3}{1} \cdot \binom{4}{2} = (3)(6) = \underline{18}$

(ii)

	$\bar{x}$			$\bar{x}$
25,57,53	45		10,53,55	39.33
25,57,55	45.67		10,53,63	42
25,57,63	48.33		10,55,63	42.67
25,53,55	44.33		19,57,55	43
25,53,63	47		19,57,55	43.67
25,55,63	47.67		19,57,63	46.33
10,57,53	40		19,53,55	42.33
10,57,55	40.67		19,53,63	45
10,57,63	43.33		19,55,63	45.67

$$\sigma_{\bar{x}} = 2.58$$

(b) $\binom{3}{2}\binom{4}{1} = 3 \cdot 4 = \underline{12}$ $\sigma_{\bar{x}} = 2.51$

	$\bar{x}$			$\bar{x}$
25,10,57	30.67		25,29,55	33
25,10,53	29.33		25,19,63	35.67
25,10,55	30		10,19,57	28.67
25,10,63	32.67		10,19,53	27.33
25,19,57	33.67		10,19,55	28
25,19,53	32.33		10,19,63	30.67

7.
(a) $n_1 = \dfrac{N_1}{N} \cdot 100 = \dfrac{10000}{30000} \cdot 300 = \underline{100}$

$$n_2 = \frac{5000}{30000} \cdot 300 = \underline{50}$$

$$n_3 = \frac{8000}{30000} \cdot 300 = \underline{80}$$

$$n_4 = \frac{7000}{30000} \cdot 300 = \underline{70}$$

(b)
$$n_1 = \frac{300(10000(15)}{10000(15)+5000(25)+8000(20)+7000(30)}$$

$$= \frac{45000000}{645000} = \underline{70}$$

$$n_2 = \frac{300(5000)(25)}{645000} = \underline{58}$$

$$n_3 = \frac{300(8000)(20)}{645000} = \underline{74}$$

$$n_4 = \frac{300(7000)(30)}{645000} = \underline{98}$$

8. (a)
$$\frac{\dfrac{\sigma}{\sqrt{400}}}{\dfrac{\sigma}{\sqrt{64}}} = \frac{\sqrt{64}}{\sqrt{400}} = \frac{8}{20} = \frac{2}{5}$$

new $\sigma_{\bar{x}}$ is 2/5 of the old $\sigma_{\bar{x}}$

(b)
$$\frac{\dfrac{\sigma}{\sqrt{100}}}{\dfrac{\sigma}{\sqrt{225}}} = \frac{\sqrt{225}}{\sqrt{100}} = \frac{15}{10} = \frac{3}{2}$$

new $\sigma_{\bar{x}}$ is $\frac{3}{2}$ of the old $\sigma_{\bar{x}}$

9. (a)

4,4	7,7	10,13	16,16	16,4	13,10
4,7	7,10	10,16	16,19	19,4	16,10
4,10	7,13	10,19	19,19	10,7	19,10
4,13	7,16	13,13	7,4	13,7	16,13
4,16	7,19	13,16	10,4	16,7	19,13
4,19	10,10	13,19	13,4	19,7	19,16

(b)

$\bar{x}$	4	5.5	7	8.5	10	11.5	13	14.5
$p(\bar{x})$	$\frac{1}{36}$	$\frac{2}{36}$	$\frac{3}{36}$	$\frac{4}{36}$	$\frac{5}{36}$	$\frac{6}{36}$	$\frac{5}{36}$	$\frac{4}{36}$

$\bar{x}$	16	17.5	19
$p(\bar{x})$	$\frac{3}{36}$	$\frac{2}{36}$	$\frac{1}{36}$

(c) $\mu_{\bar{x}} = \Sigma \bar{x}\, p(\bar{x})$

$$= 4\left(\frac{1}{36}\right) + \ldots + 19\left(\frac{1}{36}\right) = \underline{11.5}$$

$$\sigma_{\bar{x}} = (4-11.5)^2\left(\frac{1}{36}\right) + \ldots (19-11.5)^2\left(\frac{1}{36}\right)$$

$$= \underline{3.62}$$

$$\sigma_{\bar{x}} = \frac{\sigma}{\sqrt{n}} = \frac{5.12}{\sqrt{2}} = \underline{3.62}$$

10. (a) $k \dfrac{\sigma}{\sqrt{n}} = .8$

$k \dfrac{4}{\sqrt{100}} = .8 \qquad 1 - \dfrac{1}{k^2} = 1 - \dfrac{1}{4}$

$\qquad\qquad\qquad\qquad = \dfrac{3}{4} = .75$

$k(.4) = .8$

$k = 2 \qquad \underline{\text{at least 75\%}}$

(b) $z = \dfrac{\text{error}}{\sigma/\sqrt{n}}$

$z = \dfrac{-.8}{4/\sqrt{100}} = -2 \qquad z = \dfrac{.8}{4/\sqrt{100}} = 2$

$.4772 + .4772 = \underline{.9544}$

11.
(a) $z = \dfrac{\text{error}}{\sigma/\sqrt{n}}$

$z = \dfrac{-8}{35/\sqrt{49}} = \dfrac{-8}{5} = -1.6 \qquad z = \dfrac{8}{35/\sqrt{49}} = 1.6$

$.4452 + .4452 = \underline{.8904}$

(b) $z = \dfrac{-6}{-35/\sqrt{49}} = \dfrac{-6}{5} = -1.2 \qquad z = \dfrac{6}{5} = 1.2$

$.3849 + .3849 = \underline{.7698}$

12. (a) $z = \dfrac{\bar{x} - \mu}{\sigma/\sqrt{n}} = \dfrac{38 - 40}{12/\sqrt{64}} = -1.33$

$\begin{array}{r} .4032 \\ +.5000 \\ \hline .9032 \end{array}$

.4332

38 40 $\bar{x}$
-1.33 0 z

.9032

(b) $z = \dfrac{41 - 40}{12/\sqrt{64}} = .67$

$z = \dfrac{45 - 40}{12/\sqrt{64}} = 3.33$

$\begin{array}{r} .4990 \\ -.2486 \\ \hline .2504 \end{array}$

.2486

40 41   45 $\bar{x}$
0 .67   3.33 z

.2504

13. $\dfrac{\sigma}{\sqrt{n}} = \dfrac{12}{\sqrt{64}} = \dfrac{3}{2}$

14.
10,15,18	15,18,25
10,15,25	15,18,38
10,15,38	15,18,42
10,15,42	15,25,38
10,18,25	15,25,42
10,18,38	15,38,42
10,18,42	18,25,38
10,25,38	18,25,42
10,25,42	18,38,42
10,38,42	25,38,42

$\tilde{x}$	15	18	25	38
$p(\tilde{x})$	$\dfrac{4}{20}$	$\dfrac{6}{20}$	$\dfrac{6}{20}$	$\dfrac{4}{20}$

15. (a) $z = \dfrac{3.9 - 4}{.6/\sqrt{36}} = -1$

$z = \dfrac{4.2 - 4}{.6/\sqrt{36}} = 2$

$.3413 + .4772 = \underline{.8185}$

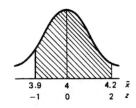

3.9   4   4.2 $\bar{x}$
-1   0   2 z

(b) $z = \dfrac{3.7 - 4}{.6/\sqrt{36}} = -3$

$.4987 + .5 = \underline{.9987}$

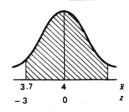

3.7   4 $\bar{x}$
-3   0 z

CHAPTER 11

MODIFIED TRUE/FALSE

1. sample value   6. true
2. population   7. true
3. true   8. decreases
4. increase   9. Type I error
5. true   10. A z value

CHAPTER 11 (continued)

1. a   6. b
2. c   7. c
3. b   8. b
4. b   9. a
5. d   10. d

COMPLETION

1. $\mu < 50$
2. α
3. $\mu_1 - \mu_2$
4. Type II
5. $n \geq .05N$
6. the center of distribution curve, the right side of test statistic numerator
7. t values
8. 13
9. the critical value
10. $\mu_1 - \mu_2 \neq 5$

PROBLEMS

1. (a) $E = z_{\alpha/2} \dfrac{\sigma}{\sqrt{n}} = 1.5 \dfrac{3.5}{\sqrt{49}} = \underline{.825 \text{ minutes}}$

    (b) $\bar{x} - z_{\alpha/2} \dfrac{\sigma}{\sqrt{n}} < \mu < \bar{x} + z_{\alpha/2} \dfrac{\sigma}{\sqrt{n}}$

    $8.4 - 1.65 \dfrac{3.5}{\sqrt{49}} < \mu < 8.4 + 1.65 \dfrac{3.5}{\sqrt{49}}$

    $8.4 - .825 < \mu < 8.4 + .825$

    $\underline{7.575 < \mu < 9.225}$

    (c) $E = 2.33 \dfrac{3.5}{\sqrt{49}} = \underline{1.165 \text{ minutes}}$

    (d) $8.4 - 2.33 \dfrac{3.5}{\sqrt{49}} < \mu < 8.4 \quad 2.33 \dfrac{3.5}{\sqrt{49}}$

    $\underline{7.235 < \mu < 9.565}$

---

2. degrees of freedom = n-1 = 16-1 = 15

    (a) $E = t_{\alpha/2} \dfrac{s}{\sqrt{n}} = 1.753 \dfrac{3.5}{\sqrt{16}}$

    $= \underline{1.534 \text{ minutes}}$

    (b) $\bar{x} - z_{\alpha/2} \dfrac{s}{\sqrt{n}} < \mu < \bar{x} + t_{\alpha/2} \dfrac{s}{\sqrt{n}}$

    $8.4 - 1.753 \dfrac{3.5}{\sqrt{16}} < \mu < 8.4 + 1.753 \dfrac{3.5}{\sqrt{16}}$

    $8.4 - 1.534 < \mu < 8.4 + 1.534$

    $\underline{6.866 < \mu < 9.934}$

(c) $E = 2.602 \dfrac{3.5}{\sqrt{16}} = \underline{2.277}$

(d) $8.4 - 2.602 \dfrac{3.5}{\sqrt{16}} < \mu < 8.4 + 2.602 \dfrac{3.5}{\sqrt{16}}$

$\underline{6.123 < \mu < 10.677}$

---

3. $n = \left[\dfrac{z_{\alpha/2} \, \sigma}{E} \right]^2 = \left[\dfrac{1.96(40)}{10} \right]^2 = 61.47$

    $\underline{62 \text{ people}}$

---

4. (a) $H_O : \mu = 60$
    $H_A : \mu < 60$

    (b) $z = \dfrac{\bar{x} - \mu}{\sigma/n}$

    $z = \dfrac{57 - 60}{15/\sqrt{100}} = -2$

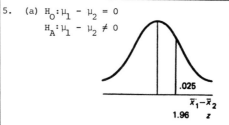

reject null hyp. conclude protection lasts less than 60 months

(c) $-1.65 \dfrac{\bar{x} - 60}{15/\sqrt{100}}$

$-2.475 = \bar{x} - 60 \quad \bar{x} = 57.525$

---

5. (a) $H_O : \mu_1 - \mu_2 = 0$
    $H_A : \mu_1 - \mu_2 \neq 0$

(b) large-sample test

$z = \dfrac{\bar{x}_1 - \bar{x}_2}{\sqrt{\dfrac{s_1^2}{n_1} + \dfrac{s_2^2}{n_2}}} = \dfrac{810 - 800}{\sqrt{\dfrac{(40)^2}{60} + \dfrac{(30)^2}{80}}} = 1.62$

do not reject null hyp. cannot say there is a difference in numbers of customers entering stores

5. (c) $H_0: \mu_1 - \mu_2 = 5$

   $H_A: \mu_1 - \mu_2 \neq 5$

   $z = \dfrac{810 - 800 - 5}{\sqrt{\dfrac{(40)^2}{60} + \dfrac{(30)^2}{80}}} = .81$

   do not reject null hyp. cannot say the difference is unequal to 5

---

6. (a) (i) rejecting null hyp. that $\mu = 60$ in favor of $\mu < 60$ when actually $\mu = 60$

   (ii) not rejecting null hyp. that $\mu = 60$ in favor of $\mu < 60$ when actually $\mu < 60$

   (b) $z = \dfrac{58 - 60}{15/\sqrt{100}} = -1.33$

   $.5 - .4082 = \underline{.0918}$

---

7. (a) $H_0: \mu \geq 30$

   $H_A: \mu < 30$

   (b) $t = \dfrac{\bar{x} - \mu_0}{s/\sqrt{n}}$

   $= \dfrac{25 - 30}{8/\sqrt{16}} = -2.5$

   $df = 15$

   .01

   -2.602 30 x
        0   t

   do not reject null hyp. cannot say that the car averages less than 30 mpg

---

8. (a) Posterior mean

   $\mu_1 = \dfrac{\dfrac{6}{1.80}(7.40) + \dfrac{1}{(.40)^2}(4.50)}{\dfrac{6}{(1.80)^2} + \dfrac{1}{(.40)^2}}$

   $= \dfrac{24.667 + 28.125}{1.852 + 6.25} = \dfrac{52.792}{8.102} = 6.52$

(b) $\dfrac{1}{\sigma_1^2} = \dfrac{6}{(1.80)^2} + \dfrac{1}{(.40)^2}$

$\dfrac{1}{\sigma_1^2} = 8.102, \quad \sigma_1^2 = .123, \quad \sigma_1 = .35$

$z = \dfrac{5 - 6.52}{.35} = \dfrac{-1.02}{.35} = -2.91$

$z = \dfrac{6 - 6.52}{.35} = \dfrac{-.52}{.35} = -1.49$

$.4982 + .4319 = .9301$

---

9. (a) $H_0: \mu_1 - \mu_2 = 0$

   $H_A: \mu_1 - \mu_2 \neq 0$

   (b)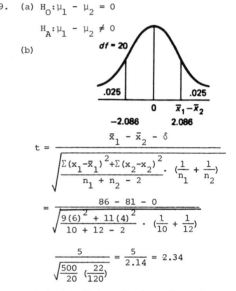

   $df = 20$

   .025   .025

   0    $\bar{x}_1 - \bar{x}_2$

   -2.086 2.086

   $t = \dfrac{\bar{x}_1 - \bar{x}_2 - \delta}{\sqrt{\dfrac{\Sigma(x_1 - \bar{x}_1)^2 + \Sigma(x_2 - \bar{x}_2)^2}{n_1 + n_2 - 2} \cdot \left(\dfrac{1}{n_1} + \dfrac{1}{n_2}\right)}}$

   $= \dfrac{86 - 81 - 0}{\sqrt{\dfrac{9(6)^2 + 11(4)^2}{10 + 12 - 2} \cdot \left(\dfrac{1}{10} + \dfrac{1}{12}\right)}}$

   $= \dfrac{5}{\sqrt{\dfrac{500}{20}\left(\dfrac{22}{120}\right)}} = \dfrac{5}{2.14} = 2.34$

   Reject null hypothesis. There is a difference in the effectiveness of the methods.

---

10. Let μ_0 = national average of housing prices

    $\bar{x}$ = average housing price in survey

    (a) $H_0: \mu = \mu_0$

    $H_A: \mu > \mu_0$

    (b) $H_0: \mu \geq \mu_0$

    $H_A: \mu < \mu_0$

CHAPTER 11 (continued)

10. (c) (i) $z = \dfrac{66000 - 64000}{5000/\sqrt{50}} = 2.83$

$.5 - .4977 = \underline{.0023}$

(ii) $z = \dfrac{66000 - 67000}{5000/\sqrt{50}} = -1.41$

$.5 - .4207 = \underline{.0793}$

11. (a) $n = \dfrac{z^2 \sigma^2}{E^2}$

$n = \dfrac{(1.65)^2 (2.5)^2}{(0.5)^2} = 68.06$

<u>69 students</u>

(b) $\bar{x} - z \dfrac{\sigma}{\sqrt{n}} < \mu < \bar{x} + z \dfrac{\sigma}{\sqrt{n}}$

$= 3.5 - 1.65 \dfrac{2.5}{\sqrt{69}} < \mu < 3.5$

$+ 1.65 \dfrac{2.5}{\sqrt{69}}$

$= 3.0 < \mu < 4.0$ with 90% confidence

12. $H_O: \mu = 15$

$H_A: \mu > 15$

$\alpha = 0.05$

$t = \dfrac{\bar{x} - \mu}{s/\sqrt{n}}$

$t = \dfrac{18 - 15}{6/\sqrt{16}} = 2$

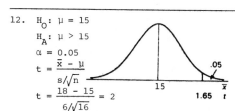

reject H_O

sufficient evidence to conclude that the drying time is greater than 15 minutes

13. $H_O: \mu_1 - \mu_2 - 0$

$H_A: \mu_1 - \mu_2 > 0$

$\alpha = 0.01$

$z = \dfrac{\bar{x}_1 - \bar{x}_2 - \delta}{\sqrt{\dfrac{\sigma_2^2}{n_1} + \dfrac{\sigma_2^2}{n_2}}}$

13. (continued)

$z = \dfrac{48 - 25 - 0}{\sqrt{\dfrac{30^2}{60} + \dfrac{20^2}{80}}}$

$= 5.14$

reject H_O

sufficient evidence to say that students who are not allowed to drink consume more

14. $z = \dfrac{\bar{x} - \mu}{\sigma/\sqrt{n}}$

$2.33 = \dfrac{\bar{x} - 50}{4/\sqrt{36}}$

$2.33(\dfrac{4}{6}) = \bar{x} - 50$

$1.55 = \bar{x} - 50$

$\bar{x} = 51.55$

15. $H_O: \mu = 30$ minutes

$H_A: \mu > 30$ minutes

CHAPTER 12
MODIFIED TRUE/FALSE
1. chi square
2. true
3. different from
4. chi-square distribution
5. sometimes
6. sometimes
7. never
8. (usually) can
9. population variances
10. never

MULTIPLE CHOICE
1. c
2. b
3. a
4. a
5. b
6. a
7. b
8. c
9. d
10. a

COMPLETION
1. s
2. n - 1
3. any number ≥ 0
4. 1.5
5. chi square
6. F ratio
7. take the square root of all terms
8. $\chi^2_{.10}$ and $\chi^2_{.90}$
9. n - 1
10. $F_{.01}$

1. (a) $df = n - 1 = 15 - 1 = 14$

$\chi^2_{.95} = 6.571, \chi^2_{.05} = 23.685$

(b) $z_{.05} = 1.65, -z_{.05} = 1.65$

(c) $df = 12$

$\chi^2_{.995} = 3.074$

$\chi^2_{.005} = 28.30$

(d) $z_{.01} = 2.33$

2. (a) $\dfrac{(n - 1)s^2}{\chi^2_{\alpha/2}} < \sigma^2 < \dfrac{(n - 1)s^2}{\chi^2_{1-\alpha/2}}$

$\dfrac{10(.6)^2}{(20.483)^2} < \sigma^2 < \dfrac{10(.6)^2}{(3.247)^2}$

$.009 < \sigma^2 < .341$

(b) $\dfrac{10(.6)^2}{(18.307)^2} < \sigma^2 < \dfrac{10(.6)^2}{(3.940)^2}$

$.011 < \sigma^2 < .232$

(c) $\sqrt{.009} < \sigma < \sqrt{.341}$

$.095 < \sigma < .584$

3. (a) $\dfrac{s}{1 + \dfrac{z_{\alpha/2}}{\sqrt{2n}}} < \sigma < \dfrac{s}{1 - \dfrac{z_{\alpha/2}}{\sqrt{2n}}}$

$\dfrac{.6}{1 + \dfrac{1.96}{\sqrt{2(50)}}} < \sigma < \dfrac{.6}{1 - \dfrac{1.96}{\sqrt{2(50)}}}$

$.502 < \sigma_2 < .746$
$.252 < \sigma^2 < .557$

(b) $\dfrac{.6}{1 + \dfrac{1.65}{10}} < \sigma < \dfrac{.6}{1 - \dfrac{1.65}{10}}$

$.515 < \sigma_2 < .719$
$.265 < \sigma^2 < .517$

(c) $.502 < \sigma < .746$

4. $\chi^2 = \dfrac{(n - 1)s^2}{\sigma^2_0} = \dfrac{14(.0324)}{(.12)^2} = 31.5$

$31.5 > 29.14$ so reject null hyp. in favor of alt. hyp. that $\sigma > .12$

5. $z = \dfrac{s - \sigma_0}{\sigma_0/\sqrt{2n}} = \dfrac{.15 - .12}{.12/\sqrt{2(50)}}$

$= \dfrac{.03}{.012} = 2.50$

$2.50 < 2.58$, so do not reject null hyp. that $\sigma = .12$

6. $\sigma \approx \dfrac{\text{Range}}{d} = \dfrac{9500 - 4000}{3.08} = \dfrac{5500}{3.08} = \underline{1786}$

7. $H_0 : \sigma = .08$
$H_A : \sigma \neq .08$
$\chi^2 = \dfrac{(n - 1)s^2}{\sigma^2_0} = \dfrac{11(.11)^2}{(.08)^2} = 20.797$

$df = n - 1 = 11 \quad 20.797 > 19.675$
reject null hyp.   Conclude that
$\sigma \neq .08$

8. (a) $F = \dfrac{9^2}{5^2} = 3.24 \qquad$ num $df = 9$
den $df = 12$

$3.24 > 2.80$ i.e., $F > F_{.05}$
reject null hypothesis

(b) $F = \dfrac{15^2}{7^2} = 4.59 \qquad$ num $df = 15$
den $df = 9$

$4.59 < 4.96$ i.e., $F < F_{.01}$
do not reject null hypothesis

9. $F = \dfrac{(.15)^2}{(.10)^2} = 2.25 \qquad$ num $df = 12$
den $df = 9$

$2.25 < 3.07$ i.e., $F < F_{.05}$

do not reject null hyp. that there is equal competition

10. $F = \dfrac{(.08)^2}{(.03)^2} = 7.11 \qquad$ num $df = 8$
den $df = 13$

$7.11 > 2.77$ i.e., $F > F_{.05}$

Reject null hyp. Conclude that the price per gallon is not equally variable in the two cities.

11. One assumption underlying the small-sample test of the difference between means requires that the variance of the two populations is equal. Then to use the standard deviation test, we would hope to be unable to reject the null hypothesis that the populations had equal variances.

12. This test is required whenever we want to test the uniformity of a product, process, or operation.

13. Since the test is two-tailed, if we used only one of the two ratios, we would want to reject the null hypothesis for either a very low or a very high ratio. But most F tables give only values of $F_{.05}$ and $F_{.01}$, so using only the larger of the two ratios (since they are reciprocals of each other) for the F value allows us to test the hypothesis using only the right hand tail.

CHAPTER 13
MODIFIED TRUE/FALSE

1.	1.96	6.	does
2.	true	7.	true
3.	true	8.	true
4.	chi-square distribution	9.	true
5.	no	10.	sample size

MULTIPLE CHOICE

1.	b	6.	d
2.	b	7.	a
3.	c	8.	c
4.	b	9.	c
5.	c	10.	c

COMPLETION

1. p

2. $\sqrt{\dfrac{p(1-p)}{n}}$

3. $\dfrac{1}{80}$, $\dfrac{79}{80}$

4. $\dfrac{1}{2}$

5. 18

6. $p_1 - p_2$

7. the number of categories minus the number of quantities estimated from the sample

---

COMPLETION (continued)

8. $E = z_{\alpha/2}\sqrt{\dfrac{\dfrac{x}{n}(1 - \dfrac{x}{n})}{n}}$

9. goodness-of-fit

10. less

PROBLEMS

1. (a) $H_O:p = .30$
   $H_A:p > .30$

   Use binomial table. Reject if $x \geq 8$. Since $x = 8$, reject null hyp. Conclude more than 30% of calls are nonbusiness.

   (b) Reject if $x = 9$. Since $x = 8$ do not reject null hyp. Cannot say more than 30% of calls are non-business.

   (c) Reject if $x = 0$ or $x \geq 8$. Since $x = 8$, reject null hyp. Conclude that more than 30% of calls are nonbusiness.

---

2. $E = z_{\alpha/2}\sqrt{\dfrac{\dfrac{x}{n}(1 - \dfrac{x}{n})}{n}}$

   $= 2.58\sqrt{\dfrac{.7(.3)}{250}} = .075$

---

3. (a) $H_O:p = .20$
   $H_A:p \neq .20$

.005   .005

-2.58   30   2.58

$z = \dfrac{x - np_0}{\sqrt{np_0(1-p_0)}}$

$= \dfrac{42 - 150(.20)}{\sqrt{150(.20)(.80)}} = 2.45 < 2.58$

Do not reject null hyp. that 20% of the time the product produces side effects.

3. (b) p = .20
        p > .20

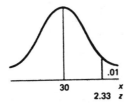

Since 2.47 > 2.33, reject null hyp. Conclude the proportion of time the product produces side effects is greater than .20.

4.

$$\frac{x}{n} - z_{\alpha/2}\sqrt{\frac{\frac{x}{n}(1 - \frac{x}{n})}{n}} < p < \frac{x}{n}$$

$$+ z_{\alpha/2}\sqrt{\frac{\frac{x}{n}(1 - \frac{x}{n})}{n}}$$

$$\frac{50}{80} = .625$$

$$.625 - 2.33\sqrt{\frac{.625(.375)}{80}} < p < .625$$

$$+ 2.33\sqrt{\frac{.625(.375)}{80}}$$

$$.625 - .126 < p < .625 + .126$$

$$\underline{.499 < p < .751}$$

5. (a)

$$n = \frac{1}{4}\left[\frac{z_{\alpha/2}}{E}\right]^2$$

$$n = \frac{1}{4}\left[\frac{2.33}{.05}\right]^2 = 542.89$$

543 graduates

(b)

$$.30 - 2.33\sqrt{\frac{.3(.7)}{543}} < p < .30$$

$$+ 2.33\sqrt{\frac{.3(.7)}{543}}$$

$$.30 < .046 < p < .30 + .046$$

$$.254 < p < .346$$

(Note that the error is .046, which is less than the required .05 that is given.)

6. (a) $H_0: P_1 - P_2 = 0$
        $H_A: P_1 - P_2 \neq 0$

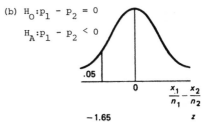

$$p = \frac{25 + 40}{60 + 80} = \frac{65}{140} = .464$$

$$z = \frac{\frac{x_1}{n_1} - \frac{x_2}{n_2}}{\sqrt{p(1-p)(\frac{1}{n_1} + \frac{1}{n_2})}}$$

$$= \frac{\frac{25}{60} - \frac{40}{80}}{\sqrt{.464(.536)(\frac{1}{60} + \frac{1}{80})}}$$

$$= -.978$$

Do not reject null hyp. that there is no difference in proportion of people watching both shows.

(b) $H_0: P_1 - P_2 = 0$
     $H_A: P_1 - P_2 < 0$

-.978 > -1.65
Do not reject null hyp. that there is no difference.

7. H_0: whether a student purchased a product is <u>independent</u> of the year in college

H_A: whether a student purchased a product is <u>dependent</u> on the year in college

$$\frac{50}{500} = .10$$

	Soph.	Jun.	Sen.	
will not	13 (10)	12 (10)	25 (30)	50
will	87 (90)	88 (90)	275 (270)	450
	100	100	300	500

7. (continued)

$$\chi^2 = \frac{(13-10)^2}{10} + \frac{(12-10)^2}{10} + \frac{(25-30)^2}{30} +$$

$$\frac{(87-90)^2}{90} + \frac{(88-90)^2}{90} + \frac{(275-270)^2}{270} =$$

$$.9 + .4 + .83 + .1 + .04 + .09 =$$

$$2.36 < 5.991$$

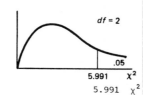

df = 2

.05

5.991 χ^2

5.991 χ^2

8.

	e	o
$210\binom{6}{0}(.4)^0(.6)^6 =$	9.80	19
$210\binom{6}{1}(.4)^1(.6)^5 =$	39.19	44
$210\binom{6}{2}(.4)^2(.6)^4 =$	65.32	68
$210\binom{6}{3}(.4)^3(.6)^3 =$	58.06	48
$210\binom{6}{4}(.4)^4(.6)^2 =$	29.03	18
$210\binom{6}{5}(.4)^5(.6)^1 =$	7.74	7
$210\binom{6}{6}(.4)^6(.6)^0 =$	.86 (8.6)	6 (13)

$$\chi^2 = \frac{(19-9.80)^2}{9.80} + \frac{(44-39.19)^2}{39.19} + \frac{(68-65.32)^2}{65.32} +$$

$$\frac{(48-58.06)^2}{58.06} + \frac{(18-29.03)^2}{29.03} + \frac{(13-8.6)^2}{8.6}$$

$$= 8.64 + .59 + .11 + 1.74 + 4.19 + 2.25$$

$$= \underline{17.52}$$

df = 6

17.52 > 12.592
Reject null hyp.
Reject claim that sample is
from binomial distribution with n=6 and p=.4

.05

12.592 χ^2

9. H_O: grade is independent of professor
   H_A: grade depends on professor

	#1	#2	#3			
A	10 (15)	12 (18)	28 (17)	50	$\frac{50}{200}$	= .25
B	15 (21)	30 (25.2)	25 (23.8)	70	$\frac{70}{200}$	= .35
C	35 (24)	30 (28.8)	15 (27.2)	80	$\frac{80}{200}$	= .40
	60	72	68	200		

$$\chi^2 = \frac{(10-15)^2}{15} + \frac{(12-18)^2}{18} + \frac{(28-17)^2}{17} +$$

$$\frac{(15-21)^2}{21} + \frac{(30-25.2)^2}{25.2} + \frac{(25-23.8)^2}{23.8}$$

$$+ \frac{(35-24)^2}{24} + \frac{(30-28.8)^2}{28.8}$$

$$+ \frac{(15-27.2)^2}{27.2}$$

$$= 1.67 + 2 + 7.12 + 1.71 + .91 +$$

$$.06 + 5.04 + .05 + 5.47 = 24.03$$

df = 4, 24.03 > 13.277. Reject null
hyp. Conclude that the grade depends
on the professor.

10. (a)

$$C = \sqrt{\frac{\chi^2}{\chi^2 + n}}$$

$$= \sqrt{\frac{13.277}{13.277 + 200}}$$

$$= \underline{.250}$$

(b) $\sqrt{\frac{k-1}{k}} = \sqrt{\frac{4-1}{4}} = \sqrt{\frac{3}{4}} = .87$

11. $H_O : p_1 - p_2 = 0$
    $H_A : p_1 - p_2 \neq 0$

$\alpha = 0.05$

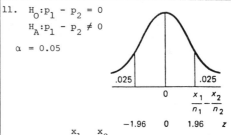

.025   .025

0    $\frac{x_1}{n_1} - \frac{x_2}{n_2}$

-1.96   0   1.96   z

$$z = \frac{\frac{x_1}{n_1} - \frac{x_2}{n_2}}{\sqrt{p(1-p)\left(\frac{1}{n_1} + \frac{1}{n_2}\right)}}$$

11. (continued)

$$p = \frac{45 + 75}{80 + 100} = \frac{120}{200} = 0.6$$

$$z = \frac{\frac{45}{80} - \frac{75}{120}}{\sqrt{.6(.4)(\frac{1}{80} + \frac{1}{120})}} = 0.884$$

do not reject H_O

Insufficient evidence to conclude that males and females differ on the issue.

12.

$$\frac{x}{n} - z\sqrt{\frac{\frac{x}{n}(1 - \frac{x}{n})}{n}} < p < \frac{x}{n} + z\sqrt{\frac{\frac{x}{n}(1 - \frac{x}{n})}{n}}$$

$$\frac{90}{120} - 2.33\sqrt{\frac{.75(.25)}{120}} < p <$$

$$\frac{90}{120} + 2.33\sqrt{\frac{.75(.25)}{120}}$$

$0.658 < p < 0.842$ with 98% confidence

13.

$$E = z\sqrt{\frac{\frac{x}{n}(1 - \frac{x}{n})}{n}}$$

$$.05 = z\sqrt{\frac{.75(.25)}{120}}$$

$$.05 = z \, (.0395)$$

$$z = 1.27$$

$$2(.398) = .796 = \underline{79.6\%}$$

14.

$$h = \frac{z^2 p(1 - p)}{E^2}$$

Choose the possible p value that is closest to $p = .5$, i.e., $p = .40$

$$n = \frac{(2.575)^2(.4)(.6)}{(.02)^2} = 3,978.375$$

$\underline{3,979 \text{ accounts}}$

---

15. H_O: Service rating is independent of annual income level.

H_A: Service rating is dependent on annual income level.

CHAPTER 14
MODIFIED TRUE/FALSE

1.	means	7.	is not
2.	true	8.	is
3.	between	9.	true
4.	different from	10.	true
5.	true	11.	true
6.	SS(Tr)		

MULTIPLE CHOICE

1.	d	7.	c
2.	b	8.	c
3.	b	9.	a
4.	d	10.	a
5.	a	11.	d
6.	d	12.	d

COMPLETION

1. $k - 1$
2. $k(n-1)$
3. error
4. two-factor ANOVA
5. SST-SS(Tr)
6. blocking factor
7. treatment
8. within
9. SST-SS(Tr)-SSB
10. SS(Tr) + SSA + SSB
11. a balanced incomplete block design
12. 3
13. 120

PROBLEMS
1. (a) 3.26

   (b) num df = 4 - 1 = 3
       den df = (3 - 1) 4 = 8 $\underline{4.07}$

   (c) 5.41
   (d) 7.59

2.

Source of Variation	Df	Sum of Squares	Mean Square	F
Treatments	4	80	20	11.998*
Error	12	20	1.667	
Total	16	100		

num df = 4
den df = 12 $F_{.01} = 5.41$

$11.988 > 5.41$ Reject null hypothesis.

3.

Source of Variation	Df	Sum of Squares	Mean Square	F
Treatments	2	10	5	1.43
Block	5	5	1	
Error	10	35	3.5	
Total	17	50		

num df = 2
den df = 10 $F_{.01} = 7.56$

1.43 < 7.56 Do not reject null hyp.

4. (a)

$$SST = 55325 - \frac{1}{4(3)}(660969)$$

$$= 55325 - 55080.75 = 244.25$$

$$SSA = \frac{1}{3}(38025 + 40000 + 42849$$

$$+ 44521) - 55080.75$$

$$= 55131.667 - 55080.75 = 50.917$$

$$SSB = \frac{1}{4}(67600 + 69169 + 84100)$$

$$- 55080.75$$

$$= 55217.25 - 55080.75 = 136.50$$

$$SSE = SST - SSA - SSB$$

$$= 244.25 - 50.92 - 136.50$$

$$= 56.83$$

Variation	Df	SS	MS	F
Treatment(A)	3	50.92	16.97	1.79
Treatment(B)	2	136.50	68.25	7.21*
Error	6	56.83	9.47	
Total	11	244.25		

(b) num df = 3
den df = 6 $F_{.05} = 4.76$

1.79 < 4.76 Do not reject null hyp. Cannot conclude that there is a difference in performance based on attitude.

(c) num df = 2
den df = 6 $F_{.05} = 5.14$

7.21 > 5.14 Reject null hyp. Conclude that there is a difference in performance based on skill level.

5. (a)

Variation	Df	SS	MS	F
Treatment	3	60	20	2.40
Block	2	90	45	5.40
Error	6	50	8.33	
Total	11	200		

(b) num df = 3
den df = 6 $F_{.05} = 4.76$

2.40 < 4.76. Do not reject null hyp.

6. (a)

$$SST = 84023 - \frac{1}{3(4)}(1006009)$$

$$= 84023 - 83834.083$$

$$= 188.92$$

$$SS(Tr) = \frac{1}{4}(120409 + 106929$$

$$+ 108241) - 83834.083$$

$$= 83894.75 - 83834.083$$

$$= 60.67$$

$$SSB = \frac{1}{3}(61009 + 61504 + 63504$$

$$+ 65536) - 83834.083$$

$$= 83851 - 83834.083 = 16.92$$

$$SSE = SST - SS(Tr) - SSB$$

$$= 188.92 - 60.67 - 16.92$$

$$= 111.33$$

Variation	Df	SS	MS	F
Treatment	2	60.67	30.34	1.63
Block	3	16.92	5.64	.30
Error	6	111.33	18.56	
Total	11	188.92		

(b) num df = 2
den df = 6 $F_{05} = 5.14$

1.63 < 5.14 Do not reject null hyp. Conclude teaching methods do not produce different achievement scores.

7. (a)

Variation	DF	SS	MS	F
Treatment A	4	60	15	7.5
Treatment B	3	40	13.33	6.67*
Error	12	24	2	
Total	19	124		

7. (continued)

(b)

(A)

num df = 4
den df = 12 $F_{.05} = 3.26$

7.5 > 3.26 Reject null hypothesis

(B)

num df = 3
den df = 12 $F_{.05} = 3.49$

6.67 > 3.49 Reject null
hypothesis

8. (a) $SST = 5459 - \frac{1}{4(3)}(60025)$

$= 5459 - 5002.08 = 456.92$

$SS(Tr) = \frac{1}{3}(16141) - 5002.08$

$= 5380.33 - 5002.08 = 378.25$

$SSE = SST - SS(Tr)$

$= 456.92 - 378.25 = 78.67$

Variation	Df	SS	MS	F
Treatment	3	378.25	126.08	12.83
Error	8	78.67	9.83	
Total	11	456.92		

(b) num df = 3
den df = 8 $F_{.01} = 7.59$

12.83 > 7.59 so reject null hyp.
Conclude that location makes a
difference in sales.

9. (a) $SST = 5783 - \frac{1}{13}(69169)$

$= 5783 - 5320.69 = 462.31$

$SS(Tr) = \frac{(90)^2}{4} + \frac{(36)^2}{3} + \frac{(53)^2}{2}$

$\frac{(84)^2}{4} - 5320.69$

$= 5625.5 - 5320.69 = 304.81$

$SSE = SST - SS(Tr)$

$= 462.31 - 304.81 = 157.50$

Variation	Df	SS	MS	F
Treatment	3	304.81	101.60	5.81
Error	9	157.50	17.5	
Total	12	462.31		

(b) num df = 3
den df = 12 $F_{.01} = 6.99$
5.81 < 6.99 so do not reject null
hyp. Conclude that location does
not affect sales.

10.

AFL	BFH	DFM	BJL	CJH
AFM	CFL	DFH	BJM	DJL
AFH	CFM	AJL	BJH	DJM
BFL	CFH	AJM	CJL	DJH
BFM	DFL	AJH	CJM	

11. $SSE = SST - SSR - SSC - SS(Tr)$

$= 3108 - 126 - 2418 - 114$

$= 450$

$F_{.05} = 19$

$MSE = \frac{450}{2} = 225$

(1) $\frac{MSR}{MSE} = \frac{63}{225} = .28 < 19$

Do not reject hyp.
Cannot conclude that sales are
affected by difference in media.

(2) $\frac{MSC}{MSE} = \frac{1209}{225} = 5.37 < 19$

Do not reject hyp.
Cannot conclude that sales are
affected by difference in location.

(3) $\frac{MS(Tr)}{MSE} = \frac{57}{225} = .25 < 19$

Do not reject hyp.
Cannot conclude that sales are
affected by difference in marketing
strategies.

12.

2	RVY	10	TVZ
5	WRT	12	SWY

13. It might be used if we want to elimi-
nate variability due to more than one
extraneous factor from the experimental
error and we want to avoid inflating
the size of the experiment beyond
practical bounds.

14. It would be desirable if we want to test
the equality among more than two means,
but we suspect that differences in
samples might be partly due to differences in an extraneous factor (or
"nuisance" factor) which were included
in the experimental error. These
differences in an extraneous factor
would be reflected by an "inflated"
error sum of squares which goes into
the denominator of the F statistic.

CHAPTER 14 (continued)

15. It is an experiment with two variables, one variable of material concern, the other an extraneous factor called a blocking factor. The design is complete, since each treatment appears the same number of times in each block.

CHAPTER 15
MODIFIED TRUE/FALSE

1. squares
2. μ_{y/x_0}
3. standard error of estimate
4. true
5. dependent
6. independent
7. smaller
8. sometimes
9. true
10. power function

MULTIPLE CHOICE

1. b
2. b
3. c
4. a
5. a
6. c
7. b
8. b
9. d
10. d

COMPLETION

1. n − 2
2. the standard error of estimate
3. $\mu_{y/x}$
4. b, a
5. greater than
6. least-squares regression
7. μ_{y/x_0}
8. is not
9. $\hat{y} = a + b_1x_1 + b_2x_2 + b_3x_3$
10. an exponential curve

PROBLEMS

1. (a)

x	x^2	x	xy
2	4	15	30
7	49	50	350
10	100	110	1100
15	225	220	3300
20	400	200	4000
54	778	595	8780

$595 = 5a + 54b$
$8780 = 54a + 778b$

$-32130 = -270a - 2916b$
$43900 = 270a + 3890b$
$1170 = 974b$
$b = 12.084$

$595 = 5a + 54(12.084)$
$695 = 5a + 652.536$
$5a = -57.536 \qquad a = 11.507$
$\hat{y} = 11.507 + 12.084x$

(b)
$$S_{xy} = 8780 - \frac{1}{5}(54)(595)$$
$$= 8780 - 6426 = 2354$$
$$S_{xx} = 778 - \frac{1}{5}(54)^2 = 5$$
$$778 - 583.2 = 194.8$$
$$b = \frac{S_{xy}}{S_{xx}} = \frac{2354}{194.8} = 12.084$$
$$a = \frac{\Sigma y - b(\Sigma x)}{n}$$
$$= \frac{595 - 12.084(54)}{5} = \frac{-57.536}{5}$$
$$= -11.507$$

(c) $\hat{y} = -11.507 + 12.084x$
$\hat{y} = -11.507 + 12.084(9) = \underline{97.249}$
$\underline{\$97,249}$

2. (a) $S_{yy} = 103,225 - \frac{1}{5}(595)^2$
$$= 32,420$$
$$S_e = \sqrt{\frac{S_{yy} - bS_{xy}}{n - 2}}$$
$$S_e = \sqrt{\frac{32,420 - 12.084(2354)}{5 - 2}}$$
$$= \sqrt{\frac{3974.264}{3}} = 36.397$$

(b) df = 5 − 2 = 3

$97.249 \pm 3.182(36.397)$
$$\frac{1}{5} + \sqrt{\frac{(9 - 10.8)^2}{194.8}}$$
97.249 ± 53.905
43.344 to 151.154
$\underline{\$43,344 \text{ to } \$151,154}$

(c) $97.249 \pm 3.182(36.397)$
$$\sqrt{1 + \frac{1}{5} + \frac{(9 - 10.8)^2}{194.8}}$$
97.249 ± 126.957
-29.708 to 224.206
$\underline{-\$29,708 \text{ to } \$224,206}$

3. (a)

x	y	x^2	xy
15	2	225	30
50	7	2500	350
110	10	12100	1100
220	15	48400	3300
200	20	40000	4000
595	54	103225	8780

3. (a) (continued)

$S_{xy} = 2354$ $S_{xx} = 32420$

$b = \dfrac{2354}{32420} = .073$

$a = \dfrac{54 - .073(595)}{5} = 2.113$

$\hat{y} = 2.113 + .073x$

(b) $\hat{y} = 2.113 + .073(40) = \underline{5.033}$

$\underline{\$5033}$

4. (a) $\Sigma x = 79.0$ $\Sigma y = 269.6$

$\Sigma xy = 1828.95$ $\Sigma x^2 = 596.5$

$S_{xy} = 1828.95 - \dfrac{1}{12}(79.0)(269.6)$

$= 54.083$

$S_{xx} = 596.5 - \dfrac{1}{12}(79.0)^2$

$= 76.417$

$b = \dfrac{54.083}{76.417} = .708$

$a = \dfrac{269.6 - .708(79.0)}{12}$

$= 17.806$

$\hat{y} = 17.806 + .708x$

(b) $\hat{y} = 17.806 + .708(5) = 21.346$

$\underline{\$21,346}$

5. (a) H_O: the population intercept of the regression line is 0

H_A: the population intercept of the regression line is not 0

calculate $S_e = 3.02$

$t = \dfrac{17.806 - 0}{3.02\sqrt{\dfrac{1}{12} + \dfrac{(6.583)^2}{76.417}}} = 7.33$

df= $12 - 2 = 10$ $7.33 > 2.28$

reject null hypothesis. Conclude $\alpha \neq 0$.

(b)

$17.806 \pm 2.228(3.02)\sqrt{\dfrac{1}{12} + \dfrac{(6.583)^2}{76.417}}$

17.806 ± 5.408

$12.40 < \alpha < 23.21$

6. (a) H_O: population slope of the regression line is 0

H_A: population slope of the regression line is more than 0

$t = \dfrac{.706 - 0}{3.02/\sqrt{76.417}} = 2.04$

df = 10 $2.06 > 1.812$

reject null hypothesis. Conclude $\beta > 0$

(b) $.706 \pm \dfrac{2.764(3.02)}{\sqrt{76.417}}$

$.706 \pm .956$

$-.250 < \beta < 1.662$

7. (a) $17.806 + .708(6) = 22.054$

$22.054 \pm 2.228(3.02)\sqrt{\dfrac{1}{12} + \dfrac{(6-6.583)^2}{76.417}}$

22.054 ± 1.99

$\underline{20.06 \text{ to } 24.04}$

(b) $22.054 \pm 2.228(3.02)\sqrt{\dfrac{1}{12} + \dfrac{(6-6.583)^2}{76.417}}$

22.054 ± 7.02

$\underline{15.03 \text{ to } 29.07}$

8.

	x	y	log y	x log y	x^2
1	-2	500	2.6990	-5.3980	4
2	-1	700	2.8451	-2.8451	1
3	0	1000	3.0000	0	0
4	1	1800	3.2553	3.2553	1
5	2	3000	3.4771	6.9542	4
			15.2765	1.9664	10

$\log a = \dfrac{15.2765}{5} = 3.0553$

$\log b = \dfrac{1.9664}{10} = .19664$

$\log \hat{y} = 3.0553 + .19664x$

$\hat{y} = 1135.80(1.57)^x$

9.

	x	y	log y	log x	$\log^2 x$	(log x)(log y)
1	500	2.6990	0	0	0	
2	700	2.8451	.3010	.0906	.8564	
3	1000	3.0000	.4771	.2276	1.4313	
4	1800	3.2553	.6021	.3624	1.9600	
5	3000	3.4771	.6990	.4886	2.4309	
		15.2765	2.0792	1.1692	6.6786	

9. (continued)

$15.2765 = 5 \log a + b(2.0792)$

$6.6786 = \log a \,(2.0792) + b(1.1692)$

$\log a = \dfrac{15.2765 - (2.0792)b}{5}$

$6.6786 = (3.0553 - .0416b)(2.0792) + 1.1692b$

$6.6786 = 6.1348 - .0865b + 1.1692b$

$.5438 = 1.0827b$

$b = \underline{.5023}$

$\log a = \dfrac{15.2765 - 2.0792(.5023)}{5} = 2.8464$

$a = 702$

$\hat{y} = 702 \; x^{.5023}$

10.

x	y	x^2	x^3	x^4	xy	x^2y
12	80	144	1728	20736	960	11520
10	100	100	1000	10000	1000	10000
8	120	64	512	4096	960	7680
6	110	36	216	1296	660	3960
4	90	16	64	256	360	1440
40	500	360	3520	36384	3940	34600

(1) $500 = 5a + 40b + 360c$

(2) $3940 = 40a + 360b + 3520c$

(3) $34600 = 360a + 3520b + 36384$

using (1) and (2)

$\begin{array}{l} -4000 = -40a -320b -2780c \\ \underline{\;\;3940 = \;\;40a +360b +3520c} \\ (*) \;\; -60 = \qquad\quad 40b + 640c \end{array}$

using (1) and (3)

$\begin{array}{l} -36000 = -360a -2880b -25920c \\ \underline{\;\;34600 = \;\;360a +3520b +36384c} \\ -1400 = \qquad\qquad 640b +10464c \end{array}$

From (x)

$\begin{array}{l} \underline{\;\;960 = \qquad\qquad - 640b -10240c} \\ -440 = 224c \end{array}$

$c = -1.964$

$\begin{array}{l} -60 = 40b +640(-1.964) \\ 1196.96 = 40b \\ b = 29.924 \end{array}$

the 1st equation

$500 = 5a + 40(29.924) + 360(-1.964)$

$500 = 5a + 489.92$

$10.08 = 5a$

$a = 2.016$

$\hat{y} = 2.016 + 29.924x - 1.964x^2$

---

11.   (a) $\Sigma x = 33.09 \qquad \Sigma y = 73.12$

$\Sigma xy = 303.1874 \quad \Sigma x^2 = 136.9911$

$\begin{aligned} S_{xy} &= 303.1874 - \tfrac{1}{8}(33.09)(73.12) \\ &= .7448 \end{aligned}$

$\begin{aligned} S_{xx} &= 136.9911 - \tfrac{1}{8}(33.09)^2 \\ &= .1226 \end{aligned}$

$b = \dfrac{.7448}{.1226} = 6.075$

$\begin{aligned} a &= \dfrac{73.12 - 6.075(33.09)}{8} \\ &= -15.988 \end{aligned}$

$\hat{y} = -15.988 + 6.075x$

(b) $S_{yy} = 673.752 - \tfrac{1}{8}(73.12)^2 = 5.4352$

$\begin{aligned} S_e &= \sqrt{\dfrac{5.4352 - 6.075(.7448)}{8 - 2}} \\ &= \underline{.390} \end{aligned}$

(c) $\begin{aligned} \hat{y} &= -15.988 + 6.075(4) \\ &= \underline{8.312 \text{ million}} \end{aligned}$

---

12.   (a) $\Sigma x_2 = 45.29 \qquad \Sigma x_2{}^2 = 270.9627$

$\Sigma x_1 y = 303.1874 \quad \Sigma y = 73.12$

$\Sigma x_2 y = 421.389 \quad \Sigma x_1{}^2 = 136.9911$

$\Sigma x_1 = 33.09 \qquad \Sigma x_1 x_2 = 188.2231$

$73.12 = 8b_0 + 33.09b_1 + 45.29b_2$

$303.1874 = 33.09b_0 + 136.9911b_1 + 188.223b_2$

$421.389 = 45.29b_0 + 188.2231b_1 + 270.9627b_2$

Solve simultaneous equations.

$b_0 = -9.87986$

$b_1 = 4.25625$

$b_2 = .24995$

$\hat{y} = -9.87986 + 4.25625x_1 + .24995x_2$

(b) $\hat{y} = -9.87986 + 4.25624(4) + .24995(7)$

$= 8.89475 \text{ millions}$

or $\underline{8,894,750}$

13. (a) $\Sigma x = 1280$ $\Sigma y = 170$

$\Sigma xy = 8660$ $\Sigma x^2 = 722400$

$S_{xy} = 86600 - \frac{1}{4}(1280)(170)$

$= 32200$

$S_{xx} = 722400 - \frac{1}{4}(1280)^2$

$= 312,800$

$b = \frac{32200}{312800} = .1029$

$a = \frac{170 - .1029(1280)}{4} = 9.572$

$\hat{y} = 9.572 + .1029x$

(b) $S_{yy} = 11100 - \frac{1}{4}(170)^2 = 3875$

$S_e = \sqrt{\frac{3875 - .1029(32200)}{4 - 2}}$

$= \underline{16.76}$

14. The relationship applies only to the range of values of x (advertising expense) on which the study is based.

15. (a) $\hat{y} = 9.572 + .1029(700) = 81.602$

$81.602 \pm 4.303(16.76)\sqrt{\frac{1}{4} + \frac{(700-320)^2}{312,800}}$

81.602 ± 60.84

$\underline{20.76 \text{ to } 142.44}$

(b) $H_O: \beta = 0$

$H_A: \beta \neq 0$

$t = \frac{.1029 - 0}{16.76/\sqrt{312,800}} = 3.43$

since t = 3.43 is not greater than 4.303, H_O cannot be rejected. There is insufficient evidence of a relation between advertising campaigns and consumer awareness.

CHAPTER 16
MODIFIED TRUE/FALSE

1. -1 and 1   6. sometimes
2. 36%   7. μ_z
3. sometimes   8. true
4. true   9. true
5. true   10. true

MULTIPLE CHOICE

1. d   6. d
2. a   7. c
3. a   8. b
4. b   9. d
5. b   10. d

COMPLETION

1. inverse   6. greater than
2. 0 and 1, inclusive   7. zero
3. ρ 8. zero
4. direct   9. one
5. .64   10. $\frac{\Sigma(y - \hat{y})^2}{\Sigma(y - \bar{y})^2}$

PROBLEMS

1. (a) $\Sigma xy = 14661$ $\Sigma x = 4685$

$\Sigma y = 24.8$ $\Sigma x^2 = 2782425$

$\Sigma y^2 = 77.66$

$S_{yy} = 77.66 - \frac{1}{8}(24.80)^2 = .78$

$S_{xx} = 2782425 - \frac{1}{8}(4685)^2$

$= 38,771.875$

$S_{xy} = 14661 - \frac{1}{8}(4685)(24.80)$

$= 137.5$

$r = \frac{S_{xy}}{\sqrt{S_{xx} \cdot S_{yy}}} = \frac{137.5}{\sqrt{(38771.875)(.78)}}$

$= .791$

(b) $r^2 = (.791)^2 = \underline{.626}$

2. $H_O: \rho = 0$

$H_A: \rho \neq 0$

$\alpha = .05$

$z = z\sqrt{n - 3}$

For r = .79   z = 1.071

$z = 1.071\sqrt{8 - 3} = 2.39 > 1.96$

Reject null hypothesis.
Conclude that there is a relationship between S.A.T. scores and college grade point averages.

3. $1.071 - \frac{1.96}{\sqrt{8}} < \mu_z < 1.071 + \frac{1.96}{\sqrt{8}}$

$1.071 - .693 < \mu_z < 1.071 + .693$

$.378 < \mu_z < 1.764$

$.36 < \rho < .94$

4. $\sqrt{\dfrac{12000}{20000}} = .775$

5. (a) $\Sigma xy = 38608 \qquad \Sigma x^2 = 43488$

$\Sigma x = 424 \qquad \Sigma y^2 = 38294$

$\Sigma y = 404$

$S_{yy} = 38294 - \dfrac{1}{10}(404)^2$

$= 21,972.4$

$S_{xx} = 43488 - \dfrac{1}{10}(424)^2$

$= 25,510.4$

$S_{xy} = 38608 - \dfrac{1}{10}(424)(404)$

$= 21,478.4$

$r = \dfrac{21478.4}{\sqrt{(25510.4)(21972.4)}} = .907$

(b) $r^2 = (.907)^2 = .823 = \underline{82.3\%}$

6. (null) There is no relationship between excess monetary growth and inflation rates.

(alt) There is such a relationship.

H_O: $\rho = .3$

H_A: $\rho \neq .3$

$z = (Z = u_z) \sqrt{n - 3}$

$= (1.528 - .310) \sqrt{10 - 3}$

$= 3.22 > 2.58$

Reject null hypothesis.
Conclude that $\rho \neq .3$

7. $1.528 - \dfrac{2.58}{\sqrt{10}} < \mu_z < 1.528 + \dfrac{2.58}{\sqrt{10}}$

$1.528 - .816 < \mu_z < 1.528 + .816$

$.712 < \mu_z < 2.344$

$.61 < \rho < .98$

8. (a) $\Sigma xy = 102.434 \qquad \Sigma x^2 = 33.9073$

$\Sigma x = 16.41 \qquad \Sigma y^2 = 313.06$

$\Sigma y = 50$

$S_{xy} = 313.06 - \dfrac{1}{8}(50)^2 = .56$

$S_{xx} = 33.9073 - \dfrac{1}{8}(16.41)^2 = .2463$

$S_{xy} = 102.434 - \dfrac{1}{8}(16.41)(50)$

$= -.1285$

8. (continued)

$r = \dfrac{-.1285}{\sqrt{(.2463)(.56)}} = \underline{.346}$

(b) $r^2 = (.346)^2 = .12 = \underline{12\%}$

9. H_O: $\rho = -.1$

H_A: $\rho \neq -.1$

$n = 8$

$z = (Z - \mu_z)\sqrt{n - 3}$

$z = [.365 - (-.1)]\sqrt{8 - 3}$

$= 1.04 < 1.96$

Do not reject null hypothesis that correlation coefficient is equal to $-.1$.

10. $\bar{y} = 9.4$

$\Sigma(\hat{y} - \bar{y})^2 = 5.0209$

$\Sigma(y - \bar{y})^2 = 5.4352$

$\sqrt{\dfrac{5.0209}{5.4352}} = \sqrt{.924} = .96$

11. (a) $S_{yy} = 600 - \dfrac{1}{13}(78)^2 = 132$

$S_{xx} = 450 - \dfrac{1}{13}(65)^2 = 125$

$S_{xy} = 500 - \dfrac{1}{13}(65)(78) = 110$

$r = \dfrac{110}{\sqrt{(125)(132)}} = \underline{.856}$

(b) $r^2 = .733 = \underline{73.3\%}$

12. H_O: $\rho = 0$

H_A: $\rho \neq 0$

$\alpha = 0.01$

$r = .86.$ Then $Z = 1293$

$z = (Z - \mu_z) \sqrt{n - 3}$

$z = (1.293 - 0) \sqrt{13 - 3} = 4.09$

Since 4.09 exceeds 2.58, the null hypothesis is rejected.

13. .75

14. .75

15. This combination of results is not possible, since the multiple correlation coefficient must always be at least as large as the simple correlation between an independent variable and the dependent variable.

CHAPTER 17

MODIFIED TRUE/FALSE

1.	true	6.	sign
2.	true	7.	smaller
3.	is not	8.	μ_u
4.	does not require	9.	true
5.	true	10.	true

MULTIPLE CHOICE

1.	b	6.	c
2.	c	7.	c
3.	d	8.	b
4.	b	9.	c
5.	a	10.	b

COMPLETION

1. $\mu = \mu_0$, $\rho = \frac{1}{2}$
2. Kruskall-Wallis
3. 10
4. randomness
5. $\frac{n(n + 1)}{2}$
6. random
7. the U test, the H test
8. is greater than 8, is greater than 8
9. 0, $n_1 n_2$, $n_1 n_2$
10. 5
11. rank correlation coefficient

PROBLEMS

1. one sample sign test

    H_O: $\mu = 15$ or $p = \frac{1}{2}$
    H_A: $\mu > 15$ or $p > \frac{1}{2}$

    Subtracting 15 from all numbers gives

    $+ - - + + + + + + - + -$ 8 plus signs

    From Table V for $n = 12$, $p = .5$:
    probability of 8 or more + signs is
    $.1208 + .0537 + .0161 + .0029 + .0002$
    $> .05$. So do not reject null hyp.
    that the average is \$15.00.

2. H_O: M = W

    H_A: M ≠ W

    M = men's average food exp.
    W = women's average food exp.

17	18	20	20	21	22
W	W	W	M	M	W
1	2	3.5	3.5	5	6

23	23	24	24	25	25
M	W	M	W	W	M
7.5	7.5	9.5	9.5	11.5	11.5

2. (continued)

26	28	28	30
M	M	M	M
13	14	15	16

W_1 = sum of women's ranks

$W_1 = 1 + 2 + 3.5 + 6 + 7.5 + 9.5 + 11.5$
$= 41$

$W_2 = 136 - 41 - 95$

$U_1 = 41 - \frac{7(8)}{2} = 13$

$U_2 = 95 - \frac{9(10)}{2} = 50$

Then U = 13

From Table VII for $n_1 = 7$, $n_2 = 9$

$U_\alpha = 15$. Since 13 < 15 reject null
hyp. that men and women have the same
average food expenditures.

3. (a) H_O: $\mu_1 = \mu_2$ or $p = \frac{1}{2}$

    H_A: $\mu_1 \neq \mu_2$ or $p \neq \frac{1}{2}$

    $+ + + + + - + - + + + +$

    10 plus signs. Probability of 10
    or more + signs if $.0161 + .003$
    $+ .000 = .019 < .05$ so reject null
    hyp. Conclude Dept. Store A has
    more sales.

    (b) H_O: $\mu_1 = \mu_2$ or $p = \frac{1}{2}$
    H_A: $\mu_1 = \mu_2$ or $p \neq \frac{1}{2}$

    two tailed

    Probability of 10 or more + signs
    is $.019 < .025$ so reject null hyp.
    Conclude that there is a differ-
    ence in sales.

4. Same hypotheses

    (a) $z = \dfrac{10 - 12(\frac{1}{2})}{\sqrt{12(\frac{1}{2})(\frac{1}{2})}} = \dfrac{4}{\sqrt{3}} = 2.31$

    $z_{.05} = 1.65$ $2.31 > 1.65$ so reject
    null hyp. Conclude Dept. Store A
    has more sales.

    (b) $z_{.025} = 1.96$ $2.31 > 1.96$
    Reject null hyp. Conclude there
    is a difference in sales.

5. n_1 = no. of M's $\qquad n_1 = 16$

$\quad n_2$ = no. of W's $\qquad n_2 = 10$

H_O: sequence is random

H_A: sequence is not random

$$\mu_u = \frac{2(16)(10)}{16 + 10} + 1 = 13.31$$

$$\sigma_u = \sqrt{\frac{1(16)(10)\{2(16)(10) - 16 - 10\}}{(16 + 20)^2(16 + 10 - 1)}}$$

$\quad = 1.70$

$$z = \frac{11 - 13.31}{1.70} = -1.36$$

$-z_{.025} = -1.96 \qquad -1.36 > -1.96$

Do not reject null hyp. Evidence that sequence is random.

6. H_O: I = II = III

$\quad H_A$: I, II, III are not all equal

H test

21	22	22	22	23	23	24
I	II	I	II	II	I	I
I	3	3	3	5.5	5.5	8

24	24	25	25	26	26	26
II	III	I	II	II	III	III
8	8	10.5	10.5	13	13	13

27	27	28	30
II	III	III	III
15.5	15.5	17	18

$R_1 = 1 + 3 + 3 + 5.5 + 8 + 10.5 = 31$

$R_2 = 3 + 5.5 + 8 + 10.5 + 13 + 15.5$
$\quad = 55.5$

$R_3 = 8 + 13 + 13 + 15.5 + 17 + 18$
$\quad = 84.5$

$n_1 = 6, \ n_2 = 6, \ n_3 = 6$

$$H = \frac{12}{(18)(19)}\left[\frac{(31)^2}{6} + \frac{(55.5)^2}{6}\right.$$

$$\left. + \frac{(84.5)^2}{6}\right] - 3(18 + 1) = 65.39 - 57$$

$\quad = 8.39$

df = k - 1 = 3 - 1 = 2

$\chi^2_{.05} = 5.991 \qquad 8.389 > 5.991$

Reject null hyp. Conclude there is a difference in gasoline economy.

7. H_O: I = II

$\quad H_A$: I $\neq$ II

60	70	73	75	80	80	80
I	I	I	I	I	I	II
1	2	3	4	6	6	6

81	82	88	88	88	89	90
I	I	I	II	II	I	I
8	9	11	11	11	13	15

90	90	91	91	93	93	95
I	II	II	I	I	II	II
15	15	17.5	17.5	19.5	19.5	22.5

95	95	95	98	99	102	105
II	II	I	II	II	II	II
22.5	22.5	22.5	25	26	27	28

$W_1 = 1 + 2 + 3 + 4 + 6 + 6 + 8 + 9 + 11$
$\quad + 13 + 15 + 15 + 17.5 + 19.5 + 22.5$
$\quad = 152.5$

$$U_1 = 152.5 - \frac{15(16)}{2} = 32.5$$

$$\mu_{u_1} = \frac{15(13)}{2} = 97.5$$

$$\sigma_{u_1} = \sqrt{\frac{15(13)(29)}{12}} = 21.71$$

$$z = \frac{U_1 - \mu_{u_1}}{\sigma_{u_1}} = \frac{32.5 - 97.5}{21.71} = 2.99$$

$z_{.005} = 2.58, \qquad 2.99 > 2.58$

Reject null hyp. Conclude that the two models have different life expectancies.

8. H_O: I = II

$\quad H_A$: I < II

The alt. hyp. is more likely to be true for low values of W_1 or high values of U_1. Then the test has a rejection region to the right.

$$z = \frac{162.5 - 97.5}{21.71} = 2.99$$

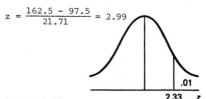

2.99 > 2.33
Reject null hyp.
Conclude that Model II has a greater life expectancy than Model I.

9. H_O: sequence is random

H_A: sequence is not random

median = 85   A = above median
            B = below median

AAABBBBBAAABBAABAABB

(A) $n_1 = 10$ (B) $n_2 = 10$

$$\mu_U = \frac{2(10)(10)}{10 + 10} + 1 = 11$$

$$\sigma_U = \sqrt{\frac{2(10)(10)(2(10)(10) - 10 - 10)}{20^2(10 + 10 - 1)}}$$

$$= 2.18$$

$U = 8$

$$z = \frac{8 - 11}{2.18} = -1.38$$

$-1.38 > -2.58$

Do not reject null hyp. evidence that sequence is random.

---

10. H_O: $\mu = 80$ or $p = 1/2$

H_A: $\mu > 80$ or $p > 1/2$

Subtract 80 from each number

+ + + + tie- - + + + + + tie- + + +
+ + - -

$x = 14$

$$z = \frac{14 - 19(1/2)}{\sqrt{19(1/2)(1/2)}} = 2.06$$

$z_{.05} = 1.65$ $2.06 > 1.65$

Reject null hyp. that the trainees average 80.

---

11. (a)

Rank of x	Rank of y	d	d^2
5	6	-1	1
3	3.5	-.5	.25
2	3.5	-1.5	2.25
7	7	0	0
6	2	4	16
1	1	0	0
8	8	0	0
4	5	-1	1
			20.5

$$r_s = 1 - \frac{6(20.5)}{8(8^2-1)} = .756$$

11. (continued)

(b) $z = r_s \sqrt{n - 1}$

$$= .756 \sqrt{8 - 1} = 2.00$$

$z_{.025} = 1.96$ $2.00 > 1.96$

Reject null hyp. Conclude that there is a relationship between S.A.T. scores and college grade point averages.

12.

$$r_s = 1 - \frac{6\Sigma(x - y)^2}{n(n^2 - 1)}$$

Ranks

x	y	x-y	$(x-y)^2$
7	3	4	16
2	1.5	0.5	0.25
4.5	12	-7.5	50.25
.	.	.	.
.	.	.	.
.	.	.	.
4.5	5	-0.5	0.25
			87.5

$$r_s = 1 - \frac{6\Sigma(x-y)^2}{n(n^2 - 1)}$$

$$= 1 - \frac{6(87.5)}{15(15^2 - 1)}$$

$$= 1 - .156 - .844$$

---

13. H_O: number of french fries is the same at restaurant and cafeteria

H_A: number of french fries is different

7	8	8	10	10	11	12	12	13
R	C	R	C	R	R	C	C	C
1	2.5	2.5	4.5	4.5	6	7.5	7.5	9.5

13	14	15	15	15	16	16	16	18
R	R	R	R	C	R	R	C	C
9.5	11	13	13	13	16	16	16	18.5

18	20
C	C
18.5	20

$W_1 = 2.5 + 4.5 + 7.5 + 7.5 + 9.5 + 13$
$\qquad + 16 + 18.5 + 18.5 + 20 = 117.5$

$$\frac{20(21)}{2} = 210$$

$$U_1 = 117.5 - \frac{10(10 + 1)}{2} = 62.5$$

$$\mu_{U_1} = \frac{10(11)}{2} = 55$$

$$\sigma_{U_1} = \sqrt{\frac{10(10)(21)}{12}} = 13.229$$

13. (continued)

$$z = \frac{U_1 - \mu_{U_1}}{\sigma_{U_1}}$$

$$= \frac{62.5 - 55}{13.229} = .57$$

Since $.57 < 1.96$, do not reject the null hypothesis. Cannot conclude that the restaurant and the cafeteria are different

---

14. H_O: arrangement is random

H_A: arrangement is not random

$\alpha = 0.05$

$n_1 = 6$, $n_2 = 10$

$u_{0.25} = 13$ $u'_{0.25} = 4$

H_O must be rejected if $u \leq 4$ or $u \geq 13$

<u>10 11</u>   <u>13 13 14</u>   <u>11</u> 9   <u>13 14 13</u>

<u>11</u>   <u>13 14</u>   <u>10</u>   <u>14 15</u>

$u = 8$

H_O cannot be rejected

Insufficient evidence to suggest that the data may not be treated as if they constitute a random sample

---

15. Use the parametric test of Chapter 11, since in the experiments for which it is applicable, it is more efficient (i.e., less wasteful of information) than the corresponding nonparametric test.